BUILDING PATTERNS
ULTIMATE GUIDE TO
Designing Clothing Patterns

Building Patterns: Ultimate Guide to Designing Clothing Patterns

Landauer Publishing, www.landauerpub.com, is an imprint of Fox Chapel Publishing Company, Inc.

Copyright © 2025 by Suzy Furrer and Fox Chapel Publishing Company, Inc.

Building Patterns is an updated and revised edition of 2012 version originally published by Apparel Arts. This version is published by Landauer, an imprint of Fox Chapel Publishing Company, Inc.

All rights reserved. No part of this book may be reproduced, stored in a retrieval system, or transmitted in any form or by any means, electronic, mechanical, photocopying, recording, or otherwise, without the prior written permission of Fox Chapel Publishing, except for the inclusion of brief quotations in an acknowledged review and the enlargement of the template patterns in this book for personal use only. The patterns themselves, however, are not to be duplicated for resale or distribution under any circumstances. Any such copying is a violation of copyright law.

Project Team

Acquisitions Editor: Amelia Johanson

Editor: Christa Oestreich

Designer: Leslie Hall

Technical Illustrations: Tria Connell, Cantürk Öz, Chelsea Raflo

Indexer: Jean Bissell

Shutterstock used: Kostikova Natalia (front cover); 9dream studio (back cover, 101, 123, 149, 177, 255); Iryna Kalamurza (liner); Ekateryna Zubal (5 top left, 179); PRO Stock Professional (5 bottom left); indira's work (5 middle); Love-Pics (5 top right); Kaspars Grinvalds (5 bottom right, 203); Fuss Sergey (9); AlexanderLipko (11, 15); malaha (14, 42); Sabelnikova Olga (23); Dmitry Galagnov (53); Shyntartanya (75); Sigridstock (79); Evgeniya369 (83); Tarzhanova (86, 247); JKstock (125); Heavenman (130, 244); Karniewska (151, 257); FOTMA (165); Iryna Imago (208); B Lamb (230); Tony_C (239); Andrius_Saz (241).

Paperback ISBN 978-1-63981-131-1

Hardcover ISBN 978-1-63981-142-7

Library of Congress Control Number: 2025936106

To learn more about the other great books from Fox Chapel Publishing, or to find a retailer near you, call toll-free at 800-457-9112 or visit us at www.FoxChapelPublishing.com.

We are always looking for talented authors.

To submit an idea, please send a brief inquiry to acquisitions@foxchapelpublishing.com.

Or write to:

Fox Chapel Publishing

903 Square Street

Mount Joy, PA 17552

Printed in China

This book has been published with the intent to provide accurate and authoritative information in regard to the subject matter within. While every precaution has been taken in the preparation of this book, the author and publisher expressly disclaim any responsibility for any errors, omissions, or adverse effects arising from the use or application of the information contained herein.

BUILDING PATTERNS
ULTIMATE GUIDE TO
Designing Clothing Patterns

Suzy Furrer

Table of Contents

Introduction 6

Chapter 1: Patternmaking Tools and Language 8
    Patternmaking Tools 10
    Patternmaking Language 17

Chapter 2: Skirts 22
    Getting Started with the Skirt Sloper 24
    Exercises 30

Chapter 3: Moulage and Bodice Slopers 52
    Drafting a Moulage for a Feminine Figure 54
    Drafting a Sloper for a Masculine Figure 72

Chapter 4: Dart Manipulation 82
    Rules and Information to Apply to Dart Manipulations 84
    Exercises 87

Chapter 5: Lines 100
    Introduction to Style Lines and Silhouettes 102
    Exercises 106

Chapter 6: Necklines 124
    Rules for Well-Fitting Necklines and Bodices 126
    Exercises 134

Chapter 7: Collars 150
    Rules for Drafting Collars 152
    Exercises 156

Chapter 8: Sleeves 178
    Introduction to Sleeve Terms and Measuring 180
    Exercises 182

Chapter 9: Pants 202
    Introduction to Pants Drafting 204
    Exercises 213

Chapter 10: Pockets..238
    Patterning Pockets..240
    Exercises..242

Chapter 11: Garments...256
    How to Work with This Chapter...258
    Exercises..259

Glossary...274

Discussion Topics..276

Index..277

Acknowledgments..279

About the Author...280

Introduction

Building Patterns was written for three types of students: those who aspire to work in the fashion industry; those who work in the fashion industry and want to sharpen their skill set; and the serious sewer, crafter, maker, or hobbyist. These groups represent different teaching opportunities, and this book speaks to all three. The skill level, questions, and expectations vary from student to student, but they all need technical and detailed instruction they can apply inside the classroom and in the design studio.

Because of the years spent refining the text in the classroom, patternmaking instructors will enjoy teaching from *Building Patterns*. In addition to detailed, vetted instruction, there are thoughtful tips on design and apparel industry practices, as well as quizzes at the end of each chapter to test the students' knowledge.

Unless specified, the exercises should be mocked up with woven fabric; however, information regarding when and how to pattern for knits is included in certain areas.

This book is divided into 11 chapters, starting with tools and ending with creating garments. The content in each chapter is fully explored before moving on. The diagrams are clear and easy to follow. With each chapter and every exercise, students build a stronger pattern-drafting foundation while gaining a deeper understanding of the art form. For those with patternmaking knowledge, the text can be used as a reference and one can pick and choose specific exercises to focus on.

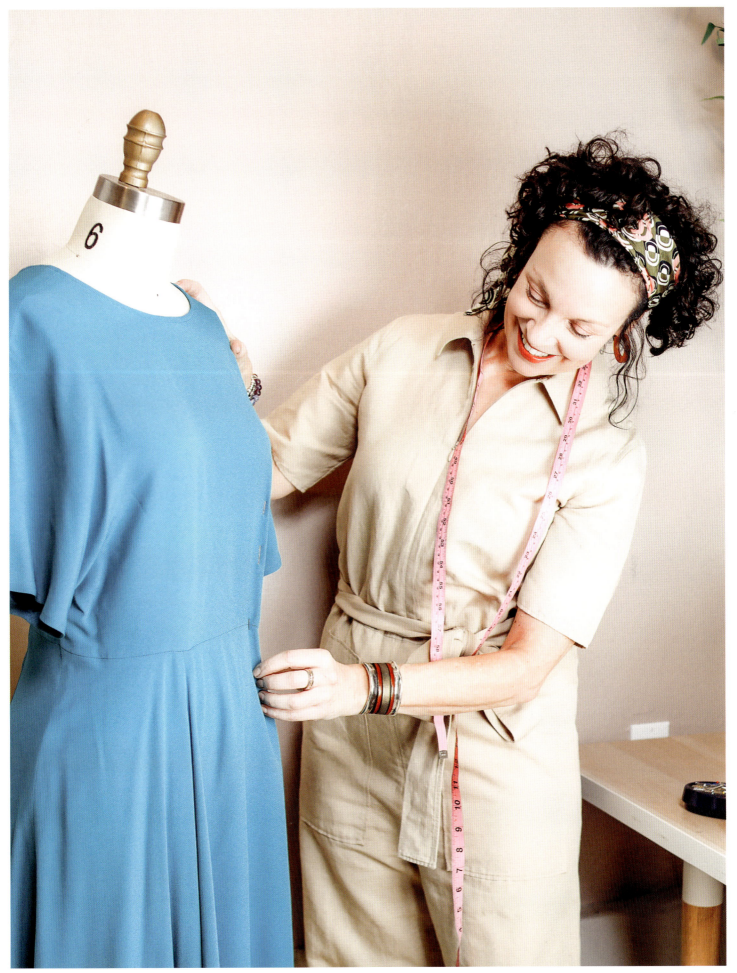

This chapter introduces students to patternmaking vocabulary and terms that will be useful for the chapters ahead. Students also gain an understanding of what is needed to build a patternmaking tool kit for the classroom or the design studio.

OBJECTIVES

Upon completion of this chapter, you will be able to

- Identify patternmaking tools and understand how to use them
- Build a patternmaking tool kit
- Understand vocabulary, terms, and phrases used in patternmaking

CHAPTER 1
Patternmaking Tools and Language

Patternmaking Tools

Figure 1.1

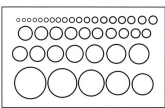

Figure 1.2

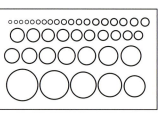

Figure 1.3

AWL

An **awl** is a pointed tool used to make holes through pattern pieces and fabric (*Fig. 1.1*). A **drill hole** is used to indicate the placement of darts points, pleats, corners, trim, belt loops, pockets, buttons, buttonholes, and other interior markings on a pattern piece or fabric piece. An **awl punch** is used in factory sewing.

CIRCLES TEMPLATE

A **circles template** (*Fig. 1.2*) is used to mark button placement and size on a pattern or is used to round pattern edges.

COMPASS

A **compass** is used to draw circles or arcs on patterns. One leg has a point at the end to secure it; the other leg has a clamp that holds a pencil (*Fig. 1.3*).

Figure 1.5

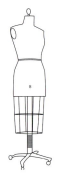

Figure 1.5

DRAFTING CURVE

Using a **drafting curve** (*Fig. 1.4*) helps you to draw professional-looking armholes, necklines, lapels, crotch seams, sleeve caps, shaped seams, and any other curve needed to complete a pattern draft. Drafting curves come in a variety of different shapes and sizes.

DRESS FORM

While a **dress form** (*Fig. 1.5*) is not necessary if you are fitting yourself or a client, it can make the fitting process easier.

ERASER

To err is human. Keep an **eraser** on hand.

Figure 1.6

Figure 1.7

FABRIC SCISSORS

Fabric scissors should be 8"–10" (20.3–25.4cm) long from the top of the handle to the tip of the blade (*Fig. 1.6*). Keep fabric scissors dedicated to fabric cutting. Using fabric scissors on paper will dull the blades. **Rotary cutters** also work well when cutting fabric.

HIP CURVE

A **hip curve** (*Fig. 1.7*) is used to shape a side seam, waistline, lapel, inseam, or other gently curving seamlines.

MUSLIN

Muslin is an inexpensive, plain-weave, unbleached fabric used for mocking up woven fabric patterns. Patterns for knit garments should be mocked up in knit fabric.

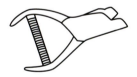

Figure 1.8

Figure 1.9

Figure 1.10

NOTCHER

A **notcher** (*Fig. 1.8*) clips a ¼" (6.4mm) notch into the edge of a pattern piece. It is used to indicate how to match pieces within a pattern. A notcher can also be used to denote seam allowances, hem allowances, fold lines, center lines, and dart legs on the perimeter of a pattern.

PAPER SCISSORS

Use **lightweight scissors** (*Fig. 1.9*) for paper cutting. Heavy paper scissors can stress the hands.

PATTERN HOOK

A **pattern hook** is a nylon cord approximately 6" (15.2cm) long with a metal hook on one end and a metal T-bar on the other (*Fig. 1.10*). It is used to hang patterns.

PATTERN RECORD CARD

A **pattern record card**, also called a cutting order, is a cover sheet for a pattern (*Fig. 1.11*). It keeps pertinent information about that pattern in one place for easy reference. A pattern record card includes the garment name or **style number**, the **season** and **year**, and **version** (noting which iteration the designer or patternmaker is working on). There is a section for **fabric** information and the planned **size range**. All the pattern pieces are listed next to columns showing how many fabric pieces to cut and out of which fabrication.

There is an area to list **trims**. Trims include zippers, buttons, bias tape, twill tape, stay tape, elastic, piping, ribbing, hooks/eyes, snaps, labels, or any other tape and hardware included on a garment that are not fabric. When listing trim, note the trim per garment not for the entire garment run. For example, one skirt might have one zipper and one hook/eye, so trims should note x1 - 9" (22.9cm) zipper and x1 hook/eye.

A **technical flat** (*Fig. 1.12*) or photograph should be included as well. Most design houses customize their pattern record card, so it is geared toward their product line.

Garment Name/Style Number	
Season/Year	
Version	
Working/Final Pattern	
Fabric	
Size Range	

Key: (1) Self | (2) Contrasting | (3) Pocketing | (4) Lining | (5) Interfacing | (6) Underlining

Pattern Pieces:	1	2	3	4	5	6

Trims:

Figure 1.11

Technical Sketch (or Photo): Front & Back View:

Figure 1.12

Figure 1.13

PATTERN PAPER

Pattern paper is lightweight and comes in large rolls. Common widths are 18", 24", and 36" (45.7, 61, and 91.4cm). Pattern paper can be clear of markings or can have a grid of dots or letters. The grid helps when drawing straight lines.

PATTERN PUNCH

A **pattern punch** has a lever and circular die-cutter (*Fig. 1.13*) and is used to punch a hole in a pattern for hanging with a pattern hook.

PATTERN STAMP

A **pattern stamp** is used to identify pattern pieces. The stamp should have a line for **season**, **style** (name or number), **piece** (front, back, sleeve, etc.), **size** (medium, etc.), and how many pieces to **cut** out of what fabric (*Fig. 1.14*). Keep this stamp at or under the dimensions of 3" x 3" (7.6 x 7.6cm).

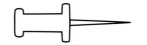

Figure 1.15

PENCILS

Mechanical pencils are ideal for drafting because the lead maintains a fine point. Regular pencils work well, but the points can become dull and thick after a few lines, which can throw off the fit of a pattern. Keep your pencils sharp if using regular pencils.

Use a **red pencil** to mark the grainline and notches, and to circle drill holes on patterns so marks are visible when cutting.

TACK

A simple **thumbtack** (*Fig. 1.15*) is used to hold the apex (point) of a dart in place when pivoting darts.

TAG

Tag is heavy manila paper that comes in rolls. It is generally available in widths of 36" and 48" (91.4 and 121.9cm). This firm paper is used to make templates and final patterns. Poster board works just as well.

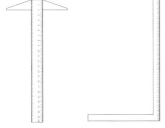

Figure 1.16

Figure 1.17

T-SQUARES AND L-SQUARES

T-squares and **L-squares** are metal rulers with arms meeting at right angles (*Fig. 1.16*). They are used to establish guidelines and right angles.

TAPE MEASURE

Tape measures are ½" x 60" (1.3 x 152.4cm) flexible measuring tools with inches and centimeters marked off (*Fig. 1.17*).

TRACING PAPER

Tracing paper can be wax or chalk paper, used to accurately transfer markings from one pattern to another or from pattern to fabric.

Season: _____
Style: _____
Piece: _____
Size: _____
Cut: _____

Figure 1.14

Figure 1.18

Figure 1.19

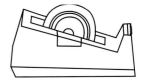

Figure 1.20

TRACING WHEEL

A **tracing wheel** can have a needle-pointed, smooth, or serrated wheel attached to a handle (*Fig. 1.18*). Use a tracing wheel with tracing paper to transfer marks from one pattern to another or from pattern to fabric. Tracing wheels are used to true darts and other folded lines.

TRANSPARENT RULER

A 2" x 18" (5.1 x 45.7cm) plastic, straight-edge **ruler** with a grid in fractions of inches or centimeters (*Fig. 1.19*) is the most important flat pattern drafting tool. It is used to draft patterns, draw grainlines and guidelines, establish angles, and more.

TRANSPARENT TAPE

Transparent tape (*Fig. 1.20*) is needed when pattern pieces are manipulated.

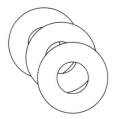

Figure 1.21

Figure 1.22

WEIGHT

A **pattern weight** (*Fig. 1.21*) is used to hold pattern pieces in place when tracing or cutting. The most economical weights to use are medium- to large-size washers from the hardware store.

YARDSTICK AND METER STICK

A **yardstick** or **meter stick** (*Fig. 1.22*) is used to mark guidelines or grainlines on long pattern pieces and for measuring fabric yardage needed for a pattern.

Patternmaking Language

DRAFTING ORDER

The order for drafting a pattern is usually front, back, sleeve, and sleeve pieces like cuffs, collar, pocket pieces, and then other details. It is best to draft a **primary pattern** and trace off the pieces, keeping the master intact so changes can easily be made. Interior pieces like linings, facings, and support pieces are not drafted until the fit has been finalized.

During the process of working out a pattern, that pattern is called a **working pattern** or a **first pattern**. Once a pattern has been fit tested and finalized, it is called a **final pattern** or a **production pattern**.

EASE

Wearing ease is added to a pattern for comfort. Wearing ease is distributed throughout a pattern. In addition to wearing ease, **design ease** can be added to achieve the look of a desired silhouette. **Negative ease** is a phrase used with knits to imply that the pattern measures less than the body circumference. This allows for the fabric to stretch around the body for a snug fit.

GRAINLINE

A **grainline** is drawn on each pattern piece to show how the piece will be placed on the fabric when cutting. The grainline is always parallel to the **selvage** edge. Selvages are the two finished edges running the length of a woven fabric. A grainline should run almost the entire length of a pattern piece.

A grainline looks like an arrow (*Fig. 1.23*). When there is an arrowhead on both ends of a grainline, the pattern can be placed in either an up or down direction on the fabric. When the line has an arrowhead only at the top or only at the bottom, let that arrowhead dictate the desired direction of the fabric nap or fabric pattern.

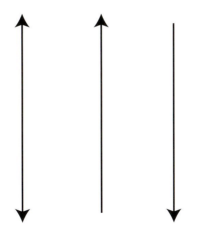

Figure 1.23

Length grain indicates the yarns parallel to the selvage in a woven fabric. These yarns are referred to as **warp yarns**. The grainline on a pattern always shows length grain. **Length grain**, also referred to as **straight grain**, is stable and strong without much give. **Cross grain** indicates the yarns perpendicular to the selvage edge. These yarns are referred to as the **weft yarns** or **filling yarns** in a woven fabric. The cross grain generally has a bit more give than the length grain.

True bias is indicated by a grainline that intersects the length and cross grains at a 45-degree angle. True bias has the maximum amount of stretch in a woven fabric. True bias will drape well and mold to the contours of the body.

Off grain is a term referring to any fabric where the length grain and cross grain have been distorted from a 90-degree angle. Sometimes this can be fixed by pulling on the fabric and steam pressing.

When choosing a length, cross, or bias grainline, consider stability, drape, fabric pattern layout, and fabric conservation (*Fig. 1.24*).

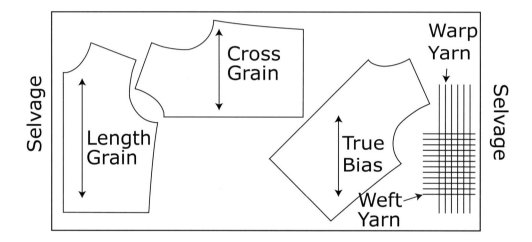

Figure 1.24

JOGGED SEAM

A **jogged seam** is an abrupt and distinct change in the seam allowance (*Fig. 1.25*). A jogged seam will alert the sewer to a change in task, such as straight seam stitching to a zipper application.

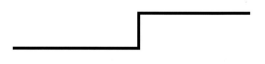

Figure 1.25

LINES AND ANGLES

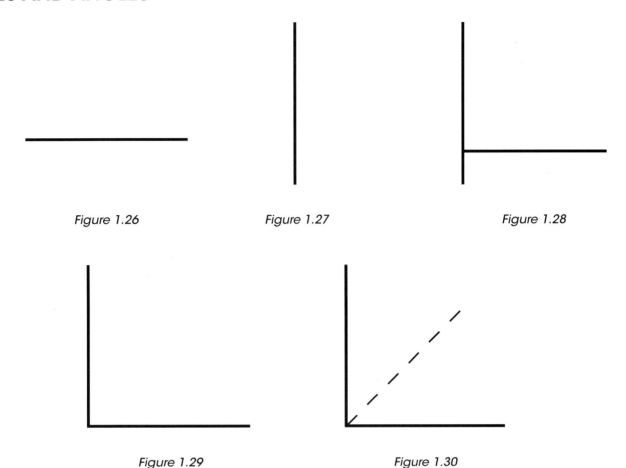

Figure 1.26   Figure 1.27   Figure 1.28

Figure 1.29   Figure 1.30

Horizontal refers to an imaginary or drawn line parallel to the floor (*Fig. 1.26*). A **vertical line** is straight up and down, perpendicular to the floor (*Fig. 1.27*). A **perpendicular line** is at a right angle to another line. (*Fig. 1.28*). A **right angle** is a line drawn perpendicular to the bottom of another line, creating a 90-degree angle (*Fig. 1.29*). The phrase "**square a line**" will also be used when a right angle is needed. A **45-degree angle** bisects a 90-degree angle (*Fig. 1.30*).

MARKING A PATTERN

In addition to marking the grainline and including information on a pattern stamp, always mark the **center front** (**CF**) and **center back** (**CB**) of a pattern. Include notches and drill holes. If a pattern is asymmetrical, each pattern piece should be noted with **correct side up** (**CSU**) or **correct side down** (**CSD**), or the word "**flip**," if the piece should be face down.

If a fabric has a plaid, stripe, or print that needs to be placed carefully, you can test it digitally. Copy a swatch of the fabric and tape or scan the fabric image to each pattern piece in the exact orientation it should appear on the garment, so the fabric pattern ends up in the correct place.

NOTCHES AND DRILL HOLES

A **notch** is a mark or set of marks on the perimeter of a pattern. A notch should be ¼" (6.4mm) long with a ⅛" (3.2mm) bar across the top (*Fig. 1.31*). Notches are a way for the patternmaker to communicate with the sewer by matching notches on corresponding pattern pieces. Notches can be used individually or in groups. For instance, two notches ¼"–½" (0.6–1.3cm) apart often denote center back. Seam and hem allowances can also be notched on the edges of a pattern piece.

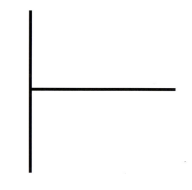

Figure 1.31

While notches are used on the edges of pattern pieces, **drill holes** are used in the interior of a pattern piece where a notch cannot reach. Drill holes should be marked by a dot with a red circle around it (*Fig. 1.32*). **Awl-punch** to make a drill hole at points, corners, dart points, pocket placement, button/buttonhole placement, and belt-loop placement. Most darts are awl-punched ½" (1.3cm) inside and away from the point. Most other drill holes are done ¹⁄₁₆"–⅛" (1.6–3.2mm) inside the seam allowance. Drill holes are another way for the patternmaker to communicate with the sewer.

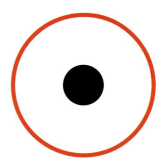

Figure 1.32

SEAM ALLOWANCE AND HEM ALLOWANCE

Seam allowance varies per garment and task. Knit garments are generally cut with ⅜" (1cm) seam allowances. Woven garments are often cut with ½" (1.3cm) seam allowances; however, ¾" (1.9cm) seam allowance behind zippers increases stability. Seam allowances at waists, waistbands, necklines, and collars are often ¼" (6.4mm) to reduce bulk. If a garment will be altered, it is best to use ¾"–1" (1.9–2.5cm) at the side seams. Note that seam allowance amounts vary even within a garment, and it is up to the patternmaker, with the help of the sewer, to determine where and how much seam allowance should be added.
Hem allowance also varies per garment. Knit garments often use ½"–1" (1.3–2.5cm) hem allowance. Woven garments that are straight or relatively straight at the base use 1½" (3.8cm). Flared pieces should not use more than 1" (2.5cm). Sheer and delicate fabrics often use baby hems of ¼"–½" (0.6–1.3cm). It is up to the patternmaker and sewer to come up with best practice.

When a pattern is still in the working pattern stage, seam and hem allowances can be left off the pattern because it is easier to make pattern changes without them. Of course, seam and hem allowances are added to the fabric when cutting mock-ups; they are just not added to the pattern until it becomes a production pattern.

SLOPER

A **sloper**, also called a **block**, is a base pattern developed for skirts, pants, bodices, sleeves, and even pocket pieces. Slopers are used as a starting point when drafting a garment. The sloper has already been fit tested, so the patternmaker only needs to design around the well-fitting sloper. Since the patternmaker does not need to start from scratch, the work time is often cut in half.

TECHNICAL FLAT

A **technical flat** shows the outline, seamlines, and all details in proportion on a scaled-down version of the garment (*Fig. 1.33*). A common scale is every 1" (2.5cm) of garment is reduced to ⅛" (3.2mm). Pants, coats, and other long garments often have a scale of ¹⁄₁₆" (1.6mm) for every 1" (2.5cm).

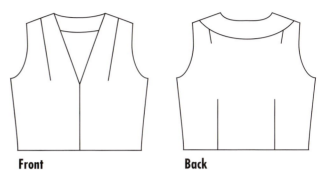

Front **Back**

Figure 1.33

TESTING A PATTERN

Test a pattern in muslin or a fabric similar to the finished garment fabric. If the finished garment is a woven fabric, test in a woven fabric. If the finished garment will be in a knit, use a knit with a similar stretch. Expect to make at least three mock-ups before cutting into the fashion fabric. With easier garments, only one mock-up might be needed. More involved garments might need multiple iterations to get it right.

TRUING A PATTERN

Truing a pattern refers to the process of establishing equal seam lengths on corresponding pattern pieces, making sure notches match, and ensuring the connections at the neck, shoulder, and side seams are smooth. Check front and back side lengths, make sure dart legs are of equal length, and recheck all measurements. Make it a habit to check and true every seam in a pattern after each draft is completed. Properly truing a pattern saves time when sewing.

 Test Your Knowledge

1. Draw an accurate example of a horizontal line, vertical line, perpendicular line, right angle, and 45-degree angle.

2. What information is included on a pattern stamp?

3. Explain the importance of a pattern record card.

4. Why is it important to have separate paper and fabric scissors?

5. What is the difference between warp yarn and weft yarn in woven fabric?

In Chapter 2, students begin to build a foundation of pattern-drafting knowledge. Basic rules for measuring, calculating, and drafting are covered. Students draft a simple skirt sloper then learn how to draft flares, pleats, wrap skirts, lining, facings, and waistbands from the sloper. Creating a knit skirt sloper is included.

OBJECTIVES

Upon completion of this chapter, you will be able to

- Demonstrate the proper use of markings on patterns
- Build a skirt sloper
- Use the skirt sloper to develop new designs

CHAPTER 2
Skirts

Getting Started with the Skirt Sloper

MEASURING FOR A SKIRT SLOPER

Accurate measuring is a key component to a well-fitting skirt sloper. Refer to the instructions and the corresponding diagram (*Fig. 2.1*).

The model should stand without shoes, feet about 4" (10.2cm) apart. They should retain their natural posture throughout the measuring process while looking straight ahead. If the arms need to be moved out of the way, have the model hold their arms out with the elbows at shoulder level.

Start the measuring process by having the model tie a ¼" (6.4mm) width elastic strip around the natural waistline. To find the natural waistline, have the model bend side-to-side to find where the body creases. Good positioning of the waist elastic is about ½"–1" (1.3–2.5cm) above the top of the navel. Check the position of the elastic frequently while measuring and readjust it if it is rolling up. The elastic is used as a measuring guide. Dress forms have twill tape pinned around the natural waistline, so an elastic is not needed.

Take snug measurements, not tight or loose. Ease will be added later.

Measuring Tip:
Small adhesive dots from an office supply store work well for marking measuring points on the body or on a dress form.

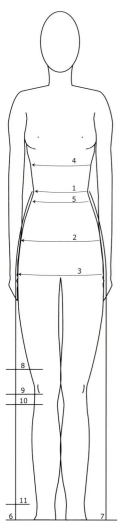

Figure 2.1

Measurements

- **Waist (1):** Measure the waist around the elastic.
- **High Hip (2):** Measure 4½" (11.4cm) down from the base of the waist elastic at the sides. Use adhesive dots to mark the depth of the high hip. Once the side depth is marked, measure the circumference of the high hip, keeping the tape measure level. Note both depth and circumference measurements.
- **Low Hip (3):** Measure 8½" (21.6cm) down from the base of the waist elastic at the sides. If the hips are wider at a point lower than 8½" (21.6cm), use that lower depth and circumference measurement. The hips are at their widest point where the rear end protrudes the most. Using adhesive dots to mark the depth at sides is helpful. Measure around the body, keeping the tape measure level. If the high-hip measurement is larger than the low-hip measurement, use the high-hip measurement for the low hip so as not to emphasize the high hip fullness. Note both depth and circumference measurements.
- **Empire Height (4):** An empire height can be 2"–4" (5.1–10.2cm) above the natural waistline. Mark the desired height at the sides from the bottom of the waist elastic and measure around the body. With the tape measure positioned, have the model take a

deep breath. If the measurement expands with the deep breath (which it usually does), use the expanded measurement. Note both height and circumference measurements.

- **Lowered Waistline (5):** Determine the desired depth at the side from the base of the waist elastic. Mark the depth. Measure around the body at the lowered-waistline depth. Note the depth and circumference measurements.
- **Skirt Length (6–11):** Measure from the base of the waist elastic to the floor on both the right side (**6**) and left side (**7**) of the body to determine if one side is longer than the other. This is common and occurs if one hip is higher or one leg is shorter. If there is a difference, take the skirt length measurements on the longer side. The longer of (**6**) or (**7**) is the full-length measurement. Take four additional length measurements. For a short skirt, take a measurement from the base of the waist elastic to the client's desired length above the knee (**8**). Measure to the middle of the kneecap (**9**). Measure below the knee 1"–4" (2.5–10.2cm) as desired, avoiding the widest part of the calf (**10**). Finally, measure to the ankle 3" (7.6cm) above the floor (or full length: 3" [7.6cm]) (**11**).

Record of Measurements

NAME: _____

DATE: _____

Waist (1): _____

High Hip (2): _____

@ a depth of: _____

Low Hip (3): _____

@ a depth of: _____

Empire (4): _____

@ a height of: _____

Lowered Waist (5): _____

@ a depth of: _____

Full Length Right Side (6): _____

Full Length Left Side (7): _____

Above Knee (8): _____

Knee Length (9): _____

Below Knee (10): _____

Ankle Length (11): _____

Practice

Use these sample measurements (fits most Women's size 8 dress forms).

Waist: 26" (66cm)

High Hip: 34" (86.4cm)

@ a depth of: 4½" (11.4cm)

Low Hip: 37" (94cm)

@ a depth of: 8½" (21.6cm)

Empire: 28" (71.1cm)

@ a height of: 3" (7.6cm)

Lowered Waist: 30" (76.2cm)

@ a depth of: 2" (5.1cm)

Full Length Right Side: 40" (101.6cm)

Full Length Left Side: 40" (101.6cm)

Above Knee: 22" (55.9cm)

Knee Length: 24" (61cm)

Below Knee: 27" (68.6cm)

Ankle Length: 37" (94cm)

CALCULATING THE MEASUREMENTS

The **waist**, **high-hip**, **low-hip**, **empire**, and **lowered-waist** circumference measurements are all divided by four. Because the sloper is symmetrical, only half the front and half the back are drafted. Half of the front or the back is one-quarter of the entire skirt. After dividing by four, ¼" (6.4mm) is added to the quotient for the front and ¼" (6.4mm) is subtracted from the quotient for the back. This redistribution allows for a flattering position of the side seam. There is more body mass in the front than the back (except at the low hip), so this calculation allows the front draft to be wider than the back draft. Of course, the low-hip area has more body mass in back, but to keep the side seam straight and consistent, and for a more flattering position of the side seam, continue with adding to the front and subtracting from the back on the low hip. The lengths are used as measured.

- -

Calculating Tip:
Download a fraction calculator app to your phone to help with the math.

- -

Skirts Calculation Worksheet

Waist: _____ + ½" (1.3cm) ease = _____ ÷ 4 = _____

    Front: _____ + ¼" (6.4mm) = _____

    Back: _____ − ¼" (6.4mm) = _____

High Hip: _____ + 1" (2.5cm) ease = _____ ÷ 4 = _____

    Front: _____ + ¼" (6.4mm) = _____

    Back: _____ − ¼" (6.4mm) = _____ (@ a depth of _____)

Low Hip: _____ + 1 ½" (3.8cm) ease = _____ ÷ 4 = _____

    Front: _____ + ¼" (6.4mm) = _____

    Back: _____ − ¼" (6.4mm) = _____

(@ a depth of _____)

Empire: _____ + ½" (1.3cm) ease = _____ ÷ 4 = _____

    Front: _____ + ¼" (6.4mm) = _____

    Back: _____ − ¼" (6.4mm) = _____

(@ a height of _____)

Lowered Waist: _____ + 0 ease = _____ ÷ 4 = _____

    Front: _____ + ¼" (6.4mm) = _____

    Back: _____ − ¼" (6.4mm) = _____

(@ a depth of _____)

Lengths (as measured)

Full Length (longer of the right and left sides): _____

Above Knee: _____

Knee Length: _____

Below Knee: _____

Ankle Length: _____

Sample Calculation Worksheet

Waist: 26" (66cm)   + ½" (1.3cm) ease = 26 ½" (67.3cm)   ÷ 4 = 6 5/8" (16.8cm)
    Front: 6 5/8" (16.8cm)   + ¼" (6.4mm) = 6 7/8" (17.5cm)
    Back: 6 5/8" (16.8cm)   − ¼" (6.4mm) = 6 3/8" (16.2cm)

High Hip: 34" (86.4cm)   + 1" (2.5cm) ease = 35" (88.9cm)   ÷ 4 = 8 ¾" (22.2cm)
    Front: 8 ¾" (22.2cm)   + ¼" (6.4mm) = 9" (22.9cm)
    Back: 8 ¾" (22.2cm)   − ¼" (6.4mm) = 8 ½" (21.6cm)
    (@ a depth of 4 ½" [11.4cm])

Low Hip: 37" (94cm)   + 1 ½" (3.8cm) ease = 38 ½" (72.4cm)   ÷ 4 = 9 5/8" (24.4cm)
    Front: 9 5/8" (24.4cm)   + ¼" (6.4mm) = 9 7/8" (25.1cm)
    Back: 9 5/8" (24.4cm)   − ¼" (6.4mm) = 9 3/8" (23.8cm)
    (@ a depth of 8 ½" [21.6cm])

Empire: 28" (71.1cm)   + ½" (1.3cm) ease = 28 ½" (72.4cm)   ÷ 4 = 7 1/8" (18.1cm)
    Front: 7 1/8" (18.1cm)   + ¼" (6.4mm) = 7 3/8" (18.7cm)
    Back: 7 1/8" (18.1cm)   − ¼" (6.4mm) = 6 7/8" (17.5cm)
    (@ a height of 3" [7.6cm])

Lowered Waist: 30" (76.2cm)   + 0 ease = 30" (76.2cm)   ÷ 4 = 7 ½" (19.1cm)
    Front: 7 ½" (19.1cm)   + ¼" (6.4mm) = 7 ¾" (19.7cm)
    Back: 7 ½" (19.1cm)   − ¼" (6.4mm) = 7 ¼" (18.4cm)
    (@ a depth of 2" [5.1cm])

Lengths (as measured)
Full Length (longer of the right and left sides): 40" (101.6cm)
Above Knee: 22" (55.9cm)
Knee Length: 24" (61cm)
Below Knee: 27" (68.6cm)
Ankle Length: 37" (94cm)

Helpful Tip:

Always highlight front and back calculations in different colors to help keep track of **front** vs. **back** calculations while drafting.

SETTING UP THE GUIDELINES

The following guidelines are needed to draft a skirt sloper. It is helpful to use the straight edge of the pattern paper as the center front (CF) and center back (CB). Go over the guidelines in red.

Front Guidelines

1. **Waist Guideline:** Perpendicular to the CF (see *Fig.* 2.2 for the location of the center front), draw a waist guideline the width of the **front low-hip calculation** (not the front waist calculation).
2. **High-Hip Guideline:** Perpendicular to the CF, draw the high-hip guideline 4½" (11.4cm) down from the waist guideline. The guideline should measure as the **front low-hip calculation** (not the front high-hip calculation).
3. **Low-Hip Guideline:** Perpendicular to the CF, draw the low-hip guideline 8½" (21.6cm) down (or as measured) from the waist guideline. The guideline should measure as the **front low-hip calculation**.
4. **Base:** Perpendicular to the CF, draw the base guideline 20" (50.8cm) down from the waist guideline. The guideline should measure as the **front low-hip calculation**.
5. Connect the open side to form a rectangle. Mark the CF and side. Label waist, high hip, low hip, and base on the corresponding lines.

Back Guidelines

1. **Waist Guideline:** Perpendicular to the CB (see *Fig.* 2.2 for the correct location of the center back), draw a waist guideline the width of the **back low-hip calculation** (not the back waist calculation).
2. **High-Hip Guideline:** Perpendicular to the CB, draw the high-hip guideline 4½" (11.4cm) down from the waist guideline. The guideline should measure as the **back low-hip calculation** (not the back high-hip calculation).
3. **Low-Hip Guideline:** Perpendicular to the CB, draw the low-hip guideline 8½" (21.6cm), or as measured, down from the waist guideline. The guideline should measure as the client's **back low-hip calculation**.
4. **Base:** Perpendicular to the CB, draw the base guideline 20" (50.8cm) down from the waist guideline. The guideline should measure as the **back low-hip calculation**.
5. Connect the open side to form a rectangle. Mark CB and side. Label waist, high hip, low hip, and base on the corresponding lines.

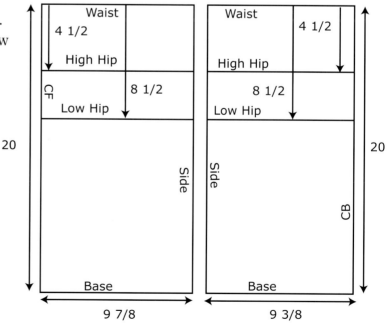

Figure 2.2

Drafting Tip:
Skirt slopers are often drafted around 20" (50.8cm) long. This is an in-between measurement, where it is easy to lengthen or shorten when drafting a garment.

DARTS

Most garments drafted for woven fabric need to have **darts** (*Fig. 2.3*). Darts and seams are used to shape fabric, so it contours to the body.

A dart will pull in fabric at the waist and release fabric at the hips. Darts can vary in width and length. Wider darts are needed when there is a bigger difference between the waist and low hip circumference. Narrower darts are needed when the difference is less. The length of a dart is dependent on the width of the dart. Wider darts need a longer **dart leg** length, and smaller darts can have a shorter length. Dart width and length charts are provided in the Skirt Sloper exercise (page 30).

The **point of a dart** (aka the **apex** or the **vanishing point**) is at the base of the **center line**. Tilting the point ¼" (6.4mm) toward the side seam is sometimes done so the fabric is released over more shapely areas of the body and to make the waist look smaller. The space in between dart legs is called the **dart bulk**. The peak or valley at the top of a dart is formed by folding the dart bulk in the direction the dart will be pressed and tracing the waistline shape over the dart bulk. This is called making the dart bulk **flush**.

Darts are not often used with knit fabrics, since knits easily stretch and contour around the body. Darts do work well on stable knits.

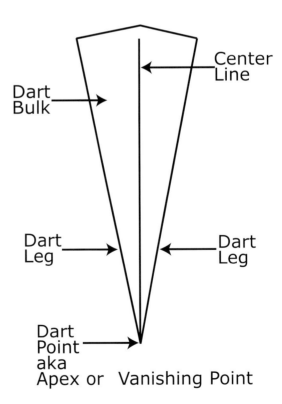

Figure 2.3

Exercises

SKIRT SLOPER
Front

1. Begin with the front skirt guidelines and mark the four corners **A**, **B**, **C**, and **D** as shown (*Fig. 2.4*).
2. **EF** = front high-hip calculation on the guideline measured from the center front
3. **GH** = front low-hip calculation on the guideline (as the skirt block width)

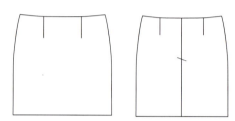

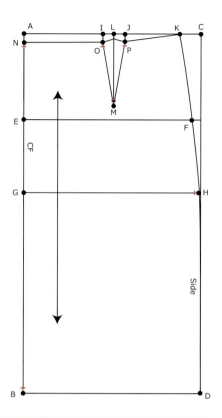

Figure 2.4

Front Dart Width Chart
If in between, round down.

- If the difference between the **full-waist** and **low-hip measurements** (with ease) is 14"–16" (35.6–40.6cm), use a 1½" (3.8cm) dart width.
- If the difference is 10"–13" (25.4–33cm), use a 1¼" (3.2cm) dart width.
- If the difference is 8"–9" (20.3–22.9cm), use a 1" (2.5cm) dart width.
- If the difference is 7" (17.8cm) or less, use a ¾" (1.9cm) dart width.

Take the difference between the full-waist and low-hip measurements with ease, not the difference between the waist and hip calculations.

4. **AI** = dart distance from center front (see Front Dart Distance Formula)
5. **IJ** = dart width (see Front Dart Width Chart)
6. **JK** = remainder of the front waist calculation after subtracting dart distance (**AI**). Make sure that **AI** + **JK** equals the front waist calculation. The dart width is excluded in measuring because it will be sewn out.
7. **L** = center of the dart width
8. **LM** = length of dart (see Dart Length Chart)

Dart Length Chart

- If the dart width is 1½" (3.8cm), use a dart length of 5¾" (14.6cm).
- If the dart width is 1¼" (3.2cm), use a dart length of 5" (12.7cm).
- If the dart width is 1" (2.5cm), use a dart length of 4½" (11.4cm).
- If the dart width is ¾" (1.9cm), use a dart length of 3½" (8.9cm).

Front Dart Distance Formula

Divide the front waist calculation in half, then add 1" (2.5cm).

For example, if the front waist calculation is 7" (17.8cm), divide by 2 = 3½" (8.9cm) + 1" (2.5cm) = 4½" (11.4cm).

Why this formula? Using it will place the front dart inside the hip bone and outside tummy. The dart position can be adjusted as desired in the fitting process, but this is a good place to start.

Design Tip:

A waistline is rarely drawn straight across at a right angle to the center front (or back). This would create wrinkles below the waist, and a straight line would visually cut the body in half.

9. **AN** = ½" (1.3cm) **waist shaping** to gently curve the waistline. **N** should be directly under **A** on the center front guideline.

10. Connect **N-K** for the waist shaping in a shallow curve. Draw a right angle at **N**, off **NE** for ¾" (1.9cm) before shaping to **K**. Squaring off for ¾" (1.9cm) will prevent the center front from coming to a point.

11. **OP** = bring dart legs **I** and **J** straight down to meet the waist shaping, keeping the dart width as **IJ**.

12. Mark **O** and **P** on the **NK** line.

13. Connect **O-M-P** for the dart legs. Make sure the dart legs are the same length by adjusting the top of the second dart leg at **P** as necessary.

14. Fold **P** toward **O** and trace the waistline over the dart bulk so the dart bulk is flush with the waistline. Pressing the dart bulk toward the side seam will create a smoother line rather than accentuating the tummy, which can happen when dart bulk is pressed toward the center front.

15. Measure **NK**, excluding the dart width **OP** (as that width will be sewn out) to check the front waist calculation. Adjust in or out at **K** if necessary.

16. Connect **K-F-H-D** for the side shape. Smooth the pattern at the high hip and low hip at side if necessary. Be conservative with smoothing. Shave off only ⅛" (3.2mm) or so.

17. Note the distance between **C** and **K**.

18. Pattern: **N-O-P-K-F-H-D-B-G-E-N**, including the dart.

19. Notch the low hip at the side. Notch vertically at the center-front waist where the fold of fabric will be. Notch the dart legs and awl-punch the dart ½" (1.3cm) up from the point. Draw a length grainline parallel to the center front. Add ½" (1.3cm) seam allowance to the waist and side, and a 1" (2.5cm) hem allowance. Drag the notches to the perimeter. Cut (1) self on fold at center front. When cutting a pattern on a center-front fold, do not add seam allowance at the fold.

20. **G** = high-hip guide at center back on the **EF** line

Tips:

- **Marking Tip:** Awl-punch ½" (1.3cm) up from the dart point. The drill hole is never on the point in case the punch damages the fabric. The sewer should be alerted to sew ½" (1.3cm) beyond the point.
- **Vocabulary Tip: Self** refers to the fashion fabric (or muslin or mock-up fabric). Two other terms used for fashion fabric are **primary** or **shell**.
- **Fitting Tip:** Any skirt pattern with a center-back seam should use back contouring to fit the curve of the spine. While it can be help to have a straight center-back seam when putting in a zipper, having this minimal amount of shaping should not affect how the zipper looks or functions.

Back

1. Begin with the back skirt block and mark the four corners **A**, **B**, **C**, and **D** as shown (*Fig. 2.5*).
2. **AE** = ⅜" (1cm) in for back contouring
3. **AF** = 7" (17.8cm)
4. Connect **E-F** for back contouring. Square down from **E** for ½" (1.3cm) before angling toward **F** to account for the waist shaping that will be added later.
5. **G** = high-hip guide at center back on the **EF** line
6. **GH** = back high-hip calculation on the guideline
7. **IJ** = back low-hip calculation on the guideline (as the skirt block)
8. Divide the back waist calculation into two parts to the nearest ⅛" (3.2mm). For example, if the back waist calculation is 6⅜" (16.2cm), then the division is 3⅛" (7.9cm) and 3¼" (8.3cm).

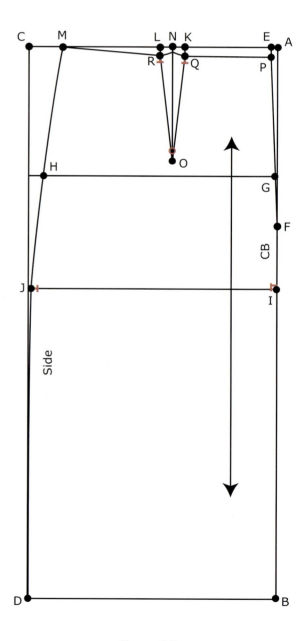

Figure 2.5

Back Dart Width Chart

- If the front dart is 1½" (3.8cm), the back dart is 1⅛" (2.9cm) (front dart, less the back contouring of ⅜" [1cm]).
- If the front dart is 1¼" (3.2cm), the back dart is ⅞" (2.2cm).
- If the front dart is 1" (2.5cm), the back dart is ⅝" (1.6cm).
- If the front dart is ¾" (1.9cm), the back dart is ⅜" (1cm).

9. **EK** = half the back waist calculation for placement of the first leg of the dart.
10. **KL** = dart width as front, less the back contouring of ⅜" (1cm) (see Back Dart Width Chart)
11. **LM** = remainder of the back waist calculation. For example, if the back waist calculation is 6⅜" (16.2cm), and **EK** is 3⅛" (7.9cm), the remainder of the back waist calculation (**LM**) is 3¼" (8.3cm). Check that **EK** + **LM** equals the back waist calculation.
12. **N** = center of the dart width
13. **NO** = length of dart (see Dart Length Chart). Round up if in between.
14. **EP** = ½" (1.3cm) waist shaping to gently curve the waistline
15. Square straight down from **E** to **P** to maintain the ⅜" (1cm) back contouring.
16. Connect **P-M** for the waist shaping in a shallow curve.
17. Draw a right angle at **P** for ¾" (1.9cm) before shaping to **M**.
18. **QR** = bring the dart legs **K** and **L** straight down to meet the waist shaping, keeping the dart width as **KL**
19. Mark **Q** and **R** on the **PM** line.
20. Connect **Q-O-R** for the dart legs.
21. Make sure the dart legs are of equal length by adjusting the top of the second dart leg at **R** as necessary.
22. Fold **Q** toward **R** and trace the waistline over the dart bulk so the dart bulk is flush with the waistline.
23. Measure **PM**, excluding the dart width **QR** (as that width will be sewn out) to check the back waist calculation. Adjust at **M** if necessary.
24. Connect **M-H-J-D** for the side shape. Smooth the pattern at the high hip and low hip at side if necessary. Shave off only ⅛" (3.2mm) or so.
25. Note the distance between **C** and **M**. If the pattern was drafted correctly, **CM** on the back should equal **CK** on the front. This allows for truing the front and back side shapes.
26. Pattern: **P-Q-R-M-H-J-D-B-I-F-G-P**, including the dart.
27. Notch the low hip at side. Double notch the low hip at center back. Notch the dart legs and awl-punch the dart ½" (1.3cm) up from the point. Draw a length grainline parallel to the lower center-back guideline. Add ½" (1.3cm) seam allowance and a 1" (2.5cm) hem allowance. Drag the notches to the perimeter. Cut (2) self.

Tips:

- **Marking Tip:** The center back is double notched at the low hip to differentiate it from the front and sides. Notch the low hip at center back, and notch ¼" (6.4mm) above that for two notches. Make sure you are double notching at the center back and not the side.
- **Cutting Tip:** In the **working pattern** stage (meaning the pattern is still being worked out), seam and hem allowances are usually left off the pattern, but they are added to the muslin when cutting. Leaving them off the pattern makes it easier to adjust. Once a pattern has been fit and perfected, then seam and hem allowances are permanently added to the pattern for a **final pattern** and notches are pulled to the perimeter of the pattern piece. Working patterns can be cut on a center-front fold. Final patterns going to factories for production are rarely cut on fold. Always make a full piece rather than have a "cut on fold" notation when making a final pattern.
- **Seam Allowance Tip:** Seam allowances are usually ⅜"–¾" (1–1.9cm). With knits, use ⅜" (1cm). With woven fabrics, use ½"–¾" (1.3–1.9cm). Bias-cut garments generally require 1" (2.5cm) seam allowances. When putting in a zipper, use a ¾" (1.9cm) seam allowance behind the zipper to support the weight of the zipper and to add stability.
- **Vocabulary Tip: Truing** means making sure seams and dart legs that will be sewn together are the same length (and shape if possible). It means notches line up and connections at the top and bottom of seams are smooth.

TRANSFERRING THE SKIRT SLOPER TO TAG

Once the sloper fit is adjusted, trace it onto tag without seam or hem allowances. It is easier to draft and adjust patterns that do not have seam and hem allowances added. Of course, seam and hem allowances will be added when the pattern is cut out of fabric, and seam and hem allowances will be added to the final pattern once the fit has been perfected.

The sloper is not a garment. It is a template. Think of the sloper as having up to 70 percent of the work done. The remaining 30 percent is about design, fabric choice, adjusting fit, silhouette, and details to reflect the designer's sketch.

Square the edges for at least ¼" (6.4mm) where you see the right-angle symbols (*Fig. 2.6*). Squaring helps with truing. Include notches on the sides of the guidelines and at the top of the dart legs. Awl-punch the vanishing point on the darts (dart lengths can vary). Add in a name and a date.

Note: waist = **W**, high hip = **HH**, low hip = **LH**, center front = **CF**, and center back = **CB**.

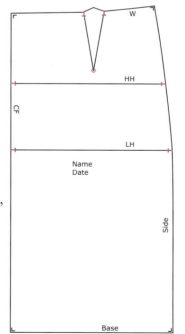
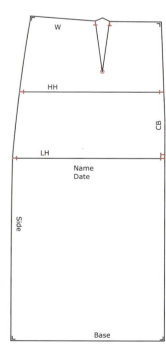

Figure 2.6

Building Patterns

Drafting a Knit Skirt Sloper

1. Start with the same waist, high-hip, and low-hip circumference measurements.
2. Subtract 2" (5.1cm) from waist, high-hip, and low-hip circumferences. Calculate using the reduced circumference measurements.
3. Subtract 1" (2.5cm) from the low-hip depth measurement.
4. Draft the front and back, skipping any references to darts and back contouring. Do include waist shaping.
5. Cut both the front and back on a center fold. Sew and test the fit in a stable knit, such as a double knit.
6. Once the fit is finalized, put it on tag to create a knit skirt sloper.

A-LINE SKIRT

The A-line skirt silhouette resembles the shape of a capital A.

Front

1. Trace the front sloper, adjust the skirt length as desired, and mark **A**, **B**, **C**, and **D** as shown (*Fig. 2.7*).
2. Redraw the dart point to the high-hip guideline That is where the flare will start.
3. Mark the dart **EFG**.
4. **H** = halfway between **B** and **D** at the base
5. Connect **G-H** (depending on where the dart is, the **GH** line could be straight up and down or slanted. Either works if **H** is centered on the base).
6. Decide on an insertion amount between 2" and 3" (5.1 and 7.6cm).
7. Cut the insertion line from **H** to **G**. Cut the dart leg from **E** to **G**, leaving a hinge of ⅛" (3.2mm).
8. Open the insertion line at **H** and insert as desired. Notice that as the insertion opens, the dart closes. Only close out the dart as much as needed to get the insertion amount. Add pattern paper to the insertion opening.

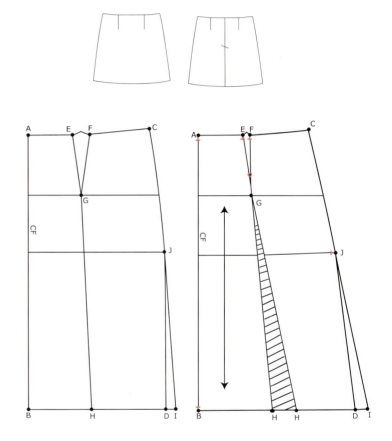

Figure 2.7

Tips:

- **Drafting Tip:** An insertion on an A-line skirt is limited to between 2" and 3" (5.1 and 7.6cm). Insertions larger than 3" (7.6cm) will create too much drape at the base, preventing the skirt from falling properly into an A-line shape.
- **Drafting Tip:** Add or shorten the length of the sloper by squaring straight up or straight down from the base.

Drafting Tip:

Extensions are half the insertion amount. For example, if an insertion is 2" (5.1cm), the extension is 1" (2.5cm). A front and back extension of 1" (2.5cm) each will create a 2" (5.1cm) extension at the side seam, matching the insertion amount.

---

9. Mark the new dart. If ¼" (6.4mm) or less of the dart width remains, shave that remainder off the side seam. If ⅜" (1cm) or more remains, mark it for sewing or add it to the back waist dart, skipping the dart in front (best option).
10. **DI** = extension as half the insertion amount
11. Connect **J-I**.
12. Measure **JD**. Measure **JI** and bring **I** up, so **JI** measures as **JD**.
13. Pattern: **A-E-F-C-J-I-H-B-A**, including the dart if it remains.
14. Notch the low hip at the side. Notch the center-front waist. Notch the top of the dart legs if the dart is included. Awl-punch ½" (1.3cm) up from the dart point if the dart is included. Draw a length grainline. Add ½" (1.3cm) seam allowance and a 1" (2.5cm) hem allowance. Drag the notches to the perimeter. Cut (1) self on fold at center front.

Back

1. Trace the back sloper, adjust the skirt length as front, and mark **A**, **B**, **C**, and **D** as shown (*Fig. 2.8*).
2. Repeat the front drafting process for the back.
3. Pattern: **A-E-F-C-J-I-H-B-A**, including the dart if it remains (because of the sway of the back, skirts fit better in back with a waist dart even if it is small. If the dart is small, add all or part of the remaining front dart width to the back dart, and skip or adjust the dart in front).
4. Notch the low hip at the side. Double notch the low hip at center back. Notch the dart legs if the dart is included. Awl-punch ½" (1.3cm) up from the dart point. Draw a length grainline parallel to center back. Add ½" (1.3cm) seam allowance and a 1" (2.5cm) hem allowance. Drag the notches to the perimeter. Cut (2) self.

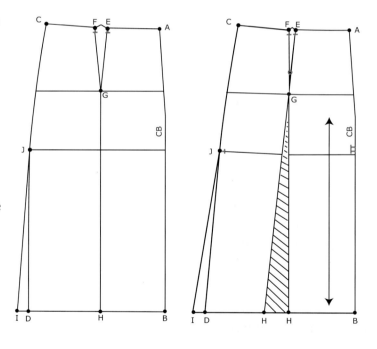

Figure 2.8

BIAS FLARE

A bias-flare skirt should be cut on a bias grainline. There are two insertions per quarter panel, each measuring between 2" and 4" (5.1 and 10.2cm) as desired. With two insertions, an extension is not needed. The darts should be manipulated out entirely.

Front

1. Trace the front sloper, adjust the skirt length as desired, and mark **A**, **B**, **C**, and **D** as shown (*Fig. 2.9*).
2. Divide the dart width into two. For example, a 1¼" (3.2cm) waist dart divided by 2 = two ⅝" (1.6cm) darts.
3. Divide the front waist calculation (excluding the dart width) into two-and-a-half parts to the nearest ⅛" (3.2mm). For example, if the waist is 6⅞" (17.5cm), the division is 2¾" (7cm) + 2¾" (7cm) + 1⅜" (3.5cm) = 6⅞" (17.5cm). The division does not have to be exact, but it should be close and should add up to the front waist calculation, excluding the dart width.

Drafting Tip:
Why two-and-a-half parts? Imagine a full front to the skirt—both the right and left sides. The middle half part becomes a full part when the skirt opens for a full right and left front.

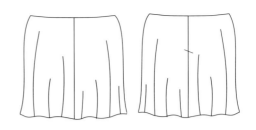
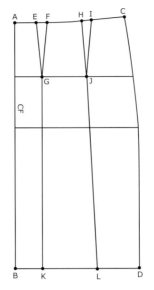
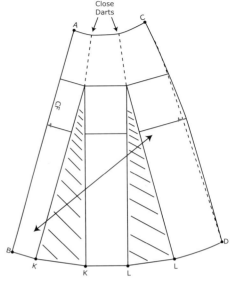

Figure 2.9

4. **AE** = the half portion of the calculation (example: 1⅜" [3.5cm])
5. **EF** = half the dart width
6. **G** = vanishing point of the first dart on the high-hip guideline, centered under the dart width
7. **FH** = full portion of the calculation (example: 2¾" [7cm])
8. **HI** = half the dart width
9. **J** = vanishing point of the second dart on the high-hip guideline, centered under the dart width
10. Divide the base (**BD**) into two-and-a-half parts. For example, if the base is 9⅞" (25.1cm), the division is 4" (10.2cm) + 4" (10.2cm) + 1⅞" (4.8cm) = 9⅞" (25.1cm). The division does not have to be exact, but it should be close and should add up to the front base calculation. Mark **K** and **L** as shown.
11. Connect **K-G** and **L-J** for the insertion lines.
12. Cut from **K** to **G** and the dart leg **E** to **G**, leaving a ⅛" (3.2mm) hinge at **G**.
13. Cut from **L** to **J** and the dart leg **H** to **J**, leaving a ⅛" (3.2mm) hinge at **J**.
14. Close out the darts completely and add pattern paper to the insertion opening. Smooth the base.
15. Straighten the side seam from the high hip to the base. Some of the low hip will be cut off; however, that is okay because of the added insertion amounts.
16. Pattern: **A-C-D-L-K-B-A**
17. Notch the low hip at the side. Draw a bias grainline at a 45-degree angle off the center front. Add 1" (2.5cm) seam allowance and a 1" (2.5cm) hem allowance. Drag the notches to the perimeter. Cut (2) self.

Seam Allowance Tip:
Bias seam allowances should be wider than the usual ½" (1.3cm) for three reasons: (1) bias stretches down, and when it stretches in length, it reduces in width; (2) it is better to sew wide bias seams because wider seams create a more stable foundation to sew a seam without puckers; and (3) wider seam allowances make it easier to adjust the fit.

Back

1. Trace the front pattern **A-C-D-L-K-B-A**, including notches and grainline. Flip the orientation.
2. Relabel it the CF (center front) as CB (center back).
3. Come in ½" (1.3cm) along the side seam from waist to base (*Fig. 2.10*). When calculating for the front and back, ¼" (6.4mm) was added to the front and ¼" (6.4mm) was subtracted from the back, creating a ½" (1.3cm) difference. Remove ½" (1.3cm) to get back to that front and back width discrepancy.
4. Notch the low hip at the side. Double notch the low hip at center back. Include the bias grainline. Add 1" (2.5cm) seam allowance and a 1" (2.5cm) hem allowance. Drag the notches to the perimeter. Cut (2) self.

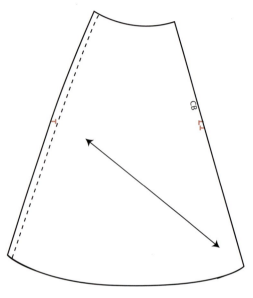

Figure 2.10

Drafting Tip:
Bias-cut garments usually work better with straight center and side seams as well as simple shapes. Keep the pattern simple and let the bias drape tell the story.

CIRCLE FLARE
The same pattern piece is used for the front and back.

Calculating for a Circle Flare
Waist measurement + ease ÷ 4" (10.2cm) + Chart (below) ÷ 2" (5.1cm) = _____.

For example: 26" (66cm) + ½" (1.3cm) ease ÷ 4" (10.2cm) = 6⅝" (16.8cm) + Chart (1⅝" [4.1cm]) = 8¼" (21cm) ÷ 2" (5.1cm) = 4⅛" (10.5cm)

1. Draw a right angle on the pattern paper marking **A** as shown (*Fig. 2.11*).
2. **AB** = as the calculation less ⅛" (3.2mm). Example: 4⅛" (10.5cm) − ⅛" (0.3cm) = 4" (10.2cm). You subtract ⅛" (3.2mm) because a circle skirt waistline has some bias stretch. The weight of a full skirt can also pull on the waistline. For both reasons, it is best to remove ⅛" (3.2mm) per quarter panel for a more secure fit at the waist.
3. **AC** = as **ABC** should be at a 45-degree angle from **A**
4. **AD** = as **AB**
5. Connect **B-C-D** for the waistline. Make sure all measurements from **A** to the waistline are as the **AB** measurement.
6. Measure **BCD**. Adjust at **D** if needed to get the correct waist calculation less ⅛" (3.2mm). Based on Step 2's example: 6⅝" (16.8cm). Mark the adjustment as **D'**. Any amount left over beyond **D'** can go into seam the allowance later.
7. **BE** = desired skirt length
8. **CF** = as **BE** for the skirt length
9. **DG** = as **BE** for the skirt length
10. Drag a line straight down from **D'** and mark **G'** at the base.
11. Connect **E-F-G'** for the base of the skirt.
12. Pattern: **B-C-D'-G'-F-E-B**
13. Draw a grainline by connecting **C-F**. Add ½" (1.3cm) seam allowance and a 1" (2.5cm) hem allowance. Cut (4) self.

Circle Flare Calculation + Addition Chart

If one-quarter of the waist measurement plus ease is:

- 6" (15.2cm), add 1½" (3.8cm)
- 6½" (16.5cm), add 1⅝" (4.1cm)
- 7" (17.8cm), add 1¾" (4.4cm)
- 7½" (19.1cm), add 1⅞" (4.8cm)
- 8" (20.3cm), add 2" (5.1cm)
- 8½" (21.6cm), add 2⅛" (5.4cm)
- 9" (22.9cm), add 2¼" (5.7cm)
- 9½" (24.1cm), add 2⅜" (6cm)
- 10" (25.4cm), add 2½" (6.4cm)

For every ½" (1.3cm) over 10½" (26.7cm), increase the chart by ⅛" (3.2mm). For every ½" (1.3cm) smaller than 6" (15.2cm), reduce the chart by ⅛" (3.2mm). Round down if the quotient does not fit neatly into the chart.

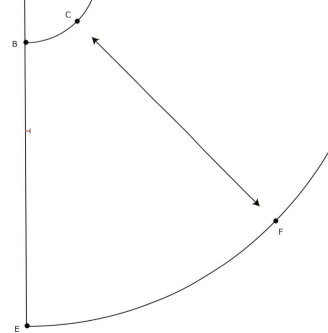

Figure 2.11

EIGHT GORE SKIRT

One pattern piece (*Fig. 2.12*) is drafted and cut eight times. Here is the formula: measurement + ease = X ÷ 8 = Y. Eight gores are common, but if ten gores are desired, divide by ten; if six gores are desired, divide by six; and so on.

> ## Sample Calculations for a Gore Skirt
>
> - Waist: 26 ½" (67.3cm) + ½" (1.3cm) ease = 27" (68.6cm) ÷ 8 = 3 ⅜" (8.6cm)
> - High Hip: 34" (86.4cm) + 1" (2.5cm) ease = 35" (88.9cm) ÷ 8 = 4 ⅜" (11.1cm) (at a depth of 4 ½" [11.4cm])
> - Low Hip: 36 ½" (92.7cm) + 1 ½" (3.8cm) ease = 38" (96.5cm) ÷ 8 = 4 ¾" (12.1cm) (at a depth of 8 ½" [21.6cm])
> - Base: 60" (152.4cm) ÷ 8 = 7 ½" (19.1cm) (designer decides on a base circumference)
>
> It is okay to round up the high hip and low hip if the calculations are in the ¹⁄₁₆" (1.6mm), but do not round up the waist or it will be too big. The high and low hip can handle more ease in exchange for easier math.

1. **AB** = skirt length as desired
2. **AC** = depth of the high hip
3. **AD** = depth of the low hip
4. **EF** = waist calculation centered over **A** (**AE** = **AF**)
5. **GH** = high-hip calculation centered over **C** (**CG** = **CH**)
6. **IJ** = low-hip calculation centered over **D** (**DI** = **DJ**)
7. **KL** = base calculation centered over **B** (**BK** = **BL**)
8. Measure **DB**. Measure **IK** and **JL**. Adjust, and mark **M** and **N** as shown (*Fig. 2.12*), so each line measures as the **DB** length. This will be more pronounced on a wider base because a slanted line will measure longer than a straight line. Redraw the base as shown.
9. Connect **E-G-I-K** and **F-H-J-L**. Fold the pattern on the **AB** line and make sure the side shapes match. Smooth out any peaks at **I** and **J** if needed.
10. Pattern: **E-A-F-H-J-N-B-M-I-G-E**
11. Notch the low hip on both sides of the pattern. Draw the length grainline. Add ½" (1.3cm) seam allowance and a 1" (2.5cm) hem allowance. Drag the notches to the perimeter. Cut (8) self.

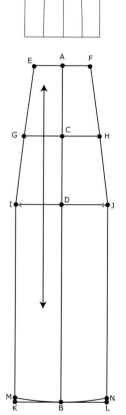

Figure 2.12

EMPIRE, PENCIL LINE, SLIT

For this exercise, combine an empire waistline with a pencil line shape at the base and a slit. Each of these three exercises can be broken out separately or combined with other skirts.

An empire line has a raised waistline 2"–4" (5.1–10.2cm) above the natural waistline. A skirt with an empire waistline is drafted with facings to finish the edge. Find the client's empire height and measurement on the record of measurements and the calculations on the worksheet.

Front

Empire

1. Trace the front sloper, adjust the skirt length as desired, and mark **A**, **B**, **C**, and **D** as shown (*Fig. 2.13*).
2. **AE** = square up for the height of the empire at center front (example: 3" [7.6cm])
3. **CF** = square up for the height of empire at side (also 3" [7.6cm]). Square a line off the high-hip guideline, and draw straight up from the waist to the empire height.
4. **EF** should mimic the shallow curve of **AC**.
5. Mark the waist dart width **G** and **H** as shown.
6. Square a line up from **G** to the empire height and mark **I**.
7. Square a line up from **H** to the empire height and mark **J**.
8. Maintain the waist calculation and the dart width on the empire line at this point.
9. Subtract the front waist calculation from the front empire calculation and note the remainder. For example, if the front waist calculation is 6⅞" (17.5cm) and the front empire calculation is 7⅜" (18.7cm), the remainder is ½" (1.3cm).
10. The remainder is taken from the dart width.
11. **IK** = half the remainder. With the example, half the remainder is ¼" (6.4mm).
12. **JL** = half the remainder as **IK** (example: ¼" [6.4mm])
13. Connect **K-G**. Connect **L-H**.
14. **M** = base of the dart
15. **N** = half **CF**
16. **NO** = ¹⁄₁₆" (1.6mm) to shape the empire side seam. Connect **F-O-C**.
17. **PQ** = draw a line 1" (2.5cm) below the waistline for the base of the facing. The entire facing consists of **E-F-O-C-Q-P-A-E**. It will sit behind the empire as a separate piece to provide stability.

Pencil Line

18. **DR** = come in 1" (2.5cm) from the side seam base for a pencil line shape. The range to come in for a pencil line is 1"–3" (2.5–7.6cm) per quarter panel. Stick to 1" (2.5cm) for shorter skirts,

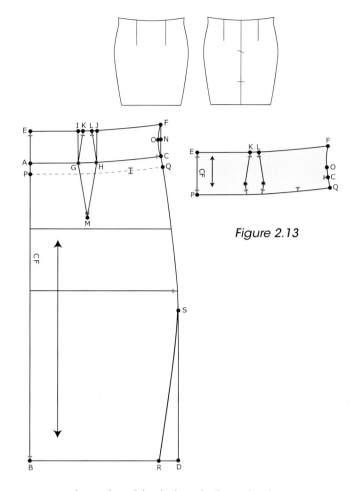

Figure 2.13

2" (5.1cm) when the skirt is just below the knee, and up to 3" (7.6cm) for longer skirts.
19. **S** = mark 2" (5.1cm) down from the low-hip guideline
20. **SR** = connect for the side seam. Smooth out the seam at **S**.
21. Front Pattern: **E-K-L-F-O-C-S-R-B-A-E**, including the dart (**K-G-M-H-L**)
22. Notch the low hip at side. Notch the center-front waist. Notch the waist at side (**C**). Notch the dart legs. Awl-punch the dart ½" (1.3cm) up from the point. Draw a length grainline. Add ½" (1.3cm) seam allowance and a 1" (2.5cm) hem allowance. Drag the notches to the perimeter. Cut (1) self on fold at center front.
23. Front Facing Pattern: **E-K-I-F-O-C-Q-P-A-E**
24. Notch the center-front waist. Notch the waist at side (**C**). Notch the beginning and end of the dart legs. Draw a length grainline. Add ½" (1.3cm) seam allowance. Drag the notches to the perimeter. Cut (1) self on fold at center front and (1) interfacing.

Drafting Tip
The remaining pattern piece below the facing can be cut from lining fabric for a lined skirt.

Back

1. Trace the back sloper. Repeat the instructions for drafting the back empire and pencil line silhouette.

Slit

2. Add a slit at the center back for ease in walking (*Fig. 2.14*).
3. **BT** = 5" (12.7cm) slit height (or longer if desired) at center back. A longer skirt needs a longer slit for ease when taking a step.
4. **BU** = ½" (1.3cm)
5. Connect **T-U**. Adding this additional ½" (1.3cm) makes the slit look straighter and will help it close completely when still.
6. **TV** = 1" (2.5cm) facing
7. **UW** = 1" (2.5cm) facing
8. Connect **T-V-W-U** for the slit facing. Mark a fold line at **TU**.

9. Back Pattern: **E-K-L-F-O-C-S-R-B-U-W-V-T-A-E**, including the dart (**K-G-M-H-L**)
10. Notch the low hip at side. Double notch the low hip at center back. Notch the waist at side (**C**). Notch the dart legs and awl-punch the dart ½" (1.3cm) up from the point. Mark **TU** as a fold line. Notch **U**. Awl-punch **T**. Draw a length grainline. Add ½" (1.3cm) seam allowance and a 1" (2.5cm) hem allowance. Drag the notches to the perimeter. Cut (2) self.
11. Back Facing Pattern: **E-K-I-F-O-C-Q-P-A-E**
12. Notch the waist at side (**C**). Double notch the center-back waist. Notch the beginning and end of the dart legs. Draw a length grainline. Add ½" (1.3cm) seam allowance around the piece. Drag the notches to the perimeter. Cut (2) self and (2) interfacing.

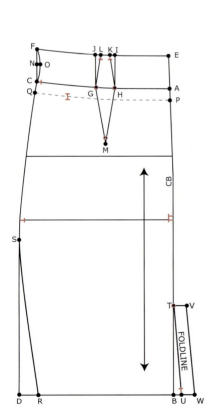

Figure 2.14

Patternmaking Tip:
Shaded pieces should have interfacing for added structure and support.

WRAP SKIRT

A wrap skirt traditionally wraps right over left.

Front

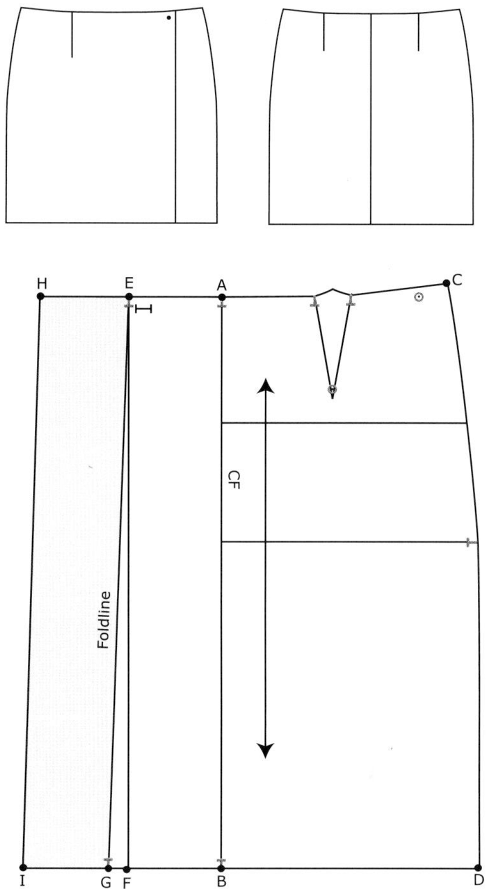

1. Trace the front sloper, adjust the skirt length as desired, and mark **A**, **B**, **C**, and **D** as shown (*Fig. 2.15*).
2. **AE** = front waist calculation, less 2" (5.1cm) for the wrap extension amount. For example, if the front waist calculation is 6⅞" (17.5cm), **AE** is 4⅞" (12.4cm) (6⅞" [17.5cm] − 2" [5.1cm] = 4⅞" [12.4cm]). It is okay to round up or down to whole numbers up for easier math. Square the extension off the center front guideline (**AB**).
3. **BF** = **AE**
4. Square **BF** off the **AB** line.
5. **FG** = ½" (1.3cm). This additional ½" (1.3cm) at the base (**FG**) helps the extension look straight. If it is not added, the extension edge will look slanted. However, if the fabric has a pattern (example: a plaid or a stripe) that will be thrown off by adding the ½" (1.3cm), leave it off.
6. Connect **E-G**.
7. Fold the pattern back at **EG**, and trace **E-A-B-F-G** for the facing. When the skirt swings open, the correct side of the self-fabric should show, not the wrong side.
8. Mark **H** and **I** as shown.
9. Mark the pattern for a button and buttonhole to hold the skirt closed. For example, if using a ¾" (1.9cm) button, mark a ⅞" (2.2cm) long buttonhole, down ¾" (1.9cm) from **E** and starting in ⅜" (1cm) from the **EG** line. The marking for the button should be down ¾" (1.9cm) from the waistline and in 2¾" (7cm) from the side of the skirt. Adjust button placement as needed when fitting the skirt.
10. Pattern: **H-E-A-C-D-B-F-G-I-H**, including the dart
11. Notch the low hip at side. Notch the fold line for the facing (**E** and **G**). Notch the center front (**A**). Notch the dart legs and awl-punch the dart ½" (1.3cm) up from the point. Draw the length grainline. Add ½" (1.3cm) seam allowance and a 1" (2.5cm) hem allowance. Drag the notches to the perimeter. Cut (2) self. Interface the facing (**H-E-G-I-H**) for stability.

Figure 2.15

Drafting Tip:

Never free-hand grainlines. Carefully mark length grainlines parallel to the center front or center back. Cross grainlines should be perpendicular to the center front or center back. Bias grainlines are drawn at a 45-degree angle off the center front or center back.

Back

1. Trace the back sloper and adjust the length as front. Mark **J**, **K**, **L**, and **M** as shown (*Fig. 16*). Other than length, no changes are needed.
2. Pattern: **J-K-M-L-J**
3. Notch the low hip at side. Double notch the low hip at center back. Notch the dart legs and awl-punch the dart ½" (1.3cm) up from the point. Draw a length grainline. Add ½" (1.3cm) seam allowance and a 1" (2.5cm) hem allowance. Drag the notches to the perimeter. Cut (2) self.

> **Design Tip:**
> To cut the back on a fold, straighten the back contouring. Square straight up from the low hip for a straight center back. However, this will increase the waist on the pattern by ⅜" (1cm), as that is the back contouring amount. Increase the back waist dart by ⅜" (1cm). When a dart is increased in width, it should be increased in length. Add 1¼" (3.2cm) to the dart length when increasing the dart width ⅜" (1cm).

INVERTED BOX PLEAT

With an inverted box pleat, the pleat is hidden on the back side of the garment. With a box pleat, the pleat is brought to the correct side of the garment and is more visible.

Front

1. Trace the front sloper, adjust the length as desired, and mark **A**, **B**, **C**, and **D** as shown (*Fig. 2.17*).
2. **E** = height of the pleat at the center front (to the low-hip guideline or as desired)
3. **BF** = ½" (1.3cm) out to help the pleat close properly when standing
4. Connect **E-F**.
5. **EG** = 3" (7.6cm) width of the pleat squared off **EF**
6. **FH** = 3" (7.6cm) width of the pleat at base squared off **EF**
7. Connect **G-H** for the center of the pleat. Fold **EF** to **GH** and trace off the shape at the base.
8. **DI** = ¾" (1.9cm) extension so there is less strain on the pleat when walking
9. **IJ** = blend the extension to the low-hip guideline at the side. If the extension blends smoothly slightly higher than the low-hip guideline, blend to that point instead.
10. Pattern: **A-C-J-I-D-B-F-H-G-E-A**, including the dart
11. Notch the low hip at side. Notch the pleat at **G**, **F**, and **H**. Awl-punch the corner of the pleat (**E**). Notch the dart legs and awl-punch the dart ½" (1.3cm) up from the point. Draw a length grainline parallel to **GH**. Add ½" (1.3cm) seam allowance and a 1" (2.5cm) hem allowance. Drag the notches to the perimeter. Cut (1) self on fold at **GH**.

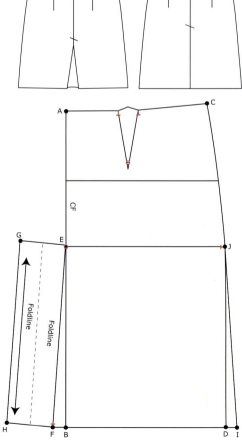

Figure 2.16

Figure 2.17

Drafting Tip:
Pleats will fall straighter and crisper when cut on the length grain.

Back
1. Trace the back sloper (**K-L-M-N**), adjust the length as front (*Fig. 2.18*).
2. **NO** = add a ¾" (1.9cm) extension
3. **OP** = blend the extension to the low hip (or wherever it blends smoothly)
4. Pattern: **K-M-P-O-N-L-K**, including the dart
5. Notch the low hip at side. Double notch the low hip at center back. Notch the dart legs and awl-punch the dart ½" (1.3cm) up from the point. Draw a length grainline. Add ½" (1.3cm) seam allowance and a 1" (2.5cm) hem allowance. Drag the notches to the perimeter. Cut (2) self.

KNIFE PLEATS
Knife pleats are a series of single pleats pressed in the same direction. Knife pleats are drafted with a distance of 1" (2.5cm) and a pleat width of 2" (5.1cm). Distance is what shows. Pleat width is double the distance and is folded behind the distance.

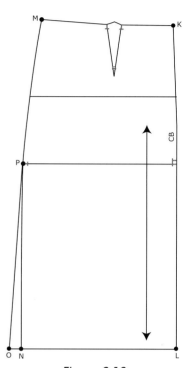

Figure 2.18

Front
1. Trace the front sloper, adjust the skirt length as desired, and mark **A**, **B**, **C**, and **D** as shown (*Fig. 2.19*).
2. **AE** = half the amount of the pleat distance at center front (example: ½" [1.3cm]). Only half the amount of the distance is needed because the skirt will be cut on a center-front fold and will open for the full 1" (2.5cm) distance.
3. **BF** = as **AE**
4. Connect **E-F**.
5. **EG** = full pleat distance (example: 1" [2.5cm])
6. **FH** = **EG**
7. Connect **G-H**.
8. **GI** = **EG**
9. **HJ** = **GI**
10. Connect **I-J**.
11. **CK** = 1½" (3.8cm) for placement of the second dart leg
12. **KL** = dart width as sloper
13. **M** = dart base centered below the **LK** dart width (check the sloper to get the dart length)

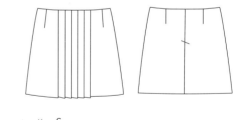

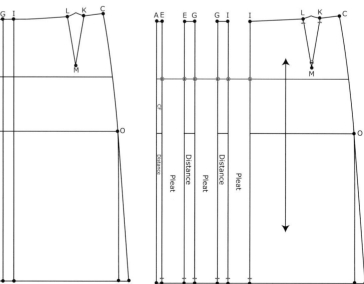

Figure 2.19

or bring the vanishing point to the high-hip guideline. Draw the dart (**LMK**). The dart is moved toward the side seam, so the dart and the pleats are not crowded together.

14. **DN** = ¾" (1.9cm) extension at side
15. **O** = blend the extension toward the low hip
16. Draw a horizontal guideline across a new sheet of pattern paper. When inserting the pleats (Step 17), align the high-hip guideline on the cut pattern pieces with the guideline drawn on the new sheet. This will allow for accurate realigning of the guidelines when folding the pleats.
17. Separate the pattern at **EF** and insert a 2" (5.1cm) pleat. Insert from the high-hip guideline to the base only.
18. Separate the pattern at **GH** and insert a 2" (5.1cm) pleat. Insert from the high-hip guideline to the base only.
19. Separate the pattern at **IJ** and insert a 2" (5.1cm) pleat. Insert from the high-hip guideline to the base only. The open space above the high-hip guideline will be sewn seams. This is done to reduce bulk over the stomach.
20. Pattern: **A-E-G-G-I-I-L-K-C-O-N-D-J-J-H-H-F-B-A**, including the dart
21. 21. Notch the low hip at side. Notch the base of the pleat fold lines (**F**, **H**, and **J**). Awl-punch the pleats on the high hip as shown. Notch the dart legs and awl-punch the dart ½" (1.3cm) up from the point. Draw the length grainline. Add ½" (1.3cm) seam allowance around the piece, including around the openings above the high-hip guideline. Drag the notches to the perimeter. Add a 1" (2.5cm) hem. Cut (1) self on fold at center front.

Back
Trace the back sloper, and adjust the length as front. Use the same instructions as those used in the Inverted Box Pleat—Back exercise (page 45).

LOWERED WAISTLINE
Front
1. Trace the front sloper, adjust the skirt length as desired, and mark **A**, **B**, **C**, and **D** as shown (*Fig. 2.20*).
2. **EF** = lower the waistline following the curve of **AC** (refer to the Skirts Calculation Worksheet)
3. **EG** = find the front lowered-waist calculation on the Worksheet. Measure from **E** to **G** along the lowered-waistline curve. Do not include the dart width. When a waistline is lowered in front, the dart is not included.
4. Blend from **G** to the low hip in a shallow curve. It is okay to cut a little of the high hip off if it makes the line smoother.
5. Pattern: **E-G-D-B-E**
6. Notch the low hip at the side. Draw the length grainline. Add ½" (1.3cm) seam allowance and a 1" (2.5cm) hem. Drag the notches to the perimeter. Cut (1) self on fold at center front.

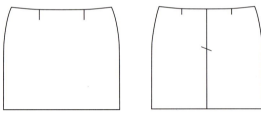

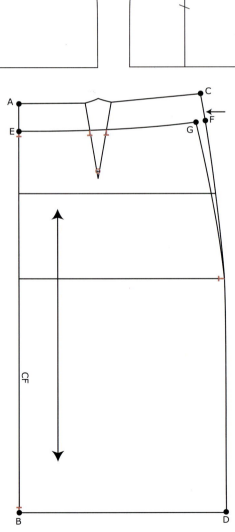

Figure 2.20

Back

1. Trace the back sloper, adjust the skirt length as front, and mark **H**, **I**, **J**, and **K** as shown (*Fig. 2.21*).
2. **LM** = lower the waistline following the curve of **HJ**
3. **LN** = measure for the back lowered-waist calculation. Find the back lowered-waist calculation on the Worksheet. Measure from **L** to **N** along the lowered-waistline curve, keeping the remaining dart width. Take the front dart out, but do not take the back dart out. The back dart is needed for the skirt to fit the sway of the back.
4. Blend from **N** to the low hip in a shallow curve. It is okay to cut a little of the high hip off if it makes the line smoother.
5. Pattern: **L-I-K-N-L**, including the dart
6. Notch the low hip at side and double notch the low hip at center back Notch the dart legs and awl-punch the dart ½" (1.3cm) up from the point. Draw the length grainline. Add ½" (1.3cm) seam allowance and a 1" (2.5cm) hem. Drag the notches to the perimeter. Cut (2) self.

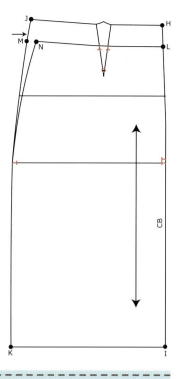

Figure 2.21

Fitting Tip:
Because the lowered waistline is sitting within the deepest part of the sway back, the back waist dart might need to be increased in width during the fitting stage for a snug fit against the waistline.

FACINGS

To clean up the waistline of a skirt, draft either facings or a waistband. Facings give a clean, minimal look while supporting the waistline, so it won't stretch out. Facings only show on the inside of a garment. Use the front and back sloper as the outside or shell of the garment. Combine this exercise with the Lining exercise (page 48).

Front

1. Trace the front sloper (**A-B-C-D**).
2. **AE** = 2" (5.1cm)
3. **CF** = 2" (5.1cm)
4. Connect **E-F** in a shallow curve for the base of the facing (*Fig. 2.22*).
5. Facing: **A-C-F-E**, including the dart if it remains
6. Cut along the **E-F** line and separate the pattern. (Save the bottom of the pattern for the lining.)
7. Fold the remaining waist dart out to reduce bulk.
8. Front Facing Pattern: **A-C-F-E-A**
9. Notch the base along **EF** to differentiate the top of the facing from the bottom. Draw a length grainline. Add ½" (1.3cm) seam allowance. Drag the notches to the perimeter. Cut (1) self on fold at center front. Cut (1) interfacing on fold. Always interface facings.

Vocabulary Tip:
Block fuse means to adhere fusible interfacing to fabric yardage and then cut pattern pieces, rather than fuse each piece individually.

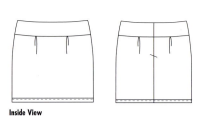
Inside View

Back
1. Repeat the instructions on the back pattern for the back facing (*Fig. 2.22*).
2. Back Facing Pattern: **A-E-F-C-A**
3. Double notch the base along **EF** to differentiate the top of the facing from the bottom. Double notch the center back. Draw the length grainline. Add ½" (1.3cm) seam allowance. Drag the notches to the perimeter. Cut (2) self. Cut (2) interfacing.

LINING
Since lining fabric is often delicate, pleating vertical darts is preferable to sewing the dart. Moving and sitting puts strain on vertical darts, so pleating lets them open and close more easily with wear without tearing apart over time.

Front
1. Front Lining Pattern: **E-F-D-B**
2. Notch the low hip at side (*Fig. 2.23*). Match a notch at the base of the front facing (along **EF**) to the top of the lining pattern (along **EF**). Notch the dart legs to show the pleat. Draw the length grainline. Add ½" (1.3cm) seam allowance and mark a ½" (1.3cm) hem allowance (most linings that hang free have a clean finish hem, which is a double ¼" [6.4mm] fold that is then stitched into place). Drag the notches to the perimeter. Cut (1) lining on fold at center front.

Back
1. Back Lining Pattern: **E-F-D-B**
2. Notch the low hip at side (*Fig. 2.23*). Double notch the low hip at center back. Match the notches at the base of the back facing (along **HI**) to the top of the lining pattern (along **HI**). Notch the dart legs to show the pleat. Draw the length grainline. Add ½" (1.3cm) seam allowance and mark a ½" (1.3cm) hem allowance for a clean finish hem. Drag the notches to the perimeter. Cut (2) lining.

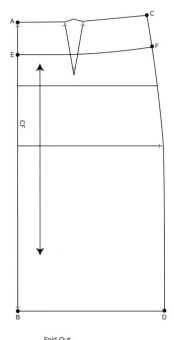
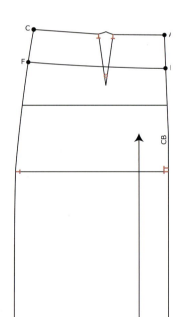
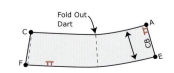

Figure 2.22

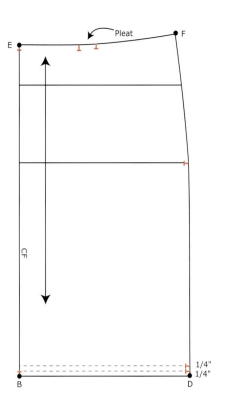
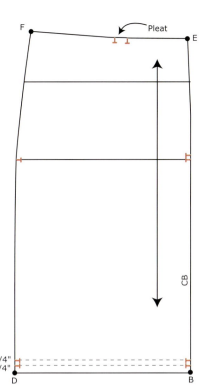

Figure 2.23

BAGGED LINING
Bagged lining means that the bottom of the lining is sewn to the top of the hem.

Front Skirt (outside of the garment)
1. Trace the front sloper, adjust the skirt length, and add a 1½" (3.8cm) hem allowance.

Back Skirt (outside of the garment)
1. Trace the front sloper, adjust the skirt length as front, and add a 1½" (3.8cm) hem allowance.

Front Bagged Lining
1. Trace the front skirt pattern, including the 1½" (3.8cm) hem. Mark **A**, **B**, **C**, and **D** (*Fig. 2.24*).
2. Remove the hem allowance: **E-F-D-B-E**

Vocabulary Tip:
A **jump pleat** is an extra 1" (2.5cm) of lining length, which absorbs the movements of the wearer. Since lining fabric does not have much give and fashion fabric often does, adding a horizontal jump pleat allows the fashion fabric to give a little.

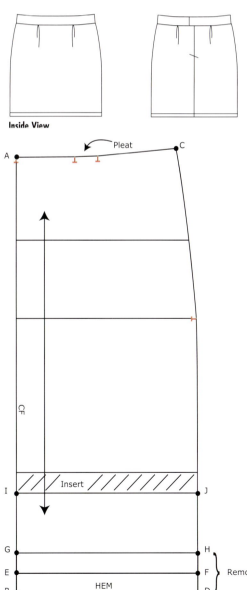

Figure 2.24

4. Remove the area the hem would sit behind: **G-H-F-E-G**
5. Mark a line 3" (7.6cm) up from **GH**, mark **I** and **J**.
6. Cut at **IJ** and insert 1" (2.5cm) across for the jump pleat. Smooth the edges. Mark the dart as a pleat.
7. Front Lining: **A-C-J-H-G-I-A**
8. Notch the low hip at side. Vertically notch the center-front waist on the fabric fold. Notch the pleat. Draw a length grainline. Add ½" (1.3cm) seam allowance, including at the base (because the base of the lining will be sewn to the bottom of the hem allowance). Drag the notches to the perimeter. Cut (1) lining on fold at center front.

Back Bagged Lining

1. Repeat the instructions for the back lining (*Fig. 2.25*).
2. Back Lining: **A-C-J-H-G-I-A**
3. Notch the low hip at side. Double notch the low hip at center back. Notch the pleat. Draw a length grainline. Add ½" (1.3cm) seam allowance, including at the base of the lining (because the base of the lining will be sewn to the bottom of the hem allowance). Drag the notches to the perimeter. Cut (2) lining.

Front Skirt (outside of the garment)

1. Notch the low hip at side. Vertically notch the center-front waist on the fabric fold. Notch the dart legs and awl-punch the dart ½" (1.3cm) above the point. Draw a length grainline. Add ½" (1.3cm) seam allowance, including at the base of the hem (because the base of the hem will be sewn to the bottom of the lining). Drag the notches to the perimeter. Cut (1) self on fold at the center front.

Back Skirt (outside of the garment)

1. Notch the low hip at side. Double notch the low hip at center back. Notch the dart legs and awl-punch the dart ½" (1.3cm) above the point. Draw a length grainline. Add ½" (1.3cm) seam allowance, including at the base of the hem (because the base of the hem will be sewn to the bottom of the lining). Drag the notches to the perimeter. Cut (2) self.

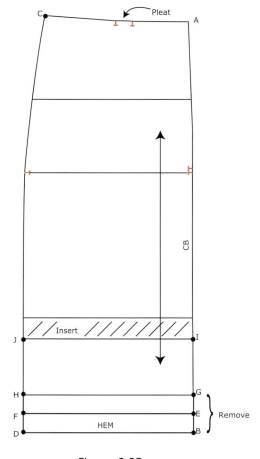

Figure 2.25

Drafting Tip:

The reason we insert 3" (7.6cm) up from the base of the lining pattern rather than just add to the length is to help maintain and match the width of the base on the self-fabric and the lining. The method is not noticeable on a straight skirt but is apparent on any skirt with a pegged base. Only bag linings on straight or pegged skirts. Flared skirt linings should hang free with a clean finish. These instructions also apply to lining dresses, jackets, and coats.

WAISTBAND

A waistband consists of two fabric layers and an interfacing support layer. It can have a seam or fold at the top edge. An extension is drafted on a waistband and closes with a button or hook/eye. A garment with a waistband can open at the front, back, or side (usually the left). This exercise will demonstrate a waistband with a button closure at the center back.

1. **AB** = back waist calculation of the skirt
2. **BC** = front waist calculation of the skirt
3. **CD** = front waist calculation
4. **DE** = back waist calculation
5. **EF** = ¾" (1.9cm) extension (or an extension as the diameter of the button)

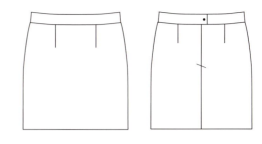

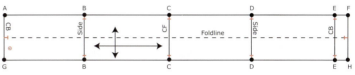

Figure 2.26

Design Tip:
The extension can be an overlap or underlap. It functions the same either way, so the choice is an aesthetic one.

6. **AG** and **FH** = two times the finished width of the waistband. Most waistbands are 1¼" (3.2cm) finished, so **AG** and **AF** should measure 2½" (6.4cm).
7. Drag the **B**, **C**, **D**, and **E** notches down to the **GH** line as shown (*Fig. 2.26*).
8. Pattern: **A-B-C-D-E-F-H-G-A**
9. Mark a fold line in the middle as shown. Notch the fold line. Notch the perimeter of the waistband at **B**, **C**, **D**, and **E** (top and bottom as shown). Mark for the button/buttonhole, snap, or hook/eye closure. Mark a length or cross grainline. Add ½" (1.3cm) seam allowance. Drag the notches to the perimeter. Cut (1) self and (1) interfacing.

Test Your Knowledge

1. Why is the front sloper ½" (1.3cm) wider than the back sloper?

2. Define insertion and extension. Why are extensions half the size of insertions?

3. Is seam allowance added to a center-front fold?

4. Describe a bagged lining and a jump pleat.

5. What is the different between a working pattern and a final pattern?

Bodice slopers are needed as a foundation to draft any upper-body garment. This chapter offers instruction on measuring and drafting a fitted womenswear moulage then adjusting that for a bodice sloper. How to measure and draft a menswear sloper is included. Knit slopers are addressed for both womenswear and menswear.

OBJECTIVES

Upon completion of this chapter, you will be able to

- Understand how to measure for a bodice sloper
- Draft a moulage and a sloper for the female figure
- Develop a sloper for the male figure

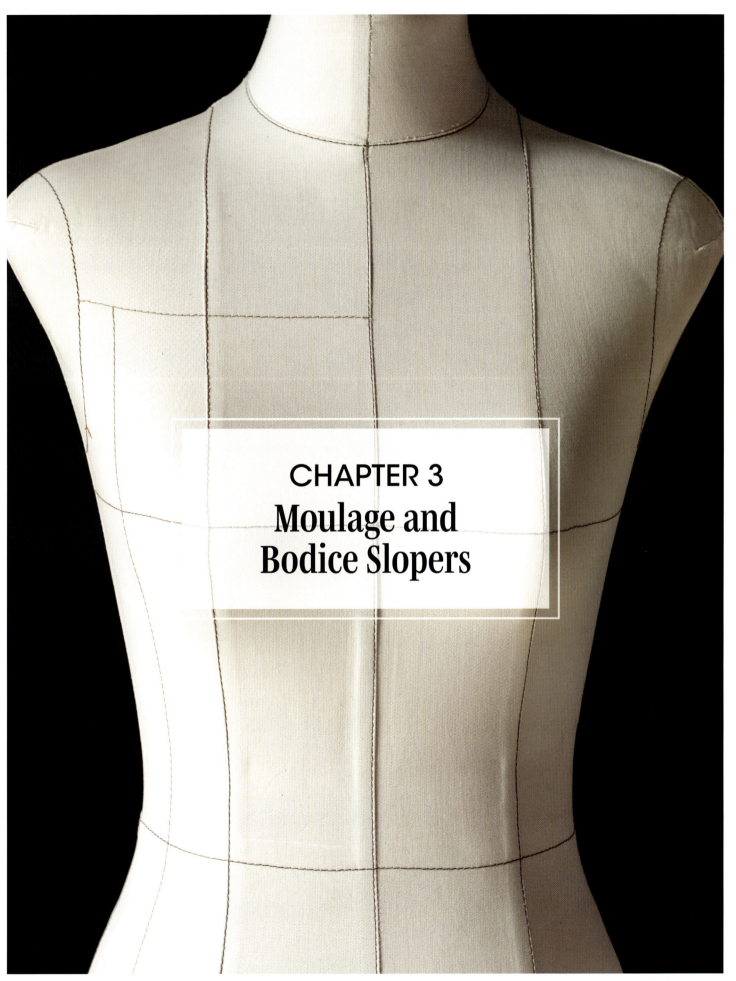

CHAPTER 3
Moulage and Bodice Slopers

Drafting a Moulage for a Feminine Figure

WHAT AND HOW TO MEASURE FOR MOULAGE

Moulage means impression or casting. You will be creating a fabric cast of the figure. Think of moulage as sculpting in fabric.

The model should wear the style of undergarments usually worn for the type of clothing being made. They should stand without shoes, feet about 4" (10.2cm) apart. The model should retain their natural posture throughout the measuring process while looking straight ahead. If the arms need to be moved out of the way, have the model hold their arms out with the elbows at shoulder level.

Start the measuring process by having the model tie a ¼" (6.4mm) width elastic around the natural waistline. To find the natural waistline, have the model bend side-to-side to find where the body creases. Good positioning of the waist elastic is about ½"–1" (1.3–2.5cm) above the top of the navel. Check the position of the elastic frequently while measuring and readjust it if it is rolling up. The elastic is used as a measuring guide. Dress forms have twill tape pinned around the natural waistline, so an elastic is not needed (*Fig. 3.1*).

- **Neck (1):** Locate the center of the dip between the collarbones at the base of the front neck. This will be referred to as the **neck point** in the following instructions. It is helpful to apply a small adhesive dot at the neck point for future measurements. Measure around the base of the neck stem. The tape measure should form a slight teardrop shape at the center-front neck point. Make sure the tape measure is snug. It can be helpful to have the model wear a thin necklace to show where the measurement should be taken at the back and sides of the neck.

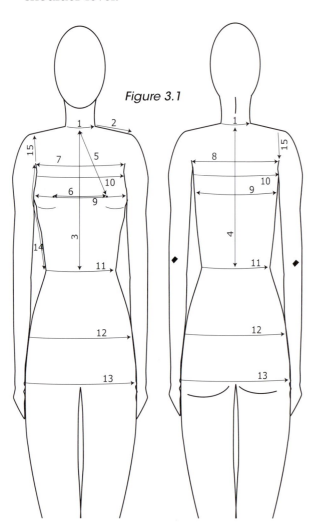

Figure 3.1

Calculation Tip:

The neckline will be divided by six for drafting. Round to the following measurements to make calculating easier:
12" (30.5cm), 12¾" (32.4cm), 13½" (34.3cm), 14¼" (36.2cm), 15" (38.1cm), 15¾" (40cm), 16½" (41.9cm), 17¼" (43.8cm), 18" (45.7cm), etc. Notice that each measuremen grows by ¾" (1.9cm) for easy calculating later.

- **Shoulder (2):** Measure the shoulder from the base of the neck stem to the outside of the collarbone. The end of the collarbone should be in line with the armhole crease.
- **Front Length (3):** Measure from the neck point to the base of the waist elastic. Pull the tape measure taut for a more accurate measurement.
- **Back Length (4):** Have the model bend their head forward with their chin toward their chest. Locate the center of the vertebrae protruding at the base of the back neck stem. It helps to add an adhesive dot here. The model should then lift their head and look forward. Measure from the center of the vertebrae to the base of the waist elastic at the center-back waistline. This measurement is often longer than the front length measurement by 1"–2" (2.5–5.1cm). If that is not the case, double-check the measurement.
- **Figure Length (5):** Ask the model if they are right- or left-handed. Take the figure length measurement on the side they favor because the muscles on that side are usually more developed, and the breast could be slightly higher and bigger. Measure from the neck point to the center of the breast (nipple).
- **Figure Breadth (6):** Measure from the center of one breast to the center of the other (nipple to nipple).

Fitting Tip:

Figuring out cup size in drafting is different from figuring out cup size in bra fitting. This cup-size formula works well, but it can be thrown off by a wide back in smaller cup sizes (A and B). If it seems way off to the model, ask what cup size they generally wear and default to that. Otherwise stick to the formula.

- **Cross Front (7):** Measure from the model's underarm crease to underarm crease. This should be a flat measurement. Do not wrap the tape under the armpit.
- **Cross Back (8):** Measure across the upper back from the model's underarm crease to underarm crease. The cross back is often wider than the cross-front measurement by 1"–2" (2.5–5.1cm). If that is not the case, double-check the measurement.
- **Full Bust (9):** Have the model lift their arms to shoulder level to position the measuring tape. Position the tape measure around the bust with the tape measure slightly higher in back so it passes around the fullest part of the breasts at the side. Dip the tape measure slightly between the breasts. The model should then lower their arms, and the measurement can be taken.
- **Upper-Bust/Cup Size (10):** Measure the circumference of the upper bust directly under the armpits. The tape measure should be snug and above the breast tissue. Note the measurement. Then, subtract this measurement from the full-bust measurement. Every 1" (2.5cm) difference equals a cup size. For example: full-bust circumference 36" (91.4cm) minus upper-bust circumference 34" (86.4cm) is a 2" (5.1cm) difference. A 2" (5.1cm) difference is a B cup. Write cup size as A, B, C, D; for every 1" (2.5cm) over D, write as D + 1" (2.5cm), D + 2" (5.1cm), etc.
- **Waist (11):** Measure the waist around the elastic.
- **High Hip (12):** Measure 4½" (11.4cm) down from the bottom of the waist elastic at the sides. Use adhesive dots to mark the depth of the high hip. Once the side depth is marked, measure the circumference of the high hip, keeping the tape measure level. Note both depth and circumference measurements.

- **Low Hip (13):** Measure 8½" (21.6cm) down from the base of the waist elastic at the sides. If the hips are wider at a point lower than 8½" (21.6cm), use that lower depth and circumference measurement. The hips are at the widest point where the rear end protrudes the most. Using adhesive dots to mark the depth at sides is helpful. Measure around the body, keeping the tape measure level. If the high-hip measurement is larger than the low-hip measurement, use the high-hip measurement for the low hip, so as to not emphasize the high-hip fullness. Note both depth and circumference measurements.
- **Side (14):** Place a ruler level under the armpit. Have the model relax their shoulder. Measure from the top of the ruler through to the base of the waist elastic.
- **Armhole (15):** Measure around the armhole on the side the model favors. The model should raise their arm to get the tape measure positioned, but the arm should be lowered to their side when taking the measurement. The tape measure should be perpendicular to the floor, as if the armpit is in a sling. Take a snug measurement.

Record of Measurements

NAME: _____

DATE: _____

Neck (1): _____

Shoulder (2): _____

Front Length (3): _____

Back Length (4): _____

Figure Length (5):

Figure Breadth (6): _____

Cross Front (7): _____

Cross Back (8): _____

Full Bust (9): _____

Upper Bust (10): _____

Waist (11): _____

High Hip (12): _____ @ a depth of: _____

Low Hip (13): _____ @ a depth of: _____

Side (14): _____

Armhole (15) _____

Practice

Use these sample measurements (fits most Women's size 8 dress forms).

Neck: 14¼" (36.8cm)

Shoulder: 4¾" (12.1cm)

Front Length: 15½" (39.4cm)

Back Length: 17" (43.2cm)

Figure Length: 8½" (21.6cm)

Figure Breadth: 8" (20.3cm)

Cross Front: 12½" (31.8cm)

Cross Back: 13¼" (33.7cm)

Full Bust: 36" (91.4cm)

Upper Bust: 34" (86.4cm)

Waist: 26" (66cm)

High Hip: 34" (86.4cm), @ a depth of: 4½" (11.4cm)

Low Hip: 37" (94cm), @ a depth of: 8½" (21.6cm)

Side: 9" (22.9cm)

Armhole: 16¾" (42.5cm)

CALCULATING THE MEASUREMENTS

The **neck** is divided by six to create a box with two parts for the front, two parts for the back, and one part each for the sides of the neck.

The **shoulder**, **front length**, and **figure length** are all used as measured.

The **back length** has ¾" (1.9cm) taken away to account for the sway of the back.

Because the garment is a mirror image from right to left sides, only half the front and half the back are drafted. Therefore, the **figure length**, **cross front**, and **cross back** are divided by two.

The **bust**, **waist**, **high-hip**, and **low-hip** circumference measurements are each divided by four because only half the front and half the back are drafted. After dividing by four, ¼" (6.4mm) is added to the quotient for the front and ¼" (6.4mm) is subtracted from the quotient for the back. There is more body mass in the front than the back, and this calculation allows the front draft to be wider than the back draft (of course, the low-hip area has more body mass in back, but to keep the side seam straight and consistent, continue with adding to the front and subtracting from the back).

Subtract ¼" (6.4mm) from the **side** measurement to lower it slightly at the deepest part of the armpit.

The **armhole** is divided by two, then ¼" (6.4mm) is subtracted from the front and ¼" (6.4mm) is added to the back. Because bodies tend to have more forward motion with the arms, the shoulders come forward slightly, creating a longer back armhole than front. However, add ¼" (6.4mm) to the front armhole and subtract ¼" (6.4mm) from the back armhole if the front length is longer than the back length.

Moulage Calculation Worksheet

Neck: _____ ÷ 6 = _____

    Front: _____ + ¼" (0.6cm) = _____

    Back: _____ + ½" (1.3cm) = _____

Shoulder: _____ (as measured)

    Front Length: _____ (as measured)

    Back Length: _____ − ¾" (1.9cm) = _____

Front Length: _____ (as measured)

Figure Breadth: _____ ÷ 2 = _____

Cross Front: _____ ÷ 2 = _____

Cross Back: _____ ÷ 2 = _____

Bust: _____ ÷ 4 = _____

    Front: _____ + ¼" (0.6cm) = _____

    Back: _____ − ¼" (0.6cm) = _____

Full Bust: _____ − Upper Bust: _____ = _____

(Every 1" [2.5cm] is a cup size) Cup Size: _____

Waist: _____ ÷ 4 = _____

    Front: _____ + ¼" (0.6cm) = _____

    Back: _____ − ¼" (0.6cm) = _____

High Hip: _____ ÷ 4 = _____ (@ a depth of: 4 ½" [11.4cm])

    Front: _____ + ¼" (0.6cm) = _____

    Back: _____ − ¼" (0.6cm) = _____

Low Hip: _____ ÷ 4 = _____ (@ a depth of: 8 ½" [21.6cm])

    Front: _____ + ¼" (0.6cm) = _____

    Back: _____ − ¼" (0.6cm) = _____

Side: _____ − ¼" (0.6cm) = _____

Armhole: _____ ÷ 2 = _____

    Front: _____ − ¼" (0.6cm) = _____

    Back: _____ + ¼" (0.6cm) = _____

Sample Calculation Worksheet

Neck: 14 1/4" (36.8cm) ÷ 6 = 2 3/8" (6cm)
   Front: 2 3/8" (6cm) + 1/4" (0.6cm) = 2 5/8" (6.7cm)
   Back: 2 3/8" (6cm) + 1/2" (1.3cm) = 2 7/8" (7.3cm)
Shoulder: 4 3/4" (12.1cm), 4 3/4" (12.1cm) (as measured)
   Front Length: 15 1/2" (39.4cm) (as measured)
   Back Length: 17" (43.2cm) − 3/4" (1.9cm) = 16 1/4" (41.3cm)
Front Length: 8 1/2" (21.6cm) (as measured)
Figure Breadth: 8" (20.3cm) ÷ 2 = 4" (10.2cm)
Cross Front: 12 1/2" (31.8cm) ÷ 2 = 6 1/4" (15.9cm)
Cross Back: 13 1/4" (33.7cm) ÷ 2 = 6 5/8" (16.8cm)
Bust: 36" (91.4cm) ÷ 4 = 9" (22.9cm)
   Front: 9" (22.9cm) + 1/4" (0.6cm) = 9 1/4" (23.5cm)
   Back: 9" (22.9cm) − 1/4" (0.6cm) = 8 3/4" (22.2cm)
Full Bust: 36" (91.4cm) − Upper Bust: 34" (86.4cm) = 2" (5.1cm)
(Every 1" [2.5cm] is a cup size) Cup Size: B
Waist: 26" (66cm) ÷ 4 = 6 1/2" (16.5cm)
   Front: 6 1/2" (16.5cm) + 1/4" (0.6cm) = 6 3/4" (17.1cm)
   Back: 6 1/2" (16.5cm) − 1/4" (0.6cm) = 6 1/4" (15.9cm)
High Hip: 34" (86.4cm) ÷ 4 = 8 1/2" (21.6cm) (@ a depth of: 4 1/2" (11.4cm])
   Front: 8 1/2" (21.6cm) + 1/4" (0.6cm) = 8 3/4" (22.2cm)
   Back: 8 1/2" (21.6cm) − 1/4" (0.6cm) = 8 1/4" (21cm)
Low Hip: 37" (94cm) ÷ 4 = 9 1/4" (23.5cm) (@ a depth of: 8 1/2" (21.6cm])
   Front: 9 1/4" (23.5cm) + 1/4" (0.6cm) = 9 1/2" (24.1cm)
   Back: 9 1/4" (23.5cm) − 1/4" (0.6cm) = 9" (22.9cm)
Side: 9" (22.9cm) − 1/4" (0.6cm) = 8 3/4" (22.2cm), 8 3/4" (22.2cm)
Armhole: 16 3/4" (42.5cm) ÷ 2 = 8 3/8" (21.3cm)
   Front: 8 3/8" (21.3cm) − 1/4" (0.6cm) = 8 1/8" (20.6cm)
   Back: 8 3/8" (21.3cm) + 1/4" (0.6cm) = 8 5/8" (21.9cm)

SETTING UP THE GUIDELINES

Set up the following guidelines to draft a moulage. It is helpful to use the straight edge of the pattern paper as the center front and center back. Go over the guidelines in red.

Front Moulage Guidelines

1. **Waist Guideline:** Perpendicular to the center front (see *Fig.* 3.2 for the location of the center front) and approximately 10" (25.4cm) up from the bottom of the paper, draw a waist guideline the width of the **front low-hip calculation** (not the front waist calculation).

2. **High-Hip Guideline:** Perpendicular to the center front, draw the high-hip guideline 4½" (11.4cm) down from the waist guideline. The guideline should measure as the **front low-hip calculation** (not the front high-hip calculation).

3. **Low-Hip Guideline:** Perpendicular to the center front, draw the low-hip guideline 8½" (21.6cm) down (or as measured) from the high-hip guideline. The guideline should measure as the **front low-hip calculation**. Close the side to form a rectangle.

4. **Front Length:** Mark the front length measurement up from the waist guideline on the center front. Perpendicular to the center front, draw a front length guideline of 4" (10.2cm) (standard length for all).

5. **Bust:** The bust guideline should be drawn perpendicular to the center front at half the front length measurement. For example, if the front length measures 15½" (39.4cm), the bust guideline is drawn 7¾" (19.7cm) up from the waist guideline and down from the front length guideline. The width of the guideline is as the **front bust calculation**.

6. **Cross Front:** The cross-front guideline should be drawn perpendicular to the center front at 3" (7.6cm) down from the front length guideline. The guideline should measure 10" (25.4cm) (standard length for all).

Back Moulage Guidelines

7. **Waist Guideline:** Perpendicular to the center back (see *Fig.* 3.2 for the location of the center back) and approximately 10" (25.4cm) up from the bottom of the paper, draw a waist guideline the width of the **back low-hip calculation** (not the back waist calculation).

8. **High-Hip Guideline:** Perpendicular to the center back, draw the high-hip guideline 4½" (11.4cm) down from the waist guideline. The guideline should measure as the **back low-hip calculation** (not the back high-hip calculation).

9. **Low-Hip Guideline:** Perpendicular to the center back, draw the low-hip guideline 8½" (21.6cm) down (or as front) from the high-hip guideline. The guideline should measure as the **back low-hip calculation**. Close the side to form a rectangle.

10. **Back Length:** Mark the back length measurement up from the waist guideline on the center back. Perpendicular to the center back, draw a back length guideline of 10" (25.4cm) (standard length for all).

11. **Bust:** The bust guideline should be drawn perpendicular to the center back at half the back length measurement. The width of the guideline is as the **back bust calculation**.

12. **Cross Back:** Divide the back length measurement into quarters. The cross-back guideline is drawn perpendicular to the center back and down one-quarter of the back length measurement from the back length guideline. For example, if the back length measurement is 16" (40.6cm), with one-quarter of 16" (40.6cm) being 4" (10.2cm), the guideline should be drawn 4" (10.2cm) down from the back length guideline. The guideline should measure 10" (25.4cm) (standard length for all).

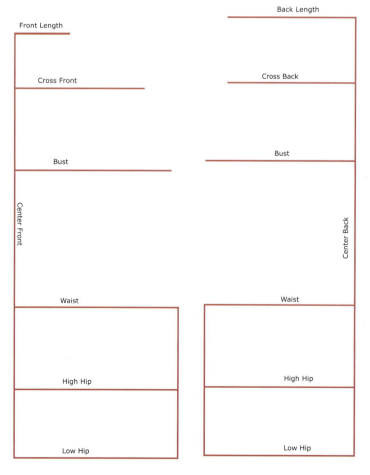

Figure 3.2

DRAFTING THE FRONT

Draft on top of the front guidelines. Note that the instructions cycle through the alphabet twice: first with uppercase letters, then with lowercase letters. Write in letters, measurements, and calculations as you draft to make it easier to double-check the work later.

Accuracy is important when drafting a moulage. Since all the measurements and calculations tie into one another, even a slight error could alter the pattern. Work carefully (*Fig. 3.3*).

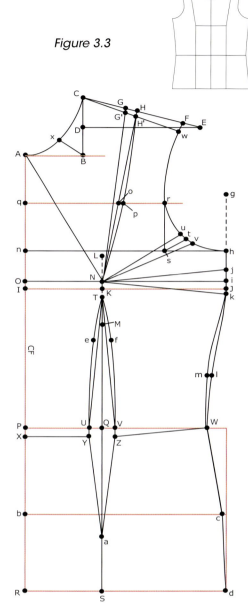

Figure 3.3

1. **AB** = front neck calculation on the front length guideline
2. **BC** = **AB** plus ⅛" (3.2mm)
3. **D** = half of **BC**
4. **DE** = 6" (15.2cm) guideline squared off **BC**
5. Connect **C-E**.
6. **CF** = shoulder width plus dart width as it falls on the **CE** line
7. **CG** = half the shoulder width (not including the dart)
8. **GH** = shoulder dart width (see Shoulder Dart Width Chart)
9. **HF** = remainder of the shoulder width
10. Check that **CG** equals **HF**.
11. **I** = bust guideline on the center-front line
12. **IJ** = front bust calculation (as the guideline)

Shoulder Dart Width Chart

- Use a ⅜" (1cm) dart width for an A cup.
- Use a ½" (1.3cm) dart width for a B cup.
- Use a ⅝" (1.6cm) dart width for a C cup.
- Use a ¾" (1.9cm) dart width for a D or larger cup

13. **IK** = half the figure breadth measurement marked on the bust guideline (**IJ**). The measurement is already halved on the calculation worksheet. Note: This is half the **figure breadth** measurement, not half the front bust calculation.
14. **LM** = square a 6" (15.2cm) guideline off **IJ** at **K**. The guideline should be 3" (7.6cm) above **K** (**L**) and 3" (7.6cm) below **K** (**M**). Draw as a dotted line.
15. **AN** = figure length measurement as it falls on the **LM** guideline. Lengthen the **LM** guideline if necessary. **N** is the high-bust point corresponding to the center of the breast. (**N** can be above, below, or directly on the bust guideline depending on the figure.)
16. **NO** = draw a line back to the center front from **N**, squaring off **LM**. Make sure **NO** is perpendicular to the center front guideline. **NO** should equal half the figure breadth.
17. **P** = waist guideline on the center-front line
18. **PQ** = as the **ON** measurement on the waist guideline
19. **R** = low-hip guideline at center front
20. **RS** = as the **ON** measurement on the low-hip guideline

Front Waist Dart Width Chart

If in between, round down.

- If the difference between the **full**-waist and low-hip measurements (with ease) is 14"–16" (35.6–40.6cm), use a 1½" (3.8cm) dart width.
- If the difference is 10"–13" (25.4–33cm), use a 1¼" (3.2cm) dart width.
- If the difference is 8"–9" (20.3–22.9cm), use a 1" (2.5cm) dart width.
- If the difference is 7" (17.8cm) or less, use a ¾" (1.9cm) dart width.

Take the difference between the full-waist and low-hip measurements with ease, not the difference between the waist and hip calculations.

21. Connect **N-Q-S**. **NQS** should be parallel to the center front.
22. **NT** = down ¾" (1.9cm) along the **NQS** line
23. **UV** = waist dart centered over **Q** (see Front Waist Dart Width Chart)
24. Make sure the dart is centered off **Q**. **UQ** should equal **QV**.
25. Measure **PU**. Subtract the **PU** measurement from the front waist calculation. For example, if the front waist calculation is 6¾" (17.1cm) and **PU** measures 3⅜" (8.6cm), that leaves 3⅜" (8.6cm) of the front waist calculation remaining.
26. **VW** = remainder of the front waist calculation. Double-check that **PU** + **VW** equals the front waist calculation. Do not include the dart width in the calculation because that will be sewn out.
27. **PX** = ½" (1.3cm) waist shaping
28. **UY** = ½" (1.3cm) waist shaping. **Y** should be directly under **U**.
29. **VZ** = ½" (1.3cm) waist shaping. **Z** should be directly under **V**.
30. Connect **X-Y** and **Z-W** for the waist shaping.
31. Connect **U-Y** and **V-Z** to maintain the dart width through the waist shaping.
32. **Sa** = 3" (7.6cm) up along the **NQS** line
33. Connect **Y-a** for the bottom of the waist dart.
34. Connect **Z-a** for the bottom of the waist dart.
35. **b** = high-hip guideline on the center-front line
36. **bc** = front high-hip calculation. Do not include the dart width that falls on the guideline because it will be sewn out. Don't let **c** fall outside of the block. Sacrificing a little of the high-hip measurement is okay. The waist and low-hip measurements are more important. It is okay is **c** is on the block.
37. **Rd** = front low-hip calculation
38. Connect **W-c-d** for the side shape.
39. Connect **T-U** for the top of the waist dart.
40. Connect **T-V** for the top of the waist dart.
41. At one-third down from **T**, bow out the dart legs **TU** and **TV** ⅜" (1cm). Mark **e** and **f**. Draw the new dart legs **T-e-U** and **T-f-V**. Bowing out the dart legs will give a tighter fit through the rib cage.
42. **Jg** = square a 5" (12.7cm) dotted guideline up from **J** off **IJ**
43. Add the side measurement to a side dart measurement. For example, if the side measurement is 9" (22.9cm) and the model is

> ### Side Dart Width Chart
> - Use a ¾" (1.9cm) dart width for an A cup.
> - Use a 1" (2.5cm) dart width for a B cup.
> - Use a 1¼" (3.2cm) dart width for a C cup.
> - Use a 1½" (3.8cm) dart width for a D cup.
>
> **For every cup size over D (as in D + 1" [2.5cm], D + 2" [5.1cm], etc.), add an additional ⅛" (3.2mm) to a 1½" (3.8cm) dart.**
>
> - Use a 1⅝" (4.1cm) dart width for a D + 1" (2.5cm) cup.
> - Use a 1¾" (4.4cm) dart width for a D + 2" (5.1cm) cup.
> - Use a 1⅞" (4.8cm) dart width for a D + 3" (7.6cm) cup.

a B cup (1" [2.5cm] side dart), add 9" (22.9cm) + 1" (2.5cm) for a 10" (25.4cm) side (see Side Dart Width Chart).

44. **Wh** = draw a temporary side line equaling the side measurement plus the dart width from **W**. Place the ruler at **W** and tilt it until it reaches the **Jg** line. Mark **h** on the **Jg** dotted guideline.

45. **i** = extend the **ON** line until it meets the side line (**Wh**). Make sure **i** is directly under **h**. Having **i** directly under **h** will reduce pulling at the side seam by giving more room to models with more full figures.

46. **ij** = half the side dart measurement. For example, if the side dart measures 1" (2.5cm), **ij** should equal ½" (1.3cm).

47. **ik** = half the side dart measurement as **ij**

48. Connect **N-j**.

49. Connect **N-k**. Measure the dart leg **Nj**. Measure the dart leg **Nk**. Extend at **k** so **Nk** equals **Nj**. Check that the **hjik** points are in a straight line.

50. **l** = 3" (7.6cm) up from **W** along the side shape

51. **lm** = ⅛" (3.2mm) in to further shape the side

52. Connect **W-m-k-i-j-h** for the final side line. The line might look awkward, but it will smooth out once the side dart is folded out. Measure the side not including the dart width. Adjust down at **h** slightly if necessary.

53. **hn** = square a line toward the center front. The **hn** guideline should be perpendicular to the center front, and it should be marked as the final bust guideline. The bust guideline follows the base of the underarm.

54. Connect **G-N-H** for the shoulder dart.

55. **o** = mark **o** where the **HN** dart leg intersects the cross-front guideline

56. **op** = ⅛" (3.2mm)

57. Connect **H-p-N** to shape this shoulder dart leg to further contour to the dip under the collarbone.

58. **q** = cross-front guideline on the center-front line

59. **qr** = cross-front calculation. Do not include the dart width when measuring because it will be sewn out

60. **rs** = square down from the **qr** line until it falls on the **nh** guideline. A right angle should be formed by **rsh**. To draw a smooth curve in the lower part of the armhole, the distance between **r** and **s** should be at least 2" (5.1cm). If the distance between **rs** needs to increase, lower the top of the side seam at **h** as much as ½" (1.3cm). If still more

distance is needed, raise the cross-front guideline until **rs** measures 2" (5.1cm).

61. **st** = 1" (2.5cm) guideline at a 45-degree angle

62. Draw in the armhole curve by connecting **h-t-r-F**.

63. **uv** = armhole dart width (see Armhole Dart Width Chart)

64. Connect **u-N-v** for the armhole dart. Center the dart over **t**.

65. Measure **F-r-u** and **v-h**, excluding the dart width because it will be sewn out.

66. Lower or raise **F** to get the correct armhole calculation (excluding the dart width), and mark the new shoulder depth (or height) **w**.

Armhole Dart Width Chart

- Use a ⅜" (1cm) dart width for an A cup.
- Use a ½" (1.3cm) dart width for a B cup.
- Use a ⅝" (1.6cm) dart width for a C cup.
- Use a ¾" (1.9cm) dart width for a D cup.

For every cup size over D, add an additional ¼" (6.4mm) to a ¾" (1.9cm) dart.

- Use a 1" (2.5cm) dart width for a D + 1" (2.5cm) cup.
- Use a 1¼" (3.2cm) dart width for a D + 2" (5.1cm) cup.
- Use a 1½" (3.8cm) dart width for a D + 3" (7.6cm) cup, etc.

Drafting Tip:

It is common to have to adjust the end of the shoulder up or down, but there are limits.
The shoulder can only be raised a maximum of ½" (1.3cm) and lowered a maximum of 1¼" (3.2cm).
If the armhole needs to be raised ¾" (1.9cm), raise it ½" (1.3cm) and let the remaining ¼" (6.4mm) go.
If the armhole needs to be dropped 1½" (3.8cm), drop 1¼" (3.2cm) and let the remaining ¼" (6.4mm) go.
Note what was dropped and it could be added to the back armhole later.

---

67. **Cw** = draw the new shoulder slope. Recenter the shoulder dart if necessary and mark **G'** and **H'** as the dart legs fall on the **Cw** line. Check that the shoulder dart legs measure the same and raise at **H'** slightly as needed.

68. **Bx** = 1¼" (3.2cm) guideline at a 45-degree angle

69. Connect **C-x-A** to shape the neckline.

70. Recheck all measurements on the draft and adjust as necessary. Remember to exclude dart widths when checking except for the dart widths falling on the bustline (**nh**). Measure straight through those.

DRAFTING THE BACK

Draft on top of the back guidelines. Record the measurements and calculations on the draft (*Fig.* 3.4).

1. **AB** = back neck calculation on the back length guideline
2. **BC** = 1⅛" (2.9cm)
3. **CD** = shoulder width plus dart width as front. **D** should fall on the back length guideline.
4. **CE** = half the shoulder width
5. **EF** = dart width as front
6. **FD** = half the shoulder width
7. **CE** should equal **FD**.
8. **G** = low-hip guideline on the center back line
9. **H** = waist guideline on the center back line
10. **I** = cross-back guideline on the center back line
11. **HJ** = ⅜" (1cm) for back contouring
12. **HK** = 7" (17.8cm) from **H** along the center back, or mark **K** 1½" (3.8cm) up from **G**
13. Connect **I-J** for the new upper center back shape.
14. **IL** = cross-back calculation on the guideline
15. **M** = bust guideline on the new center back line
16. **MN** = back bust calculation
17. **JO** = half the back waist calculation or 4" (10.2cm), whichever is smaller. Maxing out at 4" (10.2cm) will give a flattering V shape to the back seamlines.
18. **OP** = waist dart width as front less ⅜" (1cm). The waist dart width is reduced by ⅜" (1cm) because of the back contouring (**HJ**). Back waist contouring of ⅜" (1cm) and the back dart width should add up to the front dart width. For example, if using a 1¼" (3.2cm) front waist dart, use a ⅞" (2.2cm) back waist dart (⅞" [2.2cm] + ⅜" [1cm] = 1¼" [3.2cm]). This adjustment allows for the

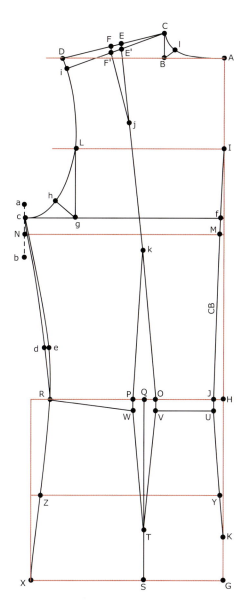

Figure 3.4

same side shape on the front and back (see Back Dart Width Chart, page 33).

19. **Q** = center of the waist dart width
20. Measure **JO**. Subtract the **JO** measurement from the back waist calculation.
21. **PR** = the remainder of the back waist calculation. Make sure **JO** plus **PR** equals the back waist calculation.
22. Measure **HQ**.
23. **GS** = **HQ** measurement
24. **S** should be directly under **Q**.
25. Connect **Q-S**.
26. **ST** = 3" (7.6cm) up along **QS**
27. **JU** = ½" (1.3cm) for waist shaping. **U** should be directly under **J**.
28. Connect **U-K**.
29. **OV** = ½" (1.3cm) for waist shaping. **V** should be directly under **O**.
30. **PW** = ½" (1.3cm) for waist shaping. **W** should be directly under **P**.
31. Connect **U-V** and **W-R** for the waist shaping.
32. Connect **V-T-W** for the bottom of the waist dart.
33. **GX** = back low-hip calculation
34. **Y** = back high-hip guideline as it falls on the **UK** line
35. **YZ** = back high-hip calculation. Do not include the dart width that falls on the guideline because it will be sewn out. Don't let **Z** fall outside of the block. Sacrificing a little of the high-hip measurement is okay. The waist and low-hip measurements are more important. It is okay is **Z** is on the block.
36. Connect **R-Z-X** for the side shape.
37. Square a 4" (10.2cm) dotted guideline off **MN** at **N** and mark **a** and **b**.
38. Mark 2" (5.1cm) above **N** (**a**) and 2" (5.1cm) below **N** (**b**).
39. **Rc** = side measurement as it falls on the **ab** guideline (no side dart in back)
40. **Rd** = 3" (7.6cm) up along the **Rc** line
41. **de** = in ⅛" (3.2mm) to shape the side
42. Connect **c-e-R**. Remeasure the side shape of **c-e-R** and adjust at **c** as needed.
43. **cf** = square a line toward the center back from **c**. The **cf** line should be marked as the new bust guideline. The **cf** line should measure as the back bust calculation. Adjust at **c** as necessary.
44. Square a line down from the cross-back guideline (**IL**) at **L** until it meets the **cf** line. Mark **g**.
45. **gh** = 1" (2.5cm) guideline at a 45-degree angle
46. Connect **D-L-h-c** for the back armhole.
47. Measure **DLhc** and lower or raise **D** to get the back armhole calculation. Just like in front, raise only as much as ½" (1.3cm) and lower only as much as 1¼" (3.2cm). If measurement was dropped from the front armhole, it can be added to the back armhole measurement.
48. **i** = adjusted end of shoulder
49. **Ci** = draw the new shoulder slope
50. Recenter the dart if necessary and mark the legs **E'** and **F'** as they fall on the **Ci** line.
51. Connect **E'-O**.
52. **E'j** = 3½" (8.9cm) for the length of the shoulder dart (first leg of the dart)
53. **F'j** = 3½" (8.9cm) (second leg of the dart). Adjust as needed at **F'** so **F'j** measures as **E'j**.
54. **k** = 1" (2.5cm) below the new bust guideline as it falls on the **E'O** line
55. Connect **k-P** for the top of the waist dart.
56. **Bl** = ½" (1.3cm) guideline for shaping the back neckline at a 45-degree angle
57. Connect **A-l-C** for the back neckline.
58. Recheck all measurements and adjust as needed. Remember to exclude the dart widths when checking the waist and shoulder.

Front and Back Patterns

1. True the front and back patterns at the neck, shoulder, base of the armhole, and along the sides.
2. Trace the front pattern (*Fig. 3.5*). (Never cut up the primary moulage pattern. It is easier to make changes if it is kept intact.) Trace the center-front panel: **A-x-C-G'-N-T-e-U-Y-a-S-R-b-X-P-I-O-n-q-A**
3. Cut away the waist shaping so the pattern is in two pieces. Cut along **ON**, hinging at **N**, and open for a center front bust dart. A center front bust dart helps to contour between the breasts. In addition, the dart seam should point to the center of the breast, which will show whether the position of the breast cup is correct (see Center-Front Bust Dart Width Chart).

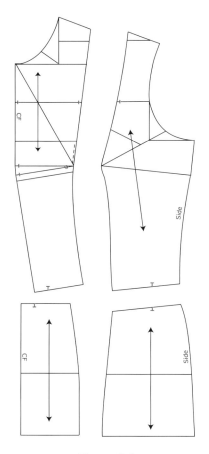

Figure 3.5

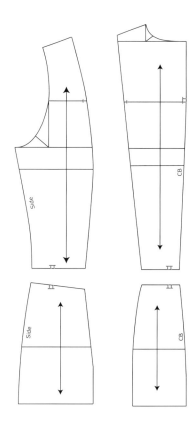

Figure 3.6

Center-Front Bust Dart Width Chart

- Use a ⅜" (1cm) dart width for an A cup.
- Use a ½" (1.3cm) dart width for a B cup.
- Use a ⅝" (1.6cm) dart width for a C cup.
- Use a ¾" (1.9cm) dart width for a D or larger cup.

4. Trace the front side panel:
H'-w-r-u-v-h-j-k-m-W-c-d-S-a-Z-V-f-T-N-p-H'

5. Fold out the armhole dart. Fold out the side dart. Cut away the waist shaping so the pattern is in two pieces.

6. Notch the cross front. Notch the waist, showing how the waist seam should sew together. Notch the legs of the center front bust dart. Mark the apex of the dart with a drill hole ½" (1.3cm) away and in the dart bulk.

7. Draw the grainlines perpendicular to the high-hip guideline on the pieces below the waist. Draw a grainline parallel to the upper center front on the center-front panel. Draw a grainline perpendicular to the waist on the front side panel.

8. Add 1" (2.5cm) seam allowance at the shoulder. Add ½" (1.3cm) seam allowance everywhere else. Drag the notches to the perimeter.

9. Cut (2) self of each piece.

10. Trace the center-back panel (*Fig. 3.6*):
A-l-C-E'-j-k-O-V-T-S-G-K-Y-U-J-M-f-I-A

11. Cut away the waist shaping so the pattern is in two pieces.

12. Trace the back side panel:
F'-i-L-h-c-e-R-Z-X-S-T-W-P-k-j-F'

13. 13. Cut away the waist shaping so the pattern is in two pieces.

14. Notch the cross back. Notch the waist, showing how the waist seam should sew together.

15. Draw grainlines perpendicular to the high-hip guideline on the pieces below the waist. Draw grainlines perpendicular to the cross-back guideline on the upper pieces.

16. Add 1" (2.5cm) seam allowance down the center back and along the shoulder seam. Add ½" (1.3cm) seam allowance everywhere else. Drag the notches to the perimeter.

17. Cut (2) self of each piece.

Drafting a Knit Bodice Sloper for the Female Figure

1. Take the same measurements, excluding figure length, figure breadth, and upper bust.
2. Subtract 2" (5.1cm) from the bust, waist, high-hip, and low-hip circumferences.
3. Subtract 1" (2.5cm) from the neck-circumference, front-length, cross-front, cross-back, side, and armhole measurements.
4. Subtract 2" (5.1cm) from the back length measurement.
5. Subtract ¾" (1.9cm) from the shoulder measurement.
6. Recalculate using the reduced measurements.
7. Draft the front and back, skipping any references to darts, waist shaping, and back contouring.
8. Trace, but no need to cut the front and back into multiple pattern pieces.
9. Cut both the front and back on a center fold. Sew and test the fit in a stable knit, such as a double knit.
10. Once the fit is finalized, put it on tag to create a knit bodice sloper. Option: Add the side dart in the front for a better fit at the bust. Also, adding in back contouring will give a better fit down the center back, but it will force a center-back seam.

Tips:

- **Seam Allowance Tip:** Adding 1" (2.5cm) seam allowance at the shoulders gives more fabric leeway to adjust the slant of the shoulder seam while fitting. Adding 1" (2.5cm) down the center back makes it easier to pin the seamline.
- **Fitting Tip:** Staystitch around the neckline and armhole on the seamlines. Then, trim the seam allowance off at the neck and armholes before fitting. If the seam allowance at the neck and armholes is not trimmed off to the staystitch, the moulage will ride up above the bust, greatly affecting the fit. Staystitch the center-back seam to show where to pin it closed (do not trim the seam allowance down the center back).

DRAFTING A SLOPER FROM MOULAGE

Ease is added to the moulage to create the bodice sloper. While not skintight like moulage, the sloper will be a close-fitting garment. Trace the moulage and adjust the areas noted (*Fig. 3.7*).

Why not go straight to sloper and skip the step of making a close-fitting moulage? Because it is important to learn how to fit the contours of the body. These skills are needed when drafting bridal, evening gowns, corsets, bras, knits, and garments made from stretch woven fabrics.

Front Sloper

1. Lower the center-front neck ¼" (6.4mm).
2. Bring the high-neck point away from the neck ¼" (6.4mm). Extend along the existing shoulder slope. Redraw the neckline squaring for ½" (1.3cm) at the center-front neck and ⅛" (3.2mm) at the high-neck point.
3. Extend the end of shoulder ¼" (6.4mm) out and ¹⁄₁₆" (1.6mm) up. Draw a new shoulder slope, recentering the dart while keeping the original dart width. The shoulder dart leg toward the armhole should be straightened, but remember the option of bowing out the dart leg for a tighter fit.
4. Extend the cross front ⅛" (3.2mm).
5. Lower the base of the armhole ½" (1.3cm). Redraw the bust guideline from the lowered base of the armhole toward the center front. Make sure the new bust guideline is perpendicular to the center front.
6. Extend the bust at side ⅜" (1cm). Redraw the armhole from the extended end of shoulder to the cross front to the new base of the armhole. Square the end of shoulder for at least 1" (2.5cm). Flatten the underarm at the bust for ½" (1.3cm).
7. Extend the waist at side ⅜" (1cm).
8. Extend the high hip ⅜" (1cm).
9. Extend the low hip at side ⅜" (1cm).
10. Draw the new side shape from the underarm to base. Square the low hip at side for 1" (2.5cm). Follow the shape of the original side. Bring the side dart legs out to the side seam but adjust the dart width back to its original moulage width.
11. Mark the high and low bust points.
12. Draw a line from the high figure point to the center front.
13. Straighten the waist dart legs to show the option of using straight legs on the waist dart for a looser fit, and include the bowed-out legs for a more fitted bodice.
14. Mark the waist-shaping depth.

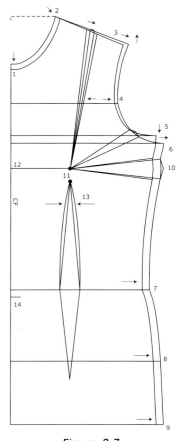

Figure 3.7

Back Sloper

1. Note the center-back neck.
2. Straighten the center back, but keep the line showing back contouring. This will show the two options of having a garment with a center-back fold or a center-back seam.
3. Bring the high-neck point away from the neck ¼" (6.4mm). Extend along the existing shoulder slope. Redraw the neckline squaring for at least ½" (1.3cm) at the center-back neck and ⅛" (3.2mm) at the high-neck/shoulder point.
4. Extend the end of shoulder ¼" (6.4mm) out and ¹⁄₁₆" (1.6mm) up. Draw a new shoulder slope, recentering the dart while keeping the original dart width. Mark for the dart, but don't draw it in yet.
5. Extend the cross back ¼" (6.4mm).
6. Lower the base of the armhole ½" (1.3cm) by squaring straight down, rather than following the shape of the side seam. Redraw the bust guideline from the lowered base of the armhole toward the center back. Make sure the new bust guideline is perpendicular to the center back.
7. Extend the bust at side ⅜" (1cm). Redraw the armhole from the extended end of shoulder to the cross back to the new base of the armhole. Square the end of shoulder for at least 1" (2.5cm) at the end of the shoulder. Flatten the underarm at the bust for ½" (1.3cm).
8. Extend the waist at side ⅜" (1cm).
9. Extend the high hip ⅜" (1cm).
10. Extend the low hip at side ⅜" (1cm). Draw the new side shape from the underarm to base. Follow the shape of the original side. Square at the low hip at side for 1" (2.5cm).
11. Connect the first leg of the shoulder dart with the first leg of the waist dart. Mark 3½" (8.9cm) down from the shoulder for the base of the shoulder dart. Draw the second leg of the shoulder dart. Make sure both legs equal 3½" (8.9cm) in length by adjusting the second leg at the shoulder. Mark the top of the waist dart at 1" (2.5cm) below the bust guideline, then draw the remainder of the dart, keeping the original width on the waist guideline, and the original length below the waist guideline.
12. Mark the waist-shaping depth.

Check: Make sure the width of the back neckline is at least ¼" (6.4mm) or wider than the width of the front neckline. (See horizontal dotted lines on the front and back slopers.) The back neckline should be slightly wider to avoid gaping at the center front (*Fig. 3.8*).

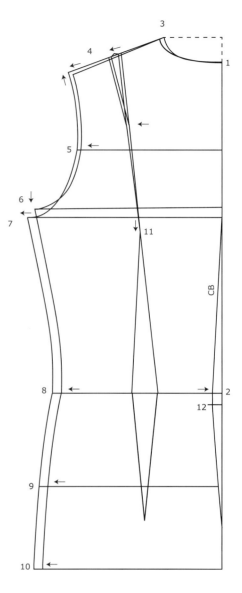

Figure 3.8

Truing Tip:

It is important to have squared edges on a sloper. Squaring edges helps the connection points between front and back pattern align more smoothly. At the center-front neck and center-back neck, square for ½" (1.3cm); square off the shoulder at the front and back high-neck/shoulder points for ⅛" (3.2mm); square off the end of shoulder down the armhole for at least 1" (2.5cm) (move the cross front or back in or out slightly for a smooth shape as needed); the base of the armholes should be flat for ½" (1.3cm) on the front and back; the front and back low hip base at side should square for 1" (2.5cm).

TRANSFERRING THE SLOPER TO TAG

Once the sloper fit is finalized, trace it onto a tag. The sloper is not a garment. It is a template. Think of the sloper as having up to 70 percent of the work done. The remaining 30 percent is about design, fabric choice, adjusting fit, silhouette, and details to reflect the designer's sketch (*Fig. 3.9*).

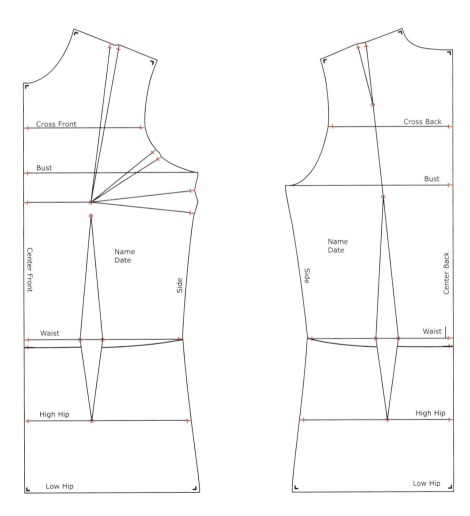

Figure 3.9

Drafting a Moulage for the Masculine Figure

WHAT AND HOW TO MEASURE FOR A SLOPER

The model should stand without shoes, feet about 4" (10.2cm) apart. They should retain their natural posture throughout the measuring process while looking straight ahead. If the arms need to be moved out of the way, have the model hold their arms out with the elbows at shoulder level.

Start the measuring process by having the model tie a ¼" (6.4mm) width elastic around the natural waistline. The natural waistline in menswear is where the model or designer prefers a pants waistband to sit. Check the position of the elastic frequently while measuring and readjust if it is rolling up. The elastic is used as a measuring guide. Dress forms have twill tape pinned around the natural waistline, so an elastic is not needed (*Fig. 3.10*).

- **Neck (1):** Locate the center of the dip between the collarbones at the base of the front neck. This will be referred to as the **neck point** in the following instructions. It is helpful to apply a small adhesive dot at the neck point for future measurements. Measure around the base of the neck stem. The tape measure should form a slight teardrop shape at the center-front neck point. Make sure the tape measure is snug. It can be helpful to have the model wear a thin necklace to show where the measurement should be taken at the back and sides of the neck.

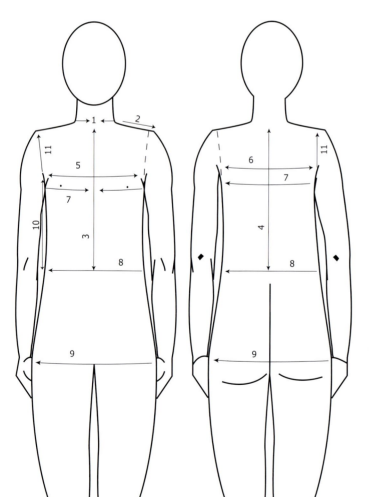

Figure 3.10

Calculation Tip:

The neckline will be divided by six for drafting. Round to the following measurements to make calculating easier: 14¼" (36.2cm), 15" (38.1cm), 15¾" (40cm), 16½" (41.9cm), 17¼" (43.8cm), 18" (45.7cm), 18¾" (47.6cm), 19½" (49.5cm), 20¼" (51.4cm), etc. Notice that each measurement grows by ¾" (1.9cm) for easy calculating later.

- **Shoulder (2):** Measure the shoulder from the base of the neck stem to the outside of the collarbone. The end of the collarbone should be in line with the armhole crease.
- **Front Length (3):** Measure from the neck point to the base of the waist elastic. Pull the tape measure taut for a more accurate measurement.
- **Back Length (4):** Have the model bend their head forward with their chin toward their chest. Locate the center of the vertebrae protruding at the base of the back neck stem. It helps to add an adhesive dot here. The model should then lift their head and look forward. Measure from the center of the vertebrae to the base of the waist elastic at the center-back waistline. This measurement is often longer than the front length measurement by 1"–2" (2.5–5.1cm). If that is not the case, double-check the measurement.
- **Cross Front (5):** Measure from the model's underarm crease to underarm crease. This should be a flat measurement. Do not wrap the tape under the armpit.
- **Cross Back (6):** Measure across the upper back from the model's underarm crease to underarm crease. The cross back is often wider than the cross-front measurement by about 1"–2" (2.5–5.1cm). If that is not the case, double-check the measurements.
- **Chest (7):** Have the model lift their arms to shoulder level to position the measuring tape. The tape measure should be level with the center of the chest (nipples). The model should then lower their arms, and the measurement can be taken.
- **Waist (8):** Measure the waist around the elastic.
- **Low Hip (9):** Measure the low hip 9" (22.9cm) down from the waist elastic. Mark the depth at the sides and measure around the body, keeping the tape measure level. Be sure to note both depth and circumference measurements.
- **Side (10):** Place a ruler level under the armpit. Have the model relax their shoulder. Measure from the top of the ruler through to the base of the waist elastic.
- **Armhole (11):** Measure around the armhole on the side the model favors. The model should raise their arm to get the tape measure positioned, but the arm should be lowered to their side when taking the measurement. The tape measure should be perpendicular to the floor as if the armpit is in a sling. Take a snug measurement.

Record of Measurements

NAME: _____

DATE: _____

Neck (1): _____

Shoulder (2): _____

Front Length (3): _____

Back Length (4): _____

Cross Front (5): _____

Cross Back (6): _____

Chest (7): _____

Waist (8): _____

Low Hip (9): _____ @ a depth of: 9" (22.9cm)

Side (10): _____

Armhole (11): _____

Practice

Use these sample measurements (fits most Men's size 36 dress forms).

Neck: 15¾" (40cm)

Shoulder: 5½" (14cm)

Front Length: 14" (35.6cm)

Back Length: 17" (43.2cm)

Cross Front: 14" (35.6cm)

Cross Back: 15½" (39.4cm)

Chest: 38" (96.5cm)

Waist: 32" (81.3cm)

Low Hip: 39" (99.1cm) @ a depth of: 9" (22.9cm)

Side: 8½" (21.6cm)

Armhole: 17½" (44.5cm)

CALCULATING THE MEASUREMENTS

Since the fit in menswear is less complicated, go straight to drafting the sloper rather than starting with a moulage. Note the ease added in the calculation sheet.

Sloper Calculation Worksheet

Neck: _____ ÷ 6 = _____

    Front: _____ + ⅜" (1cm) = _____

    Back: _____ + ⅝" (1.6cm) = _____

Shoulder: _____ (as measured)

Front Length: _____ (as measured)

Back Length: _____ − ¾" (1.9cm) = _____

Cross Front: _____ ÷ 2 = _____ + ½" (1.3cm) = _____

Cross Back: _____ ÷ 2 = _____ + ½" (1.3cm) = _____

Chest: _____ + 3" (7.6cm) ease = _____ ÷ 4 = _____

    Front: _____ + ¼" (0.6cm) = _____

    Back: _____ − ¼" (0.6cm) = _____

Waist: _____ + 3" (7.6cm) ease = _____ ÷ 4 = _____

    Front: _____ + ¼" (0.6cm) = _____

    Back: _____ − ¼" (0.6cm) = _____

Low Hip: _____ ÷ 4 = _____ (@ a depth of: 10" [25.4cm])

    Front: _____ + ¼" (0.6cm) = _____

    Back: _____ − ¼" (0.6cm) = _____

Side: _____ − 1" (2.5cm) = _____

Armhole: _____ + 2 (5.1cm) = _____ ÷ 2 = _____

    Front: _____ − ¼" (0.6cm) = _____

    Back: _____ + ¼" (0.6cm) = _____

Sample Calculation Worksheet

Neck: 15 3/4" (40cm) ÷ 6 = 2 5/8" (6.7cm)
    Front: 2 5/8" (6.7cm) + 3/8" (1cm) = 3" (7.6cm)
    Back: 2 5/8" (6.7cm) + 5/8" (1.6cm) = 3 1/4" (8.3cm)
Shoulder: 5 1/2" (14cm), 5 1/2" (14cm)   (as measured)
Front Length: 14" (35.6cm)   (as measured)
Back Length: 17" (43.2cm) − 3/4" (1.9cm) = 16 1/4" (41.3cm)
Cross Front: 14" (35.6cm) ÷ 2 = 7" (17.8cm) + 1/2" (1.3cm) = 7 1/2" (19.1cm)
Cross Back: 15 1/2" (39.4cm) ÷ 2 = 7 3/4" (19.7cm) + 1/2" (1.3cm) = 8 1/4" (21cm)
Chest: 38" (96.5cm) + 3" (7.6cm) ease = 41" (104.1cm) ÷ 4 = 10 1/4" (26cm)
    Front: 10 1/4" (26cm) + 1/4" (0.6cm) = 10 1/2" (26.7cm)
    Back: 10 1/4" (26cm) − 1/4" (0.6cm) = 10" (25.4cm)
Waist: 32" (81.3cm) + 3" (7.6cm) ease = 35" (88.9cm) ÷ 4 = 8 3/4" (22.2cm)
    Front: 8 3/4" (22.2cm) + 1/4" (0.6cm) = 9" (22.9cm)
    Back: 8 3/4" (22.2cm) − 1/4" (0.6cm) = 8 1/2" (21.6cm)
Low Hip: 37" (94cm) ÷ 4 = 40" (101.6cm)   (@ a depth of: 10" [25.4cm])
    Front: 10" (25.4cm) + 1/4" (0.6cm) = 10 1/4" (26cm)
    Back: 10" (25.4cm) − 1/4" (0.6cm) = 9 3/4" (24.8cm)
Side: 8 1/2" (21.6cm) − 1" (2.5cm) = 7 1/2" (19.1cm), 7 1/2" (19.1cm)
Armhole: 17 1/2" (44.5cm) + 2 (5.1cm) = 19 1/2" (49.5cm) ÷ 2 = 9 3/4" (24.8cm)
    Front: 9 3/4" (24.8cm) − 1/4" (0.6cm) = 9 1/2" (24.1cm)
    Back: 9 3/4" (24.8cm) + 1/4" (0.6cm) = 10" (25.4cm)

SETTING UP THE GUIDELINES

Set up the following guidelines to draft a sloper. It is helpful to use the straight edge of the pattern paper as the center-front and center-back guidelines. Go over the guidelines in red pencil.

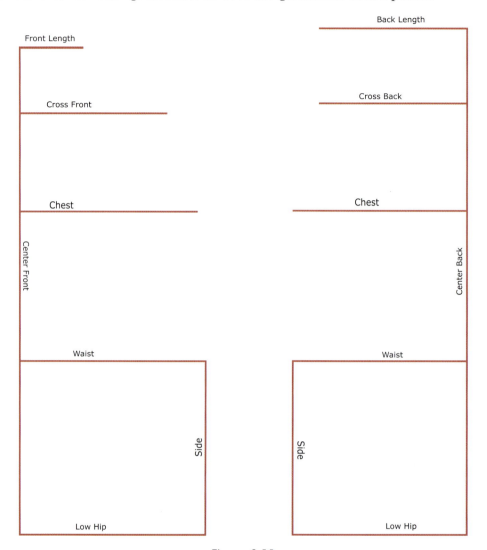

Figure 3.11

Front Guidelines

1. **Waist Guideline:** Perpendicular to the center front (see *Fig. 3.11* for placement of the center front) and about 12" (30.5cm) up from the bottom of the paper, draw a waist guideline the width of the **front low-hip calculation**.

2. **Low-Hip Guideline:** Perpendicular to the center front, draw the low-hip guideline 9" (22.9cm) down from the waist guideline. The guideline should measure as the **front low-hip calculation**.

3. **Front Length:** Mark the front length measurement up from the waist guideline. At that height and perpendicular to the center front, draw a guideline of 5" (12.7cm) (standard length for all).

4. **Chest:** The chest guideline should be drawn perpendicular to the center front guideline at half the front length measurement. The width of the guideline should be as the **front chest calculation**.

5. **Cross Front:** The cross-front guideline should be drawn perpendicular to the center front at 3½" (8.9cm) down from the front length guideline. The guideline should measure 10" (25.4cm) (standard length for all).

Back Guidelines

6. **Waist Guideline:** Perpendicular to the center back and about 12" (30.5cm) up from the bottom of the paper, draw a waist guideline the width of the **back low-hip calculation**.
7. **Low-Hip Guideline:** Perpendicular to the center back, draw the low-hip guideline 9" (22.9cm) down from the waist guideline. The guideline should measure as the **back low-hip calculation**.
8. **Back Length:** Mark the back length measurement up from the waist guideline. At that height and perpendicular to the center back, draw a guideline of 12" (30.5cm) (standard length for all).
9. **Chest:** The chest guideline should be drawn perpendicular to the center-back guideline at half the back length measurement. The width of the guideline should be as the **back chest calculation**.
10. **Cross Back:** Divide the back length measurement into quarters. The cross-back guideline should be drawn perpendicular to the center-back guideline at one-quarter of the back length measurement. For example, if the back length measurement is 16" (40.6cm), with one quarter of 16" (40.6cm) being 4" (10.2cm), draw the guideline at 4" (10.2cm) down from the center-back neck. The guideline should measure approximately 12" (30.5cm) (standard length for all).

DRAFTING THE FRONT

When drafting a sloper, accuracy is important. Since all the measurements tie into one another, even slight errors could alter the pattern. Work carefully. Remember to differentiate between measurement and calculation when reading the instructions. Draft on top of the front guidelines.

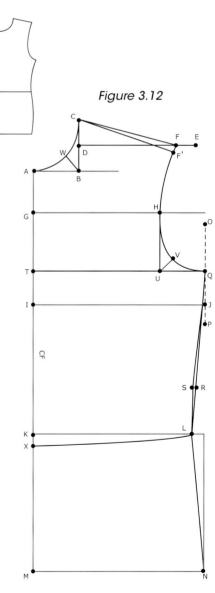

Figure 3.12

1. **AB** = front neck calculation on the front length guideline (*Fig. 3.12*)
2. **BC** = **AB** + ⅛" (3.2mm)
3. **D** = half **BC**
4. **DE** = 7" (17.8cm) guideline squared off **BC**
5. **CF** = shoulder measurement as it falls on the **DE** line
6. **GH** = cross-front calculation on the guideline
7. **IJ** = front chest calculation on the guideline
8. **KL** = front waist calculation
9. **MN** = front low-hip calculation on the guideline
10. **OP** = square a dotted guideline off **IJ** 2" (5.1cm) up from **J**. Mark **O**. Mark **P** 2" (5.1cm) below **J**.
11. **LQ** = side measurement as it falls on the **OP** guideline
12. **LR** = 3" (7.6cm) up from **L** on the **LQ** line
13. **RS** = ⅛" (3.2mm) in to shape side
14. Connect **Q-S-L** for the new side shape.
15. Connect **L-N**.
16. **QT** = Square a line back toward the center front and mark as the new chest guideline. Double-check that **QT** is squared off the center front guideline.
17. Square a line down from the cross-front guideline (**GH**) until it falls on the **QT** line and mark **U**.

18. **UV** = 1" (2.5cm) guideline at a 45-degree angle
19. Connect **Q-V-H-F** for the armhole.
20. Check the measurement of **QVHF**, and drop or raise **F** as necessary to get the correct armhole measurement. Raise the armhole above **F** a maximum of ½" (1.3cm) and lower a maximum of 1¼" (3.2cm) to get the front armhole calculation. If the armhole needs to be raised ¾" (1.9cm), raise it ½" (1.3cm) and let the remaining ¼" (6.4mm) go. If the armhole needs to be dropped 1½" (3.8cm), drop 1¼" (3.2cm) and let the remaining ¼" (6.4mm) go. If measurement was dropped from the front armhole, it can be added to the back armhole measurement. Mark **F'** if the end of shoulder was adjusted.
21. Connect **C-F'** for the new shoulder slope.
22. **BW** = 1¼" (3.2cm) guideline at a 45-degree angle to help shape the neckline
23. Connect **A-W-C** for a neckline shape.
24. **KX** = ½" (1.3cm) for optional waist shaping
25. Connect **X-L** in a shallow curve. Waist shaping is not often drafted into men's clothing, but it should be noted as an option when a waist seam or a tight fit is desired.
26. Recheck all measurements and calculations and adjust if necessary.

DRAFTING THE BACK

Note that the instructions cycle through the alphabet twice: first with uppercase letters, then with lowercase letters.

1. **AB** = back neck calculation on the back length guideline (*Fig. 3.13*)
2. **BC** = one-third **AB** + ⅛" (3.2mm)
3. **CD** = shoulder width + ¾" (1.9cm) dart width. **D** should fall on the back length guideline.
4. **CE** = half the shoulder width
5. **EF** = ¾" (1.9cm) dart width
6. **FD** = half the shoulder width. The dart width should be centered on the shoulder. **CE** should equal **FD**.
7. **G** = low-hip guideline at center back
8. **H** = waist guideline at center back
9. **I** = cross-back guideline at center back
10. **HJ** = ⅜" (1cm) back contouring
11. **HK** = 7" (17.8cm) down from **H** along center back
12. Connect **I-J** for back contouring. Back contouring helps a garment fit better along the spine.
13. **IL** = cross-back calculation on the guideline

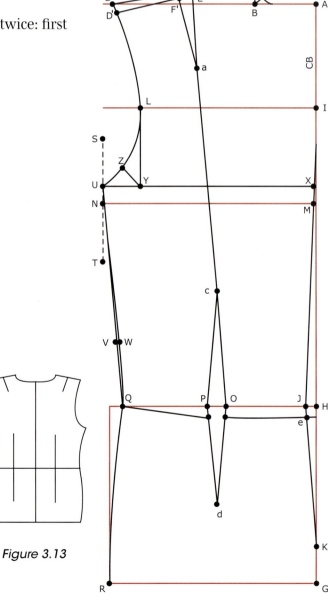

Figure 3.13

14. **M** = chest guideline at new center back on the **IJ** line
15. **MN** = back chest calculation
16. **JO** = distance from center back to the first leg of the dart. Back waist darts are centered on the waist. For example, if the back waist calculation is 8" (20.3cm), **JO** equals 4" (10.2cm).
17. **OP** = 1" (2.5cm) width for a back waist dart (standard width for all). Back waist darts are optional but encouraged for a better fit in back.
18. **PQ** = remainder of the back waist calculation. **JO** should equal **PQ**.
19. **GR** = back low-hip calculation
20. Connect **Q-R** for the side shape.
21. Square a dotted guideline off **MN**, 2" (5.1cm) up from **N** for **S**, and 2" (5.1cm) down from **N** for **T**.
22. **QU** = side measurement as it falls on the **ST** guideline
23. **QV** = 3" (7.6cm) up along the **QS** line
24. **VW** = in ⅛" (3.2mm) to shape side
25. Connect **Q-W-U** for the new side shape.
26. **UX** = square a line toward the center back from **U**, and mark as the new chest guideline.
27. **LY** = square a line down from the cross-back guideline (**IL**) until it meets the new chest guideline (**UX**), and mark **Y** as shown
28. **YZ** = 1" (2.5cm) guideline at a 45-degree angle
29. Connect **U-Z-L-D** for the armhole.
30. Check the measurement of **UZLD** and drop or raise **D** as necessary to get the correct armhole measurement. Raise the armhole above **D** a maximum of ½" (1.3cm) and lower a maximum of 1¼" (3.2cm) to get the back armhole calculation. If measurement was dropped from the front armhole, it can be added to the back armhole.
31. **D'** = adjusted end of shoulder
32. **CD'** = draw a new shoulder slope and recenter the dart if necessary. Re-mark the adjusted dart points **E'** and **F'**.
33. Connect **E'-O**.
34. **E'a** = 3¾" (9.5cm) dart length on the **E'O** line
35. Connect **F'-a** for the second dart leg.
36. Adjust at **F'** so **F'a** equals 3¾" (9.5cm). Redraw **F'** to **D'**. Fold the shoulder dart with the dart bulk toward the end of shoulder and trace off the dart bulk to true it.
37. **Bb** = ½" (1.3cm) guideline on a 45-degree angle for shaping the back neck
38. Connect **C-b-A** for the back neckline shape.
39. **Oc** = 6" (15.2cm) along the **E'O** line
40. Connect **P-c** for the second leg of the waist dart.
41. **d** = 6" (15.2cm) directly under the center of the waist dart
42. **Je** = ½" (1.3cm) for optional waist shaping
43. Connect **e-Q** in a shallow curve for waist shaping. Square the dart legs through the waist shaping.
44. Connect **O-d-P** for the lower part of the waist dart.
45. Connect **e-K** for the lower part of the back contouring.
46. Recheck all the measurements and calculations, and adjust if necessary.

Front and Back Patterns

True the back pattern to the front at the high-neck point connection and the end of shoulder connection. The sides should be the same length, but they will not be the same shape if a back waist dart was used.

1. Trace the front sloper, including the waist shaping: **A-W-C-F'-H-V-Q-S-L-N-M-X-K-I-T-G-A**. Cut the waist by separating the pattern at **KL** for the top piece and **XL** for the bottom piece.
2. Draw a length grainline perpendicular to the center front guideline on both pieces.
3. Add 1" (2.5cm) seam allowance at the shoulder and center front. Add ½" (1.3cm) seam allowance everywhere else.
4. Cut (2) self of each piece. Have the garment open at the center front or center back.
5. Trace the back sloper: **A-b-C-E'-F'-D'-L-Z-U-W-Q-R-G-K-e-J-M-I-A**, including the waist dart, shoulder dart, and waist shaping. Cut away the waist shaping by separating the pattern at **J-Q** for the top piece and **e-Q** for the bottom piece.
6. Draw a length grainline perpendicular to the low-hip guideline on the bottom piece. Draw length grainline perpendicular to the waist guideline on the upper piece.
7. Add 1" (2.5cm) seam allowance at the shoulder. Add ½" (1.3cm) seam allowance everywhere else.
8. Cut (2) self of each piece.

Truing Tip:

It is important to have squared edges on a sloper. Squaring edges helps the connection points between front and back patterns align more smoothly. At the center-front and center-back neck, square for ½" (1.3cm); square off the shoulder at the front and back high-neck/shoulder points for ⅛" (3.2mm); square off the end of shoulder all the way down to the cross front and cross back (even if that means moving the cross front and back in or out slightly; the base of the front and back armholes should be flat for ½" (1.3cm); the front and back low hip at side should square for 1" (2.5cm).

TRANSFERRING THE SLOPER TO TAG

Once the sloper fit is finalized, trace it onto tag. The sloper is not a garment. It is a template. Think of the sloper as having up to 70 percent of the work done. The remaining 30 percent is about design, fabric choice, adjusting fit, silhouette, and details to reflect the designer's sketch (*Fig. 3.14*).

Fitting Tip:

Staystitch around the neckline and armhole on the seamlines. Then, trim or clip the seam allowance at the neck and armholes before fitting. If the seam allowance at the neck and armholes is not trimmed or clipped, the sloper will ride up above the chest affecting the fit. Staystitch the center front or center-back seam to show where to pin it closed.

Drafting a Knit Bodice Sloper for the Male Figure

1. Take the same measurements.
2. Subtract 2" (5.1cm) from the chest, waist, and low-hip circumferences.
3. Subtract 1" (2.5cm) from the neck-circumference, front-length, cross-front, cross-back, side, and armhole measurements.
4. Subtract 2" (5.1cm) from the back length measurement.
5. Subtract ¾" (1.9cm) from the shoulder measurement.
6. Recalculate using the reduced measurements.
7. Draft the front and back, skipping any references to darts, waist shaping, and back contouring.
8. Trace.
9. Cut both the front and back on a center fold. Sew and test the fit in a stable knit, such as a double knit.
10. Once the fit is finalized, put it on tag to create a knit bodice sloper.

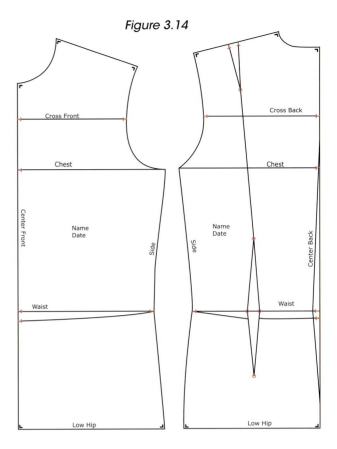

Figure 3.14

Test Your Knowledge

1. Why draft a moulage for the female form instead of going straight to sloper, as is done in menswear?

2. What is the purpose of shoulder, armhole, and side darts in a moulage?

3. How is the cup size calculated? What can throw off the formula?

4. Why is it important to square the edges of a sloper?

5. Why is working from a well-fitting sloper important?

This chapter focuses on manipulating darts to create varied seam lines in a bodice pattern. Students are encouraged to think like a designer and experiment with how different design lines influence fit and style.

OBJECTIVES

Upon completion of this chapter, you will be able to

- Rotate and combine darts for more varied and interesting garments
- Compare how different seamlines can emphasize or de-emphasize a figure
- Master manipulating dart bulk into seams, pleats, and gathers

CHAPTER 4
Dart Manipulation

Rules and Information to Apply to Dart Manipulations

BUST DARTS AND WAIST DART

The shoulder, armhole, and side darts are bust darts that build a breast cup (*Fig. 4.1*). The waist dart pulls in fullness at the waist and releases fullness above the waist at the rib cage by coming to a point.

The inside of a dart is called the **dart take-up**. A dart take-up creates **dart bulk**, which is pressed to one side. Experiment with which direction to press dart bulk. Use dart bulk to fill in any dips or hollows on the body. The bust darts and the front waist dart do not share a common **apex** (point), but since the apex of the darts are close together, they *can* be manipulated into one dart for different looks. On the back sloper, the shoulder dart and waist dart do not share a common apex. Since the apex of each dart is far apart, they *cannot* be manipulated together like in the front.

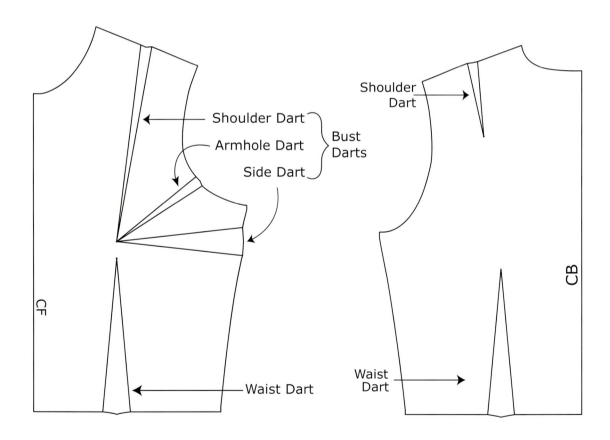

Figure 4.1

84   Building Patterns

DART EQUIVALENTS

Dart bulk resulting from a dart manipulation can be taken up by sewing the dart or in **dart equivalents**—like pleats, gathers, or in seam lines—that incorporate darts, such as princess seams.

WHEN TO USE THE FRONT HIGH OR LOW FIGURE POINT

With front dart manipulations, the **pivotal point** on a pattern is either the high or low figure point (*Fig. 4.2*). While there can be exceptions to further design and fit, if the dart or dart equivalent is manifesting above the high figure point, use the high figure point as the pivotal point. If the dart or dart equivalent is manifesting below the low figure point, use the low figure point as the pivotal point.

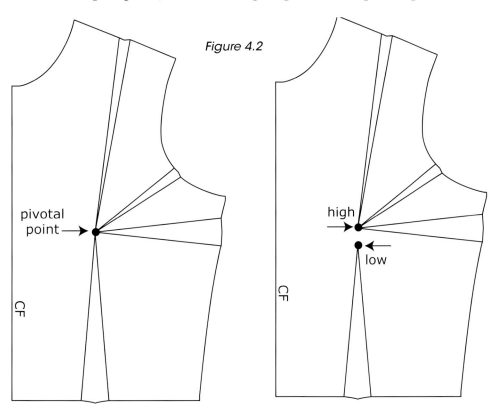

Figure 4.2

Drafting a Knit Bodice Sloper for the Male Figure

1. Use the same measurements.
2. Subtract 2" (5.1cm) from the chest, waist, and low hip circumferences.
3. Subtract 1" (2.5cm) from the neck-circumference, front-length, cross-front, cross-back, side, and armhole measurements.
4. Subtract 2" (5.1cm) from the back length measurement.
5. Subtract ¾" (1.9cm) from the shoulder.
6. Recalculate using the reduced measurements.
7. Draft the front and back patterns, skipping any references to darts, waist shaping, and back contouring.
8. Trace.
9. Cut both the front and back on a center fold. Sew and test the fit in a stable knit, such as a double knit.
10. Once the fit is finalized, put it on tag to create a knit bodice sloper.

BACKING OFF A DART

The apex of a dart can be pulled away from the high or low figure point as much as 2" (5.1cm) and still maintain the fit. Start with either the high or low figure point, manipulate the darts, then back off as desired (*Fig. 4.3*). Do not back off first then manipulate, or else the breast cup will not end up properly sized. The closer the apex stays to the pivotal points, the more fitted the garment will be at the bust. As a rule, darts are usually backed off up to 1" (2.5cm) on fitted garments and up to 2" (5.1cm) on less fitted garments. Deciding how much to back off involves experimentation.

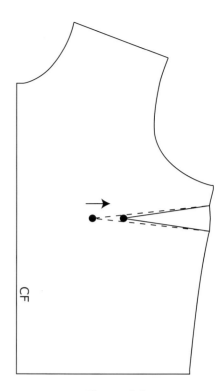

Figure 4.3

CHANGING DART BULK INTO SEAM ALLOWANCE

If a final dart manipulation opens more than 2" (5.1cm) at the perimeter of a pattern, there is the option to trim the dart bulk down to ½" (1.3cm) seam allowance on each leg. Reducing dart bulk is helpful if the dart bulk is hanging outside the perimeter of the pattern (*Fig. 4.4*).

DOUBLE-POINTED WAIST DARTS

A **double-pointed waist dart** (also called a **fish-eyed dart**), such as that found on a sloper to the low hip, cannot be manipulated with the bust darts. Double-pointed darts need to be sewn without manipulation because they do not fold out cleanly.

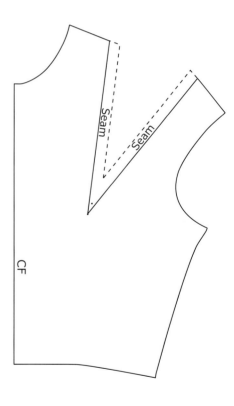

Figure 4.4

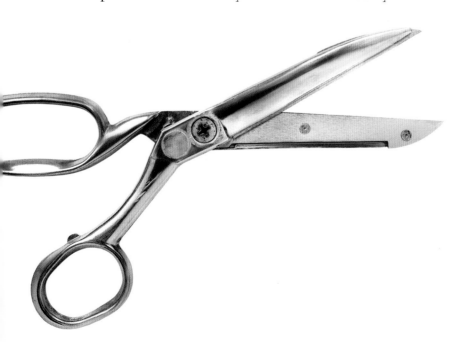

Exercises

Design Tip:
Where the dart is placed on a pattern can create a focal point. Seamlines originating above the high figure point will emphasize a bustline. Seamlines originating below the high figure point will de-emphasize a bustline.

CENTER-FRONT NECK DART

1. Trace the front sloper to the waist. Include the perimeter notches for the shoulder, armhole, side, and waist darts.
2. Mark **A**, **B**, **C**, **D**, **E**, and **F** as shown (*Fig. 4.5*).
3. Use the high figure point as the pivotal point on the pattern because the dart legs are originating above the high figure point. Mark **G**. Draw the darts to pivotal point **G**.
4. Draw a seamline as it will appear on the bodice. The beginning of the seamline for this exercise should start at **A**. The seamline will end at the pivotal point (**G**).
5. Cut the seamline from **A** to **G** and fold (manipulate) the shoulder, armhole, side, and waist darts into the slashed line. The slashed line will open and form one dart. Smooth the perimeter of the pattern where the darts were folded out.
6. Back off the dart if desired (see Backing Off a Dart).
7. Add pattern paper to the opening. Fold the new dart bulk away from the center-front neck and trace the pattern shape onto the dart bulk underneath.
8. Pattern: **A-A-B-C-D-E-F-A**, including the dart (**A-G-A**)
9. Notch the dart legs on the perimeter of the pattern. Awl-punch ½" (1.3cm) inside the dart from pivotal point (**G**). Draw the grainline parallel to the center front. Add ½" (1.3cm) seam allowance and drag the notches to the perimeter. Cut (1) self on fold at center front.

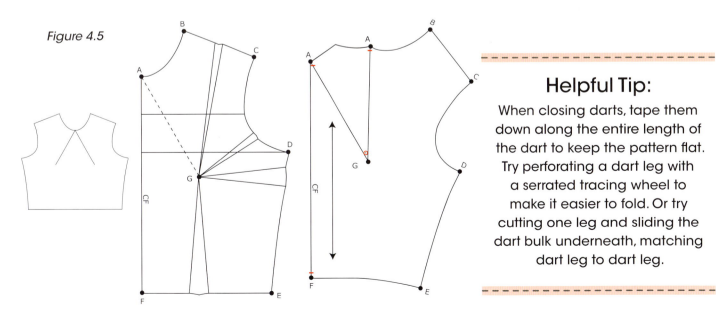

Figure 4.5

Helpful Tip:
When closing darts, tape them down along the entire length of the dart to keep the pattern flat. Try perforating a dart leg with a serrated tracing wheel to make it easier to fold. Or try cutting one leg and sliding the dart bulk underneath, matching dart leg to dart leg.

Seam Allowance Tip:
Seam allowances are added after a pattern is drafted. Hence the instructions of adding seam allowance and dragging notches to the perimeter.

FRENCH DART

1. Trace the front sloper to the waist. Include the perimeter notches for the shoulder, armhole, side, and waist darts.
2. Mark **A**, **B**, **C**, **D**, **E**, and **F** as shown (*Fig. 4.6*).
3. Using the high figure point as the pivotal point fits better with a French dart even though the dart legs are originating below the high figure point. Mark **G**. Draw the darts to pivotal point **G**.
4. Draw a seamline as it will appear on the bodice. Mark the beginning of the seamline **H**. The seamline will end at the pivotal point (**G**).
5. Cut the seamline from **H** to **G** and fold (manipulate) the shoulder, armhole, side, and waist darts into the slashed line. The slashed line will open and form one dart. Smooth the perimeter of the pattern where the darts were folded out.
6. Back off the dart if desired (see Backing Off a Dart).
7. Add pattern paper to the opening. Fold the new dart bulk away from the waist and trace the pattern shape onto the dart bulk underneath.
8. Pattern: **A-B-C-D-H-H-E-F-A**, including the dart (**H-G-H**)
9. Notch the dart legs on the perimeter of the pattern. Awl-punch ½" (1.3cm) inside the dart from pivotal point (**G**). Draw the grainline parallel to the center front. Add ½" (1.3cm) seam allowance and drag the notches to the perimeter. Cut (1) self on fold at center front.

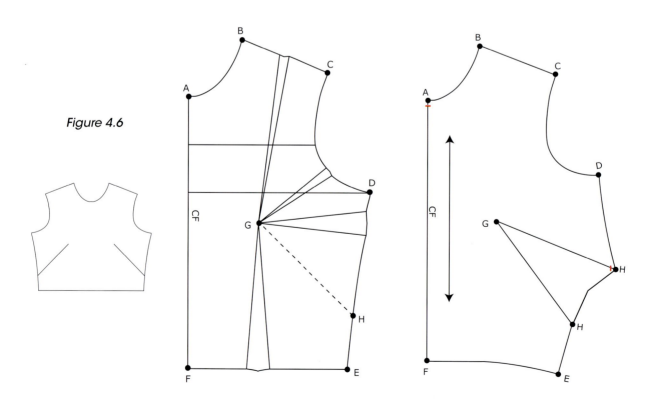

Figure 4.6

Fitting Tip:
For a more fitted French dart, bow the center of each dart leg ¼" (6.4mm) to take up more fabric.

ARMHOLE DART

1. Trace the front sloper to the waist. Include the perimeter notches for the shoulder, armhole, side, and waist darts.
2. Mark **A**, **B**, **C**, **D**, **E**, and **F** as shown (*Fig. 4.7*).
3. Use the high figure point as the pivotal point on the pattern because the dart legs are originating above the high figure point. Mark **G**. Draw the darts to pivotal point **G**.
4. Draw a seamline as it will appear on the bodice. The beginning of the seamline for this exercise should start at **H**. The seamline will end at the pivotal point (**G**).
5. Cut the seamline from **H** to **G** and fold (manipulate) the shoulder, armhole, side, and waist darts into the slashed line. The slashed line will open and form one dart. Smooth the perimeter of the pattern where the darts were folded out.
6. Back off the dart if desired (see Backing Off a Dart).
7. Add pattern paper to the opening. Fold the new dart bulk away from the base of the armhole and trace the perimeter pattern shape onto the dart bulk underneath.
8. Pattern: **A-B-C-H-H-D-E-F-A**, including the dart (**H-G-H**)
9. Notch the dart legs on the perimeter of the pattern. Awl-punch ½" (1.3cm) inside the dart from pivotal point (**G**). Draw the grainline parallel to the center front. Add ½" (1.3cm) seam allowance and drag the notches to the perimeter. Cut (1) self on fold at center front.

Figure 4.7

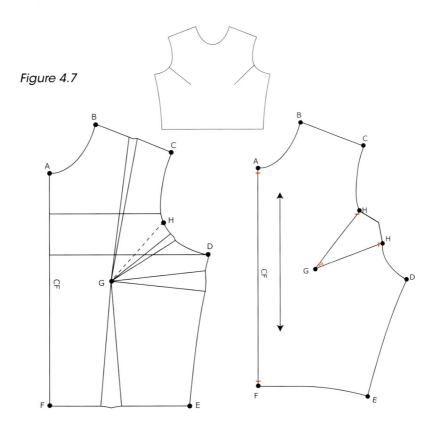

Helpful Tip:
Do not get rid of all the darts in a woven fabric garment. Darts are needed to shape fabric, so it molds to the body. Darts can be interesting and defining. The eye will register a poor fit before it registers a dart.

Y-DART

1. Trace the front sloper to the waist. Include the perimeter notches for the shoulder, armhole, side, and waist darts.
2. Mark **A**, **B**, **C**, **D**, **E**, and **F** as shown (*Fig. 4.8*).
3. Use the low figure point as the pivotal point on the pattern because the dart legs are originating below the high figure point. Mark **G**. Draw the darts to pivotal point **G**.
4. Draw a seamline as it will appear on the bodice. Mark the seam at the perimeter of the pattern **H** (for example, mark **H** 3" [7.6cm] up from the center-front base). The seamline will end at the pivotal point (**G**).
5. Cut the seamline from **H** to **G** and fold (manipulate) the shoulder, armhole, side, and waist darts into the slashed line. The slashed line will open and form one dart. Smooth the perimeter of the pattern where the darts were folded out.
6. Back off the dart if desired (see Backing Off a Dart).
7. Add pattern paper to the opening. Fold the new dart bulk toward the waist and trace the pattern shape onto the dart bulk underneath.
8. Pattern: **A-B-C-D-E-F-H-H-A**, including the dart (**H-G-H**)
9. Notch the dart legs on the perimeter of the pattern. Awl-punch ½" (1.3cm) inside the dart from pivotal point (**G**). Draw the grainline parallel to the center front. Add ½" (1.3cm) seam allowance and drag the notches to the perimeter. Cut (1) self on fold at upper center front. The lower portion of the pattern is seamed at center front.

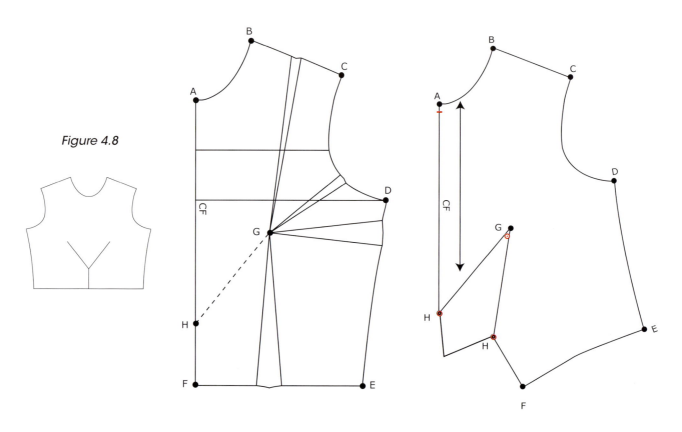

Figure 4.8

DIAMOND DARTS

1. Trace the front sloper to the waist. Include the perimeter notches for the shoulder, armhole, side, and waist darts.
2. Mark **A, B, C, D, E**, and **F** as shown (*Fig. 4.9*). Use the high figure point as the pivotal point on the pattern and mark that **G**. Draw the darts to pivotal point **G**.
3. Use the high figure point as the pivotal point on the pattern and mark that G. Draw the darts to pivotal point G.
4. Draw a diamond shape as it will appear on the bodice utilizing pivotal point **G**. Connect **A-G-F** for the diamond shape.
5. Cut the seamline **AGF** and separate the pattern into two pieces. Fold (manipulate) the shoulder, armhole, side, and waist darts. Smooth the perimeter of the pattern where the darts were folded out.
6. Center-Front Pattern: **A-G-F-A**
7. Awl-punch pivotal point (**G**). Draw the grainline parallel to the center front. Add ½" (1.3cm) seam allowance and drag the notch to the perimeter. Cut (1) self on fold at center front.
8. Side-Front Pattern: **A-B-C-D-E-F-G-A**
9. Awl-punch pivotal point (**G**). Draw the grainline parallel to the center front or squared off the base. Add ½" (1.3cm) seam allowance and drag the notches to the perimeter. Cut (2) self.

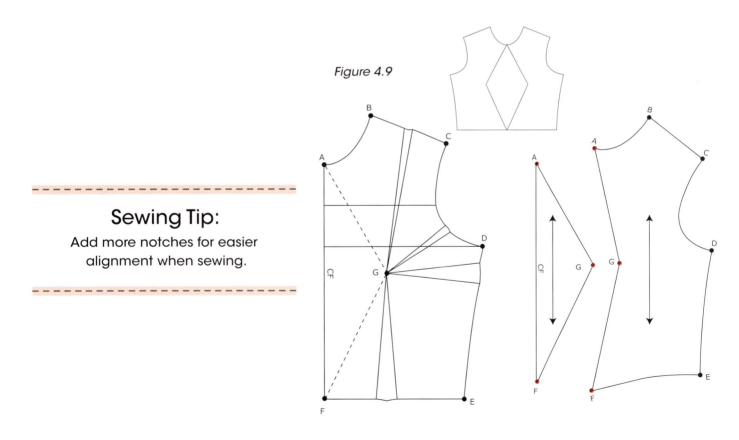

Figure 4.9

Sewing Tip:
Add more notches for easier alignment when sewing.

Design Tip:
Draft other shapes besides a diamond. If the high figure point is the pivotal point, draft in a heart, square, triangle, or rectangle. Why not add color blocking as well?

> **Design Tip:**
> This pattern can be sewn as shoulder pleats, rather than shoulder darts. Sew the dart legs down 1"–2" (2.5–5.1cm) then let the fabric fall into pleats.

ASYMMETRICAL SHOULDER DARTS

1. Trace the left and right sides of the front sloper to the waist. Include the perimeter notches for the shoulder, armhole, side, and waist darts. When a garment is asymmetrical, start with the entire front. Mark right and left side as worn. Mark **A** through **I** as shown (*Fig. 4.10*).
2. Use the high figure points as the pivotal points on the pattern because the darts are originating above the high figure points. Mark **J** and **K**. Draw the darts to points **J** and **K** as shown.
3. Draw the right-side darts to pivotal point **J**. Draw the left-side darts to pivotal point **K**.
4. Fold the shoulder darts into the side darts on the right and left sides. This will allow for a clear path to draw the cut lines emanating from the right shoulder.
5. Divide the right-side shoulder into three equal parts, or place the start of the cut lines as desired (closer to the end of shoulder or the neck). Mark **L** and **M**.
6. Connect **L-J** and **M-K**.
7. Cut **L** to **J** and fold (manipulate) the right-side darts into the opening creating a new dart (**L-J-L**).
8. Cut **M** to **K** and fold the left-side darts into the opening creating a new dart (**M-K-M**).
9. Smooth the perimeter of the pattern where the darts were closed out.
10. Back off the darts if desired (see Backing Off a Dart).
11. Add pattern paper to the openings. Fold the new dart bulks away from the center-front neck and trace the pattern shape onto the dart bulks underneath.
12. Pattern: **A-B-C-D-E-F-G-H-I-A**, including the darts (**L-J-L** and **M-K-M**).
13. Notch the dart legs on the perimeter of the pattern. Awl-punch ½" (1.3cm) inside the dart from pivotal points (**J** and **K**). Draw the grainline parallel to the center front. Add ½" (1.3cm) seam allowance and drag the notches to the perimeter. Cut (1) self.

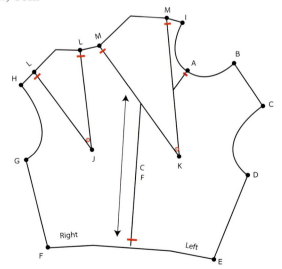

Figure 4.10

> **Production Tip:**
> Asymmetrical garments can be more expensive to produce because they involve keeping track of the right and left sides when cutting and sewing.

Helpful Tip:

Gathers cannot be drawn down to zero. Gathers need to be spread over a predetermined area.

BUST GATHERS WITH YOKE

1. Trace the front sloper to the waist. Include the perimeter notches for the shoulder, armhole, side, and waist darts.
2. Mark **A**, **B**, **C**, **D**, **E**, and **F** as shown (*Fig. 4.11*).
3. Use the low figure point as the pivotal point on the pattern because the gathers will originate below the high figure point. Mark **G**. Draw the darts to the pivotal point **G**.
4. Transfer the waist dart into the side dart by slashing one leg of the side dart and folding (manipulating) the waist dart into the side dart. This will clear a path to draw a smooth yoke seamline.
5. Draw the yoke seamline as desired. Example: Mark 4" (10.2cm) up from the center-front waist and mark **H**.
6. Mark ½" (1.3cm) on either side of the folded waist dart on the **HI** line. Mark **J** and **K** as shown. The gathers will be spread over this 1" (5.1cm) distance.
7. Cut the pattern apart at the **HI** line. Slash and open the waist dart on the top piece only. Fold the shoulder, armhole, and side darts into the remaining waist dart. The slashed line will open and form one dart. Smooth the perimeter of the pattern where the darts were folded out.
8. Add pattern paper to the dart opening. Smooth the pattern between **J** and **K**. The dart bulk will now be gathered over the **J** and **K** distance. When gathering dart bulk, there is no need to mark the dart on the pattern.
9. Top Pattern: **A-B-C-D-I-K-J-H-A**
10. Notch **J** and **K** for the gathered area. Awl-punch **H**. Draw the grainline parallel to the center front. Add ½" (1.3cm) seam allowance and drag the notches to the perimeter. Cut (1) self on fold at center front.
11. Yoke Pattern: **H-I-E-F-H**
12. Awl-punch **H**. Draw the grainline parallel to the center front. Add ½" (1.3cm) seam allowance and drag the notches to the perimeter. Cut (1) self on fold at center front.

Figure 4.11

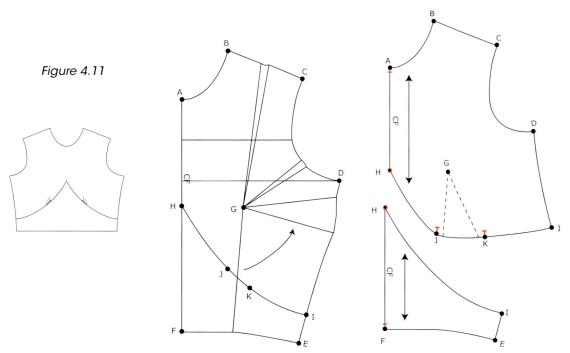

HORIZONTAL GATHERS AT WAIST DART

1. Trace the front sloper to the waist. Include the perimeter notches for the shoulder, armhole, side, and waist darts.
2. Mark **A**, **B**, **C**, **D**, **E**, and **F** as shown (*Fig. 4.12*).
3. Use the low figure point as the pivotal point on the pattern because the gathers will originate below the high figure point. Mark **G**. Draw the darts to the pivotal point **G**.
4. Mark the waist dart legs **H** and **I** as shown.
5. Cut one leg of the waist dart and fold (manipulate) the shoulder, armhole, and side darts into the waist dart. Smooth the perimeter of the pattern where the darts were folded out. Cut away the waist dart bulk.
6. Divide the **GI** measurement into four equal parts. Draw slash lines from the **GI** line to the side squaring off the **GI** line as shown.
7. Cut the slash lines from the **GI** line, hinging at the side. Insert 1½" (3.8cm), or as desired, into each slash line on the **GI** line to zero at the side.
8. Smooth the pattern along **GI** and **DE**.
9. Pattern: **A-B-C-D-E-I-G-H-F-A**
10. Notch halfway along **GH** and halfway along **GI**. Match these notches when sewing. Awl-punch pivotal point (**G**). *The fabric will need to be slashed to G to gather up to G.* Draw the grainline parallel to the center front. Add ½" (1.3cm) seam allowance and drag the notches to the perimeter. Cut (1) self on fold at center front.

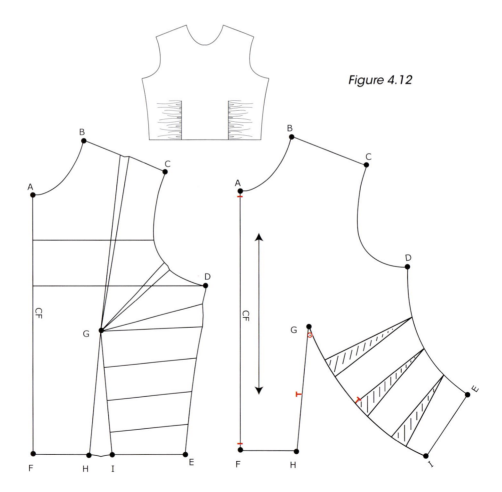

Figure 4.12

Building Patterns

Fitting Tip:

Remove ¼" (6.4mm) along the side seam from underarm to waist on the front and back to make the garment more fitted. Horizontal gathers need to fit snug against the body for a more flattering look.

SHOULDER PLEATS

1. Trace the front sloper to the waist. Include the perimeter notches for the shoulder, armhole, side, and waist darts.
2. Mark **A**, **B**, **C**, **D**, **E**, and **F** as shown (*Fig. 4.13*).
3. Use the high figure point as the pivotal point on the pattern because the pleats are originating from above the high figure point. Mark **G**. Draw the darts to pivotal point **G**.
4. Temporarily fold (manipulate) the shoulder dart into the side dart.
5. Measure the shoulder width and divide it into four equal parts. Mark **H**, **I**, and **J**.
6. Draw lines from **H**, **I**, and **J** to pivotal point **G**. Slash those lines and manipulate the armhole, side, and waist darts into the slash lines. Make the open spaces even. Add pattern paper behind the openings. Fold the pleats (**H** to **H**, **I** to **I**, and **J** to **J**) with the bulk toward the end of shoulder and trace the shoulder line over the dart bulk.
7. Open the pleats.
8. Smooth the perimeter of the pattern where the darts were folded out.
9. Pattern: **A-B-H-H-I-I-J-J-C-D-E-F-A**
10. Notch the pleats on the perimeter of the pattern (**HH**, **II**, **JJ**). Awl-punch 1" (2.5cm) down the legs of the pleats to show where to stop sewing down the pleats and release them. Draw the grainline parallel to the center front. Add ½" (1.3cm) seam allowance and drag the notches to the perimeter. Cut (1) self fold at center front.

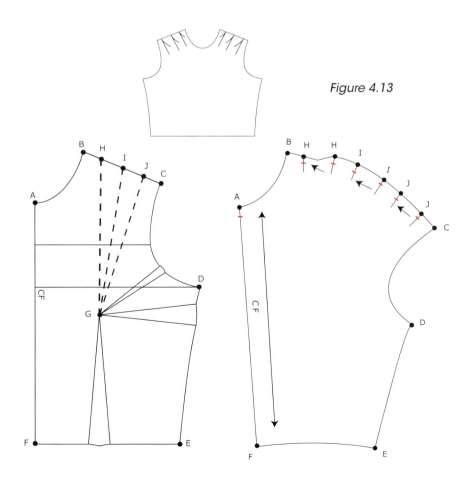

Figure 4.13

Marking Tip:
When pleating dart bulk, there is no need to mark the entire dart on the pattern. Just notch the width at the perimeter of the pattern and draw an arrow showing the direction the pleat is to be folded.

NECKLINE GATHERS

1. Trace the front sloper to the waist. Include the perimeter notches for the shoulder, armhole, side, and waist darts.
2. Mark **A**, **B**, **C**, **D**, **E**, and **F** as shown (*Fig. 4.14*).
3. Use the high figure point as the pivotal point on the pattern because the gathers will originate above the high figure point. Mark **G**. Draw the darts to the pivotal point **G**.
4. Measure ½" (1.3cm) from the center-front neck along the neckline and mark **H**. Measure 1" (2.5cm) from **H** along the neckline and mark **I**. Measure 1" (2.5cm) from **I** along the neckline and mark **J**. Connect **H**, **J**, and **I** to the pivotal point (**G**).
5. Slash the seamlines (**HG**, **IG**, and **JG**) and fold (manipulate) shoulder, armhole, side, and waist darts into the slashed lines. The slashed lines will open to form three darts. Distribute the fullness evenly between the three darts. Add pattern paper to the openings. Blend the neckline. Cut off part of the original neckline to get a smooth line as shown (**AJ**).
6. Note on the pattern that **AJ** should be gathered to 2½" (6.4cm). No need to draw in the darts since the dart bulk will be gathered.
7. Smooth the perimeter of the pattern where the darts were folded out.
8. Pattern: **A-J-B-C-D-E-F-A**
9. Notch **J** and **A** on the perimeter of the pattern to denote the gathered area. Draw the grainline parallel to the center front. Add ½" (1.3cm) seam allowance and drag the notches to the perimeter. Cut (1) self on fold at center front.

Design Tip:
Design a lowered neckline before starting the draft. Experiment with design while you learn.

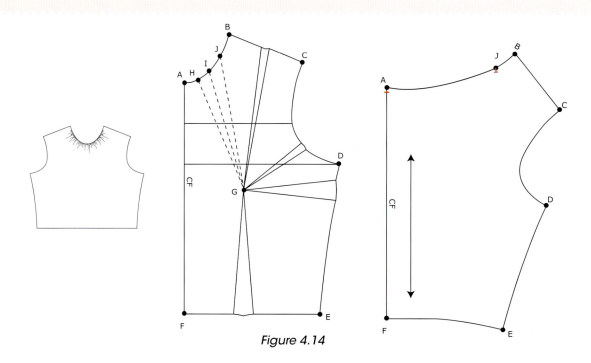

Figure 4.14

BACK DART MANIPULATIONS

Transferring the Position of the Back Darts

1. Trace the back sloper to the waist. Include the shoulder and waist darts.
2. Draw a seamline, starting anywhere on the perimeter of the pattern, and have it end at the point of the shoulder dart (*Fig. 4.15*).
3. Slash the line and fold (manipulate) the shoulder dart into the opening. Add pattern paper behind the opening.
4. Fold and trace the pattern shape over the new dart bulk to true it.
5. Smooth the pattern where the shoulder dart was folded out. Notch the legs of the dart and awl-punch ½" (1.3cm) inside the point.
6. Repeat the process with the waist dart.

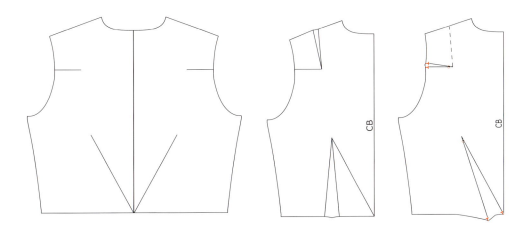

Figure 4.15

Design Tip:

Often the back of a garment is there to support the design and structure of the front. Let the back be the star sometimes by creating interesting dart manipulations on back patterns.

Shaving the Darts

Another way to manipulate back darts is to shave them off. This is often done on patterns for knit garments.

Fitting Tip:

Fit is compromised when shaving darts off woven fabric garments because the ability to contour to the curves of the body is lost without darts.

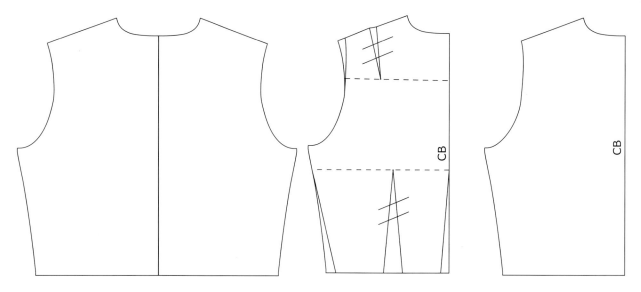

Figure 4.16

1. **Shoulder Dart:** Trace the back sloper to the waist, including the shoulder and waist darts. Measure the width of the shoulder dart, and mark that same width in from the end of shoulder. Blend from that mark to zero at the cross-back guideline in the armhole (or wherever it blends smoothly).
2. **Waist Dart:** Measure the waist dart width and split it in half. Take half the amount of the waist dart off at the waist at side and the other half off at the center-back waist, provided the garment has a center-back seam. If the garment does not have a center-back seam, take the entire dart width off the side seam. Blend to zero; level with the apex of the dart, at side, and center back as shown (*Fig. 4.16*).

Ignoring the Darts

Ignoring the shoulder and waist darts (*Fig. 4.17*) is also an option. If the shoulder dart is ignored, the shoulder measurement is extended by the width of the dart, giving a slightly dropped shoulder look. If the waist dart is ignored, the waist is increased by the width of the waist darts, giving a less-fitted look to a garment. If the shoulder and waist darts are ignored on the back, they are generally ignored on the front as well, and looseness at the waist is carried throughout the garment. Cross out darts so they are not mistakenly marked and sewn.

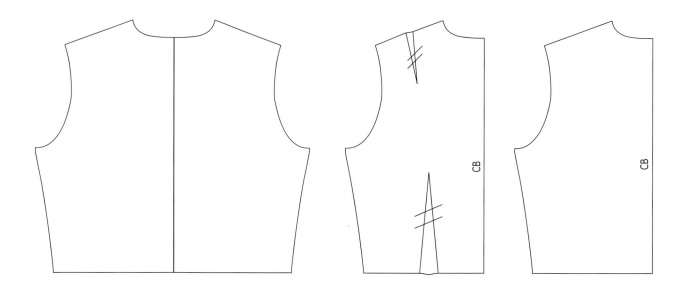

Figure 4.17

Fabric Tip:
Darts are often ignored or shaved off in knit garments. Knit fabric stretches, which helps the fabric contour around the body. Woven fabrics need darts to help contour.

DART MANIPULATION FOR SKIRTS
Front and/or Back

1. Trace the skirt sloper. Mark **A**, **B**, **C**, **D**, **E**, **F**, and **G** as shown (*Fig. 4.18*).
2. Draw the desired seamline as it will appear on the skirt. The base of the dart and the end of the seamline must be the same point (**E**). The beginning of the seamline can fall anywhere on the perimeter of the pattern. Mark **H**.
3. Slash the seamline from **H** to **E** and fold (manipulate) out the dart. The slashed line will open. Add pattern paper behind the opening, fold the new dart with the bulk down toward the base of the pattern, and trace the shape of the skirt onto the dart bulk underneath.
4. Pattern: **A-B-H-H-C-D-A**, including the dart (**H-E-H**)
5. Notch the dart legs and awl-punch the dart ½" (1.3cm) up from the base inside the dart bulk. Draw the grainline parallel to the center front. Add ½" (1.3cm) seam allowance and drag the notches to the perimeter. Cut (1) self on fold at center front. Cut (2) self for the back.

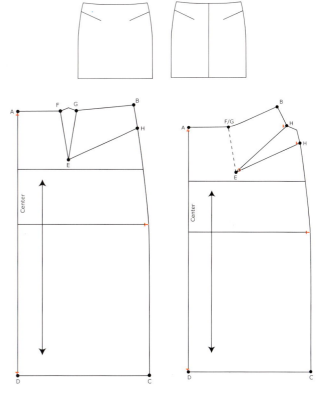

Figure 4.18

 Test Your Knowledge

1. Which three darts make up the breast cup?
2. Can a double-pointed dart be transferred to another dart? Why or why not?
3. If a dart is originating from the center-front neck, will that emphasize or de-emphasize a bustline?
4. What would be the reason to change dart bulk into seam allowance?
5. Which of the exercises above was your favorite? Which was your least favorite? What would you do differently to align the pattern with your style?

This chapter covers silhouettes and interior seamlines on bodice patterns. Exercises include princess seams; empire lines; and shift, smock, and trapeze outlines. Lines encourages students to experiment with silhouette and interior seamlines to influence shape and fit.

OBJECTIVES

Upon completion of this chapter, you will be able to

- Understand how interior seamlines can influence the fit of a garment

- See how exterior seamlines affect the silhouette of a garment

- Gain a further understanding of how to work with a bodice sloper

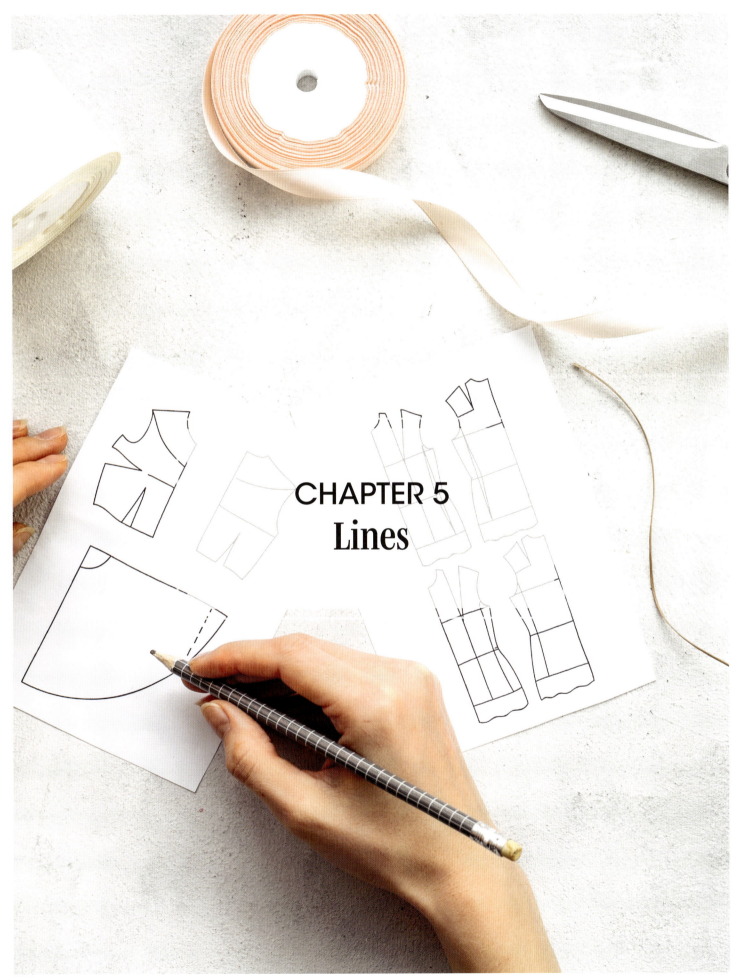

CHAPTER 5
Lines

Introduction to Style Lines and Silhouettes

DART-EQUIVALENT VS. NONDART-EQUIVALENT STYLE LINES

Lines refers to the interior style lines of a garment. There are two types of style lines: **dart equivalent** and **nondart equivalent**. **Silhouette** refers to the exterior outline of a garment.

Dart-equivalent style lines cross over or near the bust points and/or dart points. The darts are folded into a seam or absorbed into the seamline. Dart-equivalent style lines control the fit of a garment. Dart-equivalent style lines are functional and decorative. The dart manipulations done in the previous chapter are dart-equivalent style lines. Princess seams are also dart-equivalent style lines.

Nondart-equivalent style lines do not control the fit of a garment. They are purely decorative seamlines. Color-blocked seams are an example of nondart-equivalent style lines.

WHEN TO USE AN ARMHOLE DART AND DECIDING BUST EASE

The armhole dart is taken (meaning sewn or manipulated out) if a garment is sleeveless. In addition to taking the dart, sleeveless garments should have no more than 1" (2.5cm) ease added to the bust circumference for a close fit that does not gape under the arm.

When a garment has sleeves, 2" (5.1cm) or more ease should be added to the bust circumference to move the arms comfortably in a woven fabric garment. Half the armhole dart width is folded out (manipulated) and the other half is left in for extra ease to move the arms easily. Manipulating half the dart width helps build the proper cup size. However, the entire armhole dart width can be left in (ignored) for a looser fit. Manipulating the armhole dart in the exercises ahead is optional.

DRAFTING RULES FOR PRINCESS SEAMS

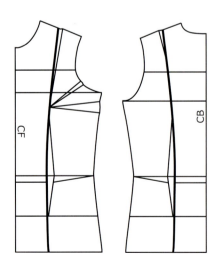

Figure 5.1

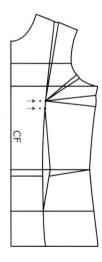

Figure 5.2

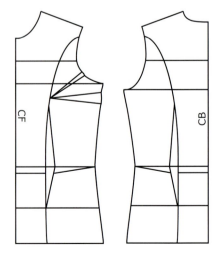

Figure 5.3

102 Building Patterns

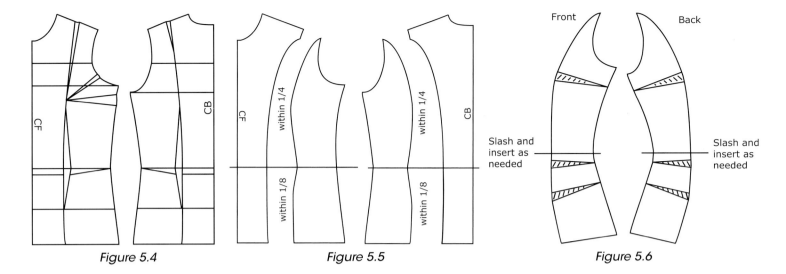

Figure 5.4   *Figure 5.5*   *Figure 5.6*

The following rules apply when drafting princess seams.

Smooth Seamlines (*Fig. 5.1*). When drawing a princess seam on a pattern, make sure the line is smooth. It does not have to be straight, just smooth. The way the line looks at the edge of the center-front and center-back panels is how the finished seamline will look.

High and Low Figure Points/Pivotal Points (*Fig. 5.2*). A princess seam does not have to cross the high figure point. But the further a seam is from the high figure point, the less fitted the garment will be at the bust. If drafting a loose jacket or coat, moving the pivotal point over as much as 2" (5.1cm) toward the side is not unusual. If drafting a fitted dress or blouse, stay closer to the original pivotal point (within 1" [2.5cm]). After manipulating the shoulder and armhole darts into the side dart, draw the princess seam and move the high figure point/pivotal point over to the newly drawn princess seamline. The low figure point will also be dragged to the seamline.

Forming Waist Darts to Seamlines (*Fig. 5.3*). If the seamline is curved, redraw the waist dart so it forms to the seam as shown. The smoothest seamlines usually occur when the entire waist dart is taken toward the side panel. But a waist dart can also be centered over the seamline. Experiment.

Waist Shaping (*Fig. 5.4*). Waist shaping is drawn below the waist guideline. When drafting waist shaping in a princess line pattern, draw a solid ½" (1.3cm) block from the center front or center back to the first leg of the dart. Mark ½" (1.3cm) at the second leg of the dart and blend to zero at the side seam. If a solid ½" (1.3cm) block is not drawn from the center front or back to the first leg of the dart, the center front or back guideline will be skewed when the waist shaping is folded out.

Seam Lengths Should Be Within ⅜" (1cm) (*Figs. 5.5–5.6*). Check the lengths of adjoining princess seams after drafting. Curved princess seams incorporating the waist dart can result in seams of different lengths. Always measure the inside edge of the pattern pieces from the waist notch up and then from the waist notch down. Note the waist up and the waist down measurements separately. The total difference between the seams should be no more than ⅜" (1cm). From waist down, there can be a ⅛" (3.2mm) difference. From waist up, there can be a ¼" (6.4mm) difference. Adjust the side panels to the center panels. Meaning, don't change anything on the center-back and center-front panels. Alter the side panels so they are within ⅛" (3.2mm) below the waist and ¼" (6.4mm) above. Notch the waist after folding out the waist shaping so it is clear where to start measuring.

Note the location of the slash and insertion lines on *Fig. 5.5*. Above the waist in front, insert as needed level with the high figure point. Insert at the same level on the back. Below the waist, insert as needed within 2" (5.1cm) of the waist guideline on the front and back. If more than ¼" (6.4mm) needs to be added below the waist, add it in equal ¼" (6.4mm) to sections about 1¼" (3.2cm) apart so the insertions are spread over the piece. The insert is a wedge shape with a hinge at the side seam. Smooth the pattern pieces after inserting.the center-back and center-front panels. Alter the side panels so they are within ⅛" (3.2mm) below the waist and ¼" (6.4mm) above. Notch the waist after folding out the waist shaping so it is clear where to start measuring.

Note the location of the slash and insertion lines on *Fig. 5.5*. Above the waist in front, insert as needed level with the high figure point. Insert at the same level on the back. Below the waist, insert as needed within 2" (5.1cm) of the waist guideline on the front and back. If more than ¼" (6.4mm) needs to be added below the waist, add it in equal ¼" (6.4mm) to sections about 1¼" (3.2cm) apart so the insertions are spread over the piece. The insert is a wedge shape with a hinge at the side seam. Smooth the pattern pieces after inserting.

BACK CONTOURING

If using a center-back seam, utilize back contouring by coming in ⅜" (1cm) at the center-back waist and blending to zero at the cross back and to zero at 7" (17.8cm) below the waist (as was done in the back moulage instructions). The waist dart can be reduced in width by ⅜" (1cm), so the back waist calculation is not compromised. If a tighter fit is desired, use back contouring but do not reduce the waist dart. Back contouring allows the garment to fit closer to the body along the spine (*Fig. 5.7*).

WAIST SHAPING AT THE NECK AND SHOULDER

If unable to take waist shaping conventionally at the waist with a princess line or a waist seam, the waist shaping can be taken at the neck and shoulder. Waist shaping is taken with a fitted or semifitted garment to prevent wrinkling at the curve of the waist. There is no need to take waist shaping on loose garments because the fabric hangs away from the body. Taking waist shaping at the neck and shoulder lifts the garment up at the neck and shoulder pulling waist winkles up and out. It is done before drafting any other part of the pattern.

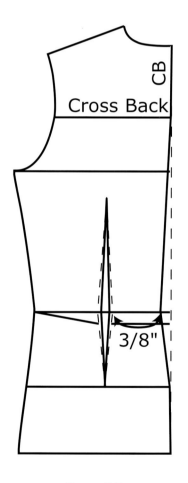

Figure 5.7

Front and Back

1. Trace the sloper and mark **A**, **B**, **C**, **D**, **E**, and **F** as shown (*Fig. 5.8*).
2. **AG** = ½" (1.3cm) drop at the center-front or center-back neck
3. **BH** = ½" (1.3cm) drop at the high-neck point (square straight down)
4. **CI** = ¼" (6.4mm) drop at the end of shoulder (square straight down)
5. **DJ** = ¼" (6.4mm) drop at the underarm (square straight down)
6. Make sure all the above drops are taken straight down from the original point, not along the slope of the neckline, shoulder, or side.
7. Connect **G-H** for the new neckline (trace the sloper neckline to get the proper shape).
8. Connect **H-I** for the new shoulder (trace the sloper shoulder to get the proper shape).
9. Connect **I-J** for the new armhole (trace the sloper armhole to get the proper shape).
10. In **front**, drop the figure points (high and low) ⅜" (1cm) to correspond with the amount dropped directly above on the shoulder. Redraw the darts to the new lowered figure points.
11. In **back**, lower the points of the shoulder and waist darts ⅜" (1cm) to correspond to the amount dropped directly above on the shoulder. Redraw the darts to the new lowered points.

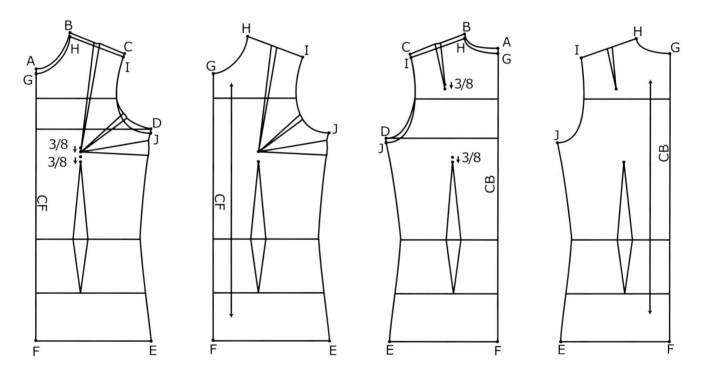

Figure 5.8

Exercises

PRINCESS LINE TO THE SHOULDER

A princess seam line to the shoulder begins anywhere on the shoulder and ends anywhere at the base of the garment. The seam incorporates the shoulder, armhole, side, and waist darts. The princess line to shoulder is a dart-equivalent style line. Princess seamlines on the front and back shoulder should line up.

Front

1. Trace the front sloper, including the darts and waist shaping. Mark **A**, **B**, **C**, **D**, **E**, and **F** as shown (*Fig. 5.9*).
2. Manipulate the shoulder and armhole darts (both noted as dotted lines, showing they were folded out) into the side dart to get them out of the way when drawing the princess seam.
3. Indicate the desired placement of the seam on the shoulder. Commonly, the seam is in the center of the shoulder, but it can be anywhere on the shoulder. Starting the seam closer to the end of shoulder will make the shoulders look broader. Starting closer to the neck makes the shoulders look narrower. Mark **G**.
4. Indicate the desired placement of the seam at the base. It can fall anywhere on the base as designed. Mark **H**.
5. Draw the desired princess seamline from **G** to **H**. The diagram shows the princess seam crossing the high figure point, but the line can be moved toward the side seam. The line can be straight up and down or curved (see Drafting Rules for Princess Seams—Smooth Seamlines).
6. Mark the new pivotal point on the princess line if it moved from the high figure point and draw the side dart to the new pivotal point (see Drafting Rules for Princess Seams—High and Low Figure Points/Pivotal Points).
7. Redraw the waist dart so it forms to the side of the **GH** line as shown or center it over the line

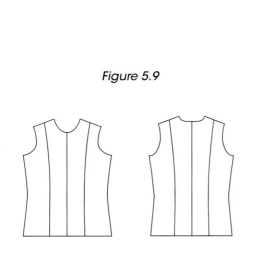

Figure 5.9

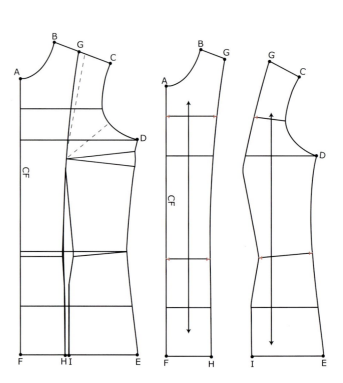

(see Drafting Rules for Princess Seams—Forming Waist Darts to Seamlines).

8. **HI** = ¼" (6.4mm) to create a channel below the dart. Figure out where on the waist dart the width is ¼" (6.4mm). From that ¼" (6.4mm) width, draw down to the base, keeping a ¼" (6.4mm) channel. Removing ¼" (6.4mm) between the seams creates a smoother fit below the dart through to the low hip in front.
9. Cut the pattern apart on the **GH** seamline.
10. Cut the waist dart away.
11. Fold the side dart out.
12. Fold the waist shaping out on the center-front and side panel pieces (see Drafting Rules for Princess Seams—Waist Shaping).
13. Measure the princess seamlines. Adjust as necessary to keep the difference to no more than ⅜" (1cm) (see Drafting Rules for Princess Seams—Seam Lines Should be Within ⅜" [1cm]).
14. Smooth the pattern by trimming or filling in any points or dips that are not part of the design.
15. Center-Front Panel: **A-B-G-H-F-A**
16. Notch the waist and cross front at the center front and on the princess seam. Draw the grainline parallel to the center front. Add ½" (1.3cm) seam allowance and a 1½" (3.8cm) hem. Drag the notches to the perimeter. Cut (2) self or cut (1) self on fold at center front.
17. Side-Front Panel: **G-C-D-E-H-G**
18. Notch the waist on the princess seam and the side. Notch the cross front on the princess seam. Draw the grainline perpendicular to the low-hip guideline. Add ½" (3.8cm) seam allowance and a 1½" (3.8cm) hem. Drag the notches to the perimeter. Cut (2) self.

Fitting Tip:
Drafting a channel below the waist is only done in front because there is a hollow where the legs meet the torso. The adjustment is not done on the back because a rear end fills out the fabric. There is no hollow on the back side.

Back

1. Trace the back sloper, including the darts and waist shaping. Mark **J**, **K**, **L**, **M**, **N**, and **O** as shown (*Fig. 5.10*). Utilize back contouring if the garment will have a center-back seam (see Back Contouring).
2. **P** = placement of the princess seam on the shoulder. Match it to **G** on the front.
3. **Q** = placement of the seam at the base. **Q** should be similarly placed as **H** on the front.
4. Draw the desired princess seamline from **P** to **Q** (see Drafting Rules for Princess Seams—Smooth Seamlines).
5. Redraw the waist dart and the shoulder dart so they form to the **PQ** seam as shown. Both the shoulder and waist dart should be placed toward the side panel or centered over the line (see Drafting Rules for Princess Seams—Forming Waist Darts to Seamlines).
6. Cut the pattern apart on the **PQ** seamline. Cut the shoulder and waist darts away.
7. Fold the waist shaping out (see Drafting Rules for Princess Seams—Waist Shaping).
8. Measure the princess seamlines. Adjust as necessary to keep the difference to no more than

⅜" (1cm) (see Drafting Rules for Princess Seams—Seam Lines Should be Within ⅜" [1cm]).

9. Smooth the pattern by trimming or filling in any obvious points or dips.

10. True the front and back patterns at the shoulders and sides. Check that the connections at the high-neck/shoulder point, end of shoulder, underarm, and base at side are smooth.

11. Center-Back Panel: **J-K-P-Q-O-J**

12. Double notch the waist and cross back at the center back, and single notch on the princess seam at the waist and cross back. Draw the grainline parallel to the original (straight, not contoured) center back. Drag the notches to the perimeter. Add ½" (1.3cm) seam allowance and a 1½" (3.8cm) hem. Cut (2) self.

13. Side-Back Panel: **P-L-M-N-Q-P**

14. Align the notches at the waist and cross back on the princess seam. Notch waist at side. Draw the grainline perpendicular to the low-hip guideline. Add ½" (1.3cm) seam allowance and a 1½" (3.8cm) hem. Drag the notches to the perimeter. Cut (2) self.

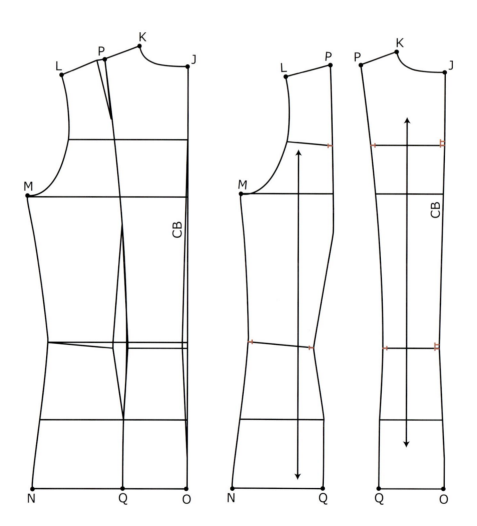

Figure 5.10

Building Patterns

PRINCESS LINE TO THE ARMHOLE

A princess seam to the armhole begins in the armhole and ends at the base of the garment. The seam incorporates the shoulder, armhole, side, and waist darts. The waist shaping is folded out. A princess seam to the armhole is a dart-equivalent style line. The seam can start anywhere in the armhole, however traditionally, the front seam starts at the cross-front guideline and the back seam starts at the cross-back guideline.

Front

1. Trace the front sloper, including the darts and waist shaping. Mark **A**, **B**, **C**, **D**, **E**, and **F** as shown (*Fig. 5.11*).
2. Manipulate the shoulder and armhole darts (both noted as a dotted lines, showing they were folded out) into the side dart to get them out of the way when drawing the princess seam.
3. Indicate the desired placement of the seam in the armhole. Mark **G**.
4. Indicate the desired placement of the seam at the base. Mark **H**.
5. Draw the desired princess seamline from **G** to **H**. The diagram shows the princess seam crossing outside the high figure point, but it is up to the designer where the line crosses (see Drafting Rules for Princess Seams—Smooth Seamlines).
6. Mark the new pivotal point on the princess line if it moved from the high figure point, and draw the side dart to the new pivotal point (see Drafting Rules for Princess Seams—High and Low Figure Points/Pivotal Points).
7. Redraw the waist dart so it forms to the side of the **GH** line as shown or center the dart over the line (see Drafting Rules for Princess Seams—Forming Waist Darts to Seamlines).
8. **HI** = ⅜" (1cm) to create a channel below the dart as was done in Princess Line to the Shoulder (page 109).
9. Cut the pattern apart on the **GH** seamline.

Figure 5.11

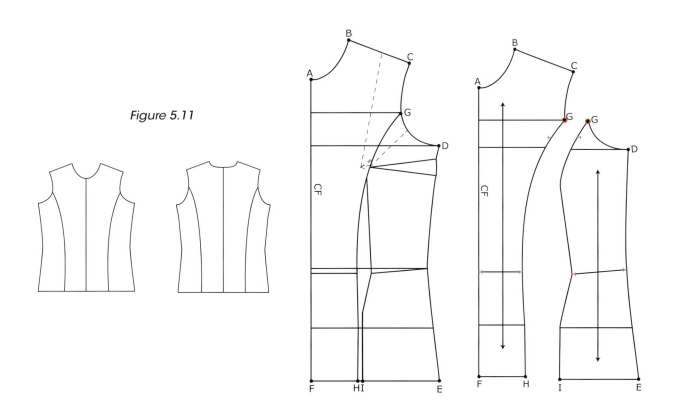

Fitting Tip:
The closer the princess line is to the high figure point, the more fitted the garment will be through the bust.

---

10. Cut the waist dart away.
11. Fold the side dart out.
12. Fold the waist shaping out on the center front and side panel pieces (see Drafting Rules for Princess Seams—Waist Shaping).
13. Measure the princess seamlines. Adjust as necessary to keep the difference to no more than ⅜" (1cm) (see Drafting Rules for Princess Seams—Seam Lines Should be Within ⅜" [1cm]).
14. Smooth the pattern by trimming or filling in any points or dips that are not part of the design.
15. Center-Front Panel: **A-B-C-G-H-F-A**
16. Notch the waist at center front and side. Notch 3" (7.6cm) below the cross front on the princess seam. Awl-punch **G**. Draw the grainline parallel to the center front. Add ½" (1.3cm) seam allowance and a 1½" (3.8cm) hem. Drag the notches to the perimeter. Cut (2) self or cut one on fold at center front.
17. Side-Front Panel: **G-D-E-H-G**
18. Notch the waist on the princess seam and the side. Notch 3" (7.6cm) below the cross front on the princess seam. Draw the grainline perpendicular to the low-hip guideline. Add ½" (1.3cm) seam allowance and a 1½" (3.8cm) hem. Drag the notches to the perimeter. Cut (2) self.

Marking Tip:
Whenever a pattern piece comes to a point or has a corner, awl-punch the point or corner. Awl-punching will allow the sewer to construct pointed and cornered pieces more accurately.

Back
1. Trace the back sloper, including the darts and waist shaping. **Mark J**, **K**, **L**, **M**, **N**, and **O** as shown (*Fig. 5.12*). Utilize back contouring if the garment will have a center-back seam (see Back Contouring).
2. **P** = placement of the princess seam in the armhole
3. **Q** = placement of the seam at the base. **Q** should be similarly placed as **H** on the front.
4. Draw the desired princess seamline from **P** to **Q** (see Drafting Rules for Princess Seams—Smooth Seamlines).
5. Redraw the waist dart so it forms to the **PQ** seam as shown. Place the waist dart so it is toward the side panel or center it over the line (see Drafting Rules for Princess Seams—Forming Waist Darts to Seamlines).
6. Cut the pattern apart on the **PQ** seamline. Cut waist dart away.
7. Fold the waist shaping out (see Drafting Rules for Princess Seams—Waist Shaping).

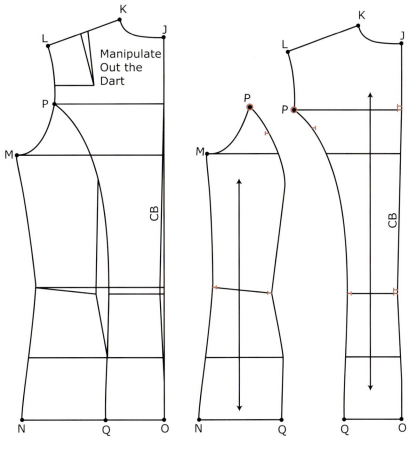

Figure 5.12

Drafting Tip:

Sewing the back shoulder dart would not look compatible with the curve of the princess line to the armhole. Manipulate the shoulder dart out of the pattern by shaving the width off the end of the shoulder; or manipulating it into the armhole (see *Fig. 5.12*), and then lower the end of the shoulder the amount the dart opens; or ease the dart width into the front shoulder when sewing. Any of these options will give the back shoulder a cleaner line that will not visually conflict with the back princess seam line into the armhole.

8. Measure the princess seamlines. Adjust as necessary to keep the difference to no more than ⅜" (1cm) (see Drafting Rules for Princess Seams—Seam Lines Should be Within ⅜" [1cm]).

9. Smooth the pattern by trimming or filling in any obvious points or dips.

10. True the front and back patterns at the shoulders and sides. Check that the connections at the high-neck/shoulder point, end of shoulder, underarm, and base at side are smooth.

11. Center-Back Panel: **J-K-L-P-Q-O-J**

12. 1 Double notch the waist and cross back at the center back, and single notch on the princess seam at the waist and cross back. Draw the grainline parallel to the original (straight, not contoured) center back. Add ½" (1.3cm) seam allowance and a 1½" (3.8cm) hem. Drag the notches to the perimeter. Cut (2) self.

13. Side-Back Panel: **P-M-N-Q-P**

14. Align the notches at the waist and cross back with the center-back panel. Notch waist at side. Draw the grainline perpendicular to the low-hip guideline. Add ½" (1.3cm) seam allowance and a 1½" (3.8cm) hem. Drag the notches to the perimeter. Cut (2) self.

DOUBLE PRINCESS LINES

A double princess seam garment has both a princess seam to the shoulder and a princess seam to the armhole in the same quarter panel. In all, there are eight princess seams within the same garment.

Fitting Tip:
The more seam lines there are in a pattern, the more opportunities there are to refine the fit. Subtle refinements over multiple seam lines fit better than chunky adjustments over fewer seams. Multiple subtle seam and dart refinements are what help corsets fit so smoothly to the body.

Front

1. Begin by tracing the front sloper then manipulating the armhole dart into the side dart (*Fig. 5.13*).
2. Draft a princess seam to the shoulder, putting half the waist dart width in the princess seam. Try something different by placing the shoulder dart next to the princess line, so it can be cut away later rather than manipulating it. The shoulder dart can be manipulated out or cut away with the princess seam.
3. Draft a princess seam to the armhole, putting the other half of the waist dart width in that princess seam. Seam placement is as desired, but centering the line over the remaining base and waist is a good place to start. Be sure the seam squares straight through the side dart, so when that dart is folded out, the seam does not have a jog in it.
4. Cut the pattern apart on the princess seams, and cut the waist and shoulder darts away. Fold out the side dart. Fold out the waist shaping. It helps to add **F1** (on the center-front panel), **F2** (on the middle panel), and **F3** (on the side panel) to keep track of the pieces.
5. Check the princess seam lengths and adjust as necessary (see Drafting Rules for Princess Seams—Seam Lines Should be Within ⅜" [1cm]). **F2** needs to be adjusted to **F1**, and **F3** needs to be adjusted to **F2**.
6. Notch at the waist on all the pieces. Awl-punch at the points of the princess seam to the armhole. Draw length grainlines on all pieces. Add ½" (1.3cm) seam allowance and a 1½" (3.8cm) hem. Drag the notches to the perimeter. Cut (2) self or (1) self on fold at center.

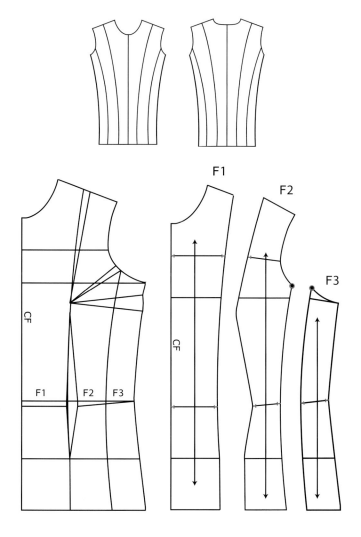

Figure 5.13

Back

1. Begin by tracing the back sloper (*Fig. 5.14*). Utilize back contouring if the garment will have a center-back seam (see Back Contouring).
2. Draft a princess seam to the shoulder, matching the seam at the shoulder to the front. Put half the waist dart width against the princess seam. Put the full shoulder dart against the princess seam.
3. Draft a princess seam to the armhole, putting the other half of the waist dart width against that princess seam.
4. Cut the pattern apart on the princess seams, and cut the waist and shoulder darts away. Fold out the waist shaping. Add **B1** (on the center-back panel), **B2** (on the middle panel), and **B3** (on the side panel) to keep track of the pieces.
5. Check the princess seam lengths and adjust as necessary (see Drafting Rules for Princess Seams—Seam Lines Should be Within ⅜" [1cm]). **B2** needs to be adjusted to **B1**, and **B3** needs to be adjusted to **B2**.
6. Notch at the waist on all the pieces. Double notch center back at the cross back and waist. Awl-punch at the points of the princess seam to the armhole. Draw length grainlines on all pieces. Add ½" (1.3cm) seam allowance and a 1½" (3.8cm) hem. Drag the notches to the perimeter. Cut (2) self.

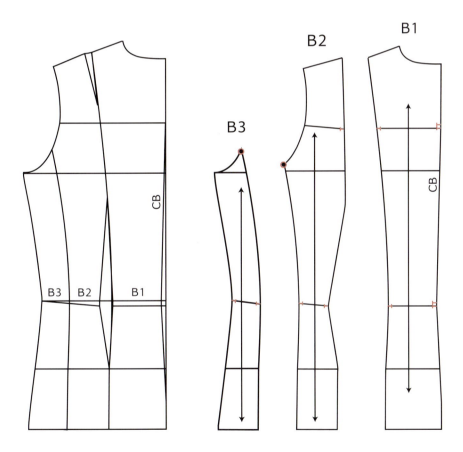

Figure 5.14

PRINCESS LINE/SIDE PANEL

Side panels remove a traditional side seam by merging side pieces. Side panels are often used on garments that are semifitted or loosely fitted.

Front and Back

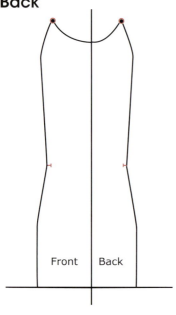
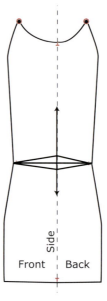
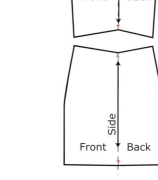

Figure 5.15   *Figure 5.16*

1. Trace pattern piece **F3** and **B3** (front and back side panels), including the notches and drill holes.
2. Draw a vertical guideline down the middle of a new piece of pattern paper. The guideline should be slightly longer than the length of the side seam.
3. Draw a horizontal guideline off the base of the vertical guideline.
4. Place the underarm points touching against the vertical guideline. These points need to touch, or the garment will be too big at the bust and armhole. Place the base of the front and back side panels against the horizontal guideline. To keep the base straight on the horizontal guideline, there might be slight overlapping at the hips of pieces **F3** and **B3**. Or the pieces might tip up at the bottom edges. If that happens, straighten the base line from the edge to edge.
5. Notice that there is a gap in the middle of **F3** and **B3**. This gap will create a loose look and feel (*Fig. 5.15*).
6. Draw the waist guideline across the piece from waist notch to waist notch.
7. Mark ¼" (6.4mm) above the middle of the horizontal waist guideline and ¼" (6.4mm) below. Blend to zero at the seams on the edge of the pattern piece for a horizontal **fish-eyed** (aka **double-pointed**) **dart**. This dart will allow the side panel to contour to the waistline curve.
8. Cut the fish-eyed dart away. There are now two pattern pieces for the side panel (*Fig. 5.16*). Notch to help line up the pieces when sewing.
9. **Upper Side Piece:** Notch on the vertical guideline under the arm. Notch to line up the upper and lower side pieces on the waistline. Awl-punch the princess seam points. Draw a length grainline. Add ½" (1.3cm) seam allowance. Drag the notches to the perimeter. Cut (2) self.
10. **Lower Side Piece:** Notch to line up with the upper-side-piece notch on the waistline. Draw a length grainline. Drag the notches to the perimeter. Add ½" (1.3cm) seam allowance and a 1½" (3.8cm) hem. Cut (2) self.
11. Sew **F1, F2, B1,** and **B2** pattern pieces to the side panels and refine the fit as needed.

Design Tip:
With so many vertical seamlines, it helps to add a horizontal seamline at the waist to break up the visual monotony. Adding a hidden pocket into the horizontal waist seam would make the garment more versatile.

EMPIRE LINE

An empire line crosses under the bust horizontally. The line can be straight or curved. The fit can be snug or loose. An empire line is a dart-equivalent style line.

Front

1. Trace the front sloper, including the darts and waist shaping. Mark **A**, **B**, **C**, **D**, **E**, and **F** as shown (*Fig. 5.17*).
2. Manipulate the shoulder and armhole darts into the side dart, using the low figure point as the pivotal point.
3. Indicate the desired placement of the empire seam at the center front. Commonly, the seam is placed 3"–4" (7.6–10.2cm) above the waist but under the breast tissue. Mark **G**.
4. Indicate the desired placement of the seam at the side. Mark **H**.
5. Draw the desired empire seam line from **G** to **H**. The line can be designed straight or curved.
6. **GI** = ½" (1.3cm) waist shaping. Take the waist shaping under the empire seam.
7. Connect **I-H** in the same shape as **G-H** for the waist shaping as shown.
8. Cut the pattern along the **GH** line and cut the waist shaping away at the **IH** line.
9. Manipulate the side dart into what is remaining of the waist dart on the top piece. The remaining waist dart can be pleated, gathered, sewn as a dart, or taken in a princess seam.
10. The remaining dart on the bottom piece is sewn. Make sure the bottom piece is trued to the top piece by adjusting the seam in at **H**, so the top and bottom pieces fit together.
11. Front Top Piece: **A-B-C-D-H-G-A**, including the dart (or pleat or gather)
12. Notch the center front at the neck and base. Notch arbitrarily along the empire line. Awl-punch and notch the dart or mark for gathers or for a pleat. Draw the grainline parallel to the center front. Add ½" (1.3cm) seam allowance. Drag the notches to the perimeter. Cut (1) self on fold.
13. Front Bottom Piece: **I-H-E-F-I**, including the dart
14. Notch the center of the piece, top, and bottom. Include a notch along the empire line to match the front top piece. Notch the waist at side. Awl-punch and notch the dart. Draw the grainline parallel to the center front. Add ½" (1.3cm) seam allowance and a 1½" (3.8cm) hem. Drag the notches to the perimeter. Cut (1) self on fold.

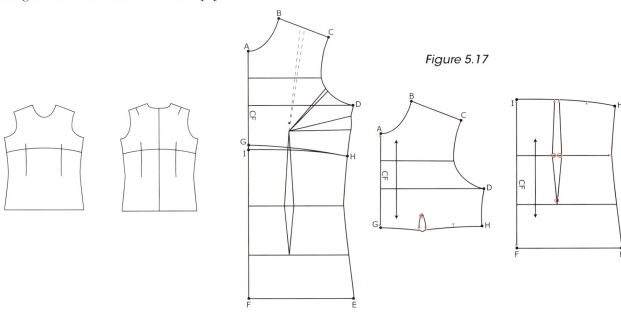

Figure 5.17

Back

1. Trace the back sloper, including the darts and waist shaping. Mark **J**, **K**, **L**, **M**, **N**, and **O** as shown (*Fig. 5.18*). Utilize back contouring if the garment will have a center-back seam (see Back Contouring).
2. Indicate the desired placement of the seam at the center back. Mark **P**.
3. Indicate the desired placement of the seam at the side. Mark **Q**. Figure out where to position **Q** by temporarily attaching **DH** from the front to the back side seam, to find a smooth transition point between front and back.
4. Draw the desired empire seamline from **P** to **Q**.
5. **PR** = ½" (1.3cm) waist shaping
6. Connect **R-Q** in the same shape as **PQ** for the waist shaping as shown.
7. Cut the pattern along the **PQ** line and cut the waist shaping away at the **QR** line.
8. Keep the remaining dart in the top piece and sew it as a dart.
9. The remaining dart on the bottom piece is also sewn. Make sure the bottom piece is trued to the top piece by adjusting the side seam in at **Q**, so the top and bottom pieces fit together.
10. True the front and back patterns at the shoulders and sides. Check that the connections at the high-neck/shoulder point, end of shoulder, underarm, and base at side are smooth.
11. Back Top Piece: **J-K-L-M-Q-P**, including the dart
12. Double notch at the cross back. Notch arbitrarily along the empire line. Awl-punch and notch the dart. Draw the grainline perpendicular to the guidelines. Add ½" (1.3cm) seam allowance. Drag the notches to the perimeter. Cut (2) self.
13. Back Bottom Piece: **R-Q-N-O-R**, including the dart
14. Double notch the waist at the center back. Include a notch along the empire line to match the back top piece. Notch the waist at side. Awl-punch and notch the dart. Draw the grainline perpendicular to the guidelines. Add ½" (1.3cm) seam allowance and a 1½" (3.8cm) hem. Drag the notches to the perimeter. Cut (2) self.

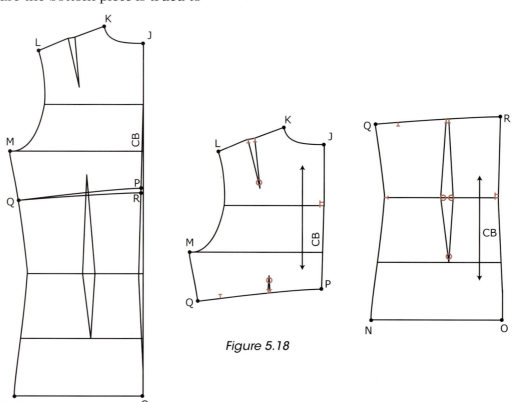

Figure 5.18

SHIFT DRESS

A shift dress is fitted through the bustline, fairly fitted through the waist, and has an A-line skirt base. Waist shaping should be taken through the neck and shoulder since the garment does not have a waist seam or a princess seam. A shift dress has a French dart and a center-front seam. It can be cut on the length or bias grainline (length for more structure and bias for a softer look) and is sleeveless.

Front

1. Trace the sloper and extend the length as a rectangle from the low-hip guideline (example: add 15" [38.1cm] in length from the low-hip guideline).
2. Take the waist shaping at the neck and shoulder (see Waist Shaping at the Neck and Shoulder).
3. Mark **A**, **B**, **C**, **D**, **E**, and **F** as shown (*Fig. 5.19*).
4. Using the high figure point as a pivotal point, manipulate the shoulder, armhole, and side darts into a French dart.
5. Mark **G** midway between **F** and **E** at the base.
6. Connect **G** to the bottom of the waist dart.
7. Cut from **G** to the base of the dart and open 1½" (3.8cm) at the base for a flare insertion. It will be necessary to crease the pattern at the side (see crease on *Fig. 5.19*) to open the pattern for the flare insertion.

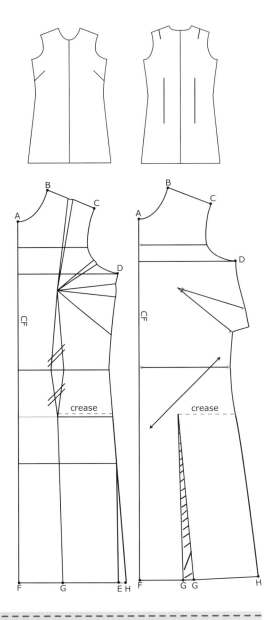

Figure 5.19

Fitting Tip:

Because some of the side length was absorbed by the crease, the side base might have to be lengthened in the first fitting. However, because the garment is cut on bias, the side seam could also easily stretch, which could balance out this issue. Add a hem allowance of 2" (5.1cm) rather than the usual 1" (2.5cm) on flares, so there is enough fabric to adjust as needed. Pay close attention to leveling out the base in the first fitting.

---

8. **EH** = ¾" (1.9cm) extension at side (half the width of the insertion)
9. Blend the extension from **H** to the low-hip guideline at side.
10. The waist dart will not be sewn. Draw lines through it, so it does not mistakenly get marked and sewn.
11. Front Pattern: **A-B-C-D-H-F-A**, including the French dart
12. Notch the waist at the side and center front. Notch the cross front at the center front. Awl-punch and notch the French dart. Draw a bias grainline. Add 1" (2.5cm) seam allowances at sides and center front, ½" (1.3cm) everywhere else, and a 2" (5.1cm) hem. Drag the notches to the perimeter. Cut (2) self.

Cutting Tip:
Many bias-cut garments have center-front, center-back, and seemingly randomly placed seams because full width pattern pieces don't always fit on the fabric at a 45-degree angle.

Back
1. Trace the back sloper, including the darts. Extend the base as front.
2. Take the waist shaping at the neck and shoulder (see Waist Shaping at the Neck and Shoulder). Utilize back contouring (see Back Contouring).
3. Mark **I**, **J**, **K**, **L**, **M**, and **N** as shown (*Fig. 5.20*).
4. Mark **O** midway between **N** and **P** at the base.
5. Connect **O** to the bottom of the waist dart.
6. Cut from **O** to the base of the dart and open 1½" (3.8cm) at the base for a flare insertion. It will be necessary to crease the pattern at the side (see crease on *Fig. 5.20*) to open the pattern for the flare insertion.
7. **MP** = ¾" (1.9cm) extension at side (half the width of the insertion)
8. Blend the extension from **P** to the low-hip guideline at side.
9. The waist dart can or cannot be sewn. Not sewing the waist dart in front works well for this silhouette, but sewing the waist dart in back offers a better fit.
10. True the front and back patterns at the shoulders and sides. Check that the connections at the high-neck/shoulder point, end of shoulder, underarm, and base at side are smooth.
11. Back Pattern: **I-J-K-L-P-O-N-I**
12. Notch the waist at the side and double notch the waist and cross back at center back. Mark the back dart with drill holes if it will be used. Otherwise cross out the waist dart. Notch and awl-punch the shoulder dart. Draw a bias grainline. Add 1" (2.5cm) seam allowances at sides and center back, ½" (1.3cm) everywhere else, and a 2" (5.1cm) hem. Drag the notches to the perimeter. Cut (2) self.

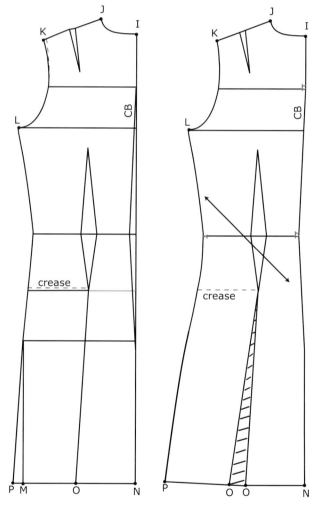

Figure 5.20

118   Building Patterns

SMOCK DRESS

A smock dress is fitted from the shoulder to the high figure point, and falls loosely from there. Waist shaping is not needed because the garment is full. Often, the top pattern piece is cut on the length grain for structure and the bottom piece is cut on bias so the fabric drapes.

Front

1. Trace the front sloper, including the shoulder, armhole, and side darts (exclude the waist dart). Extend the length as a rectangle from the low-hip guideline (example: add 15" [38.1cm] in length from the low-hip guideline).
2. Mark **A**, **B**, **C**, **D**, **E**, and **F** as shown (*Fig. 5.21*).
3. Draw a line from the center front through the high figure point to the side seam. The line should be perpendicular to the center front. Mark **G** and **H**.
4. Redraw the side dart width below **H** and draw to the high figure point.
5. Divide the **FE** line into two and a half parts. Mark **J** and **K**. For example, if **FE** measures 10" (25.4cm), two and a half parts is 2" (5.1cm), 4" (10.2cm), and 4" (10.2cm). The half part is closest to the center front, so when the garment opens, there will be a full part at the center front.
6. Divide the **GI** line into two and a half parts. Mark **L** and **M**.
7. Connect **J-L** and connect **K-M**.
8. Cut along the **GH** line. Cut the side dart away.
9. Fold the shoulder and the armhole darts out of the top piece.
10. Cut from **J**, hinging at **L**. Cut from **K**, hinging at **M**. Insert equally as desired (example: 3" [7.6cm] insertions).
11. Top Front Pattern: **A-B-C-D-H-G-A**
12. Arbitrarily notch along **GH**. Draw a length grainline. Add ½" (1.3cm) seam allowances. Drag the notches to the perimeter. Cut (1) self on fold.
13. Front Base Pattern: **G-L-M-I-E-K-J-F-G**
14. Notch along the **GI** line corresponding to the notch on the top pattern.
15. Notch the waist at the center front and side. Draw a bias grainline. Add 1" (2.5cm) seam allowances at sides and center front, ½" (1.3cm) everywhere else, and a 1" (2.5cm) hem. Cut (2) self.

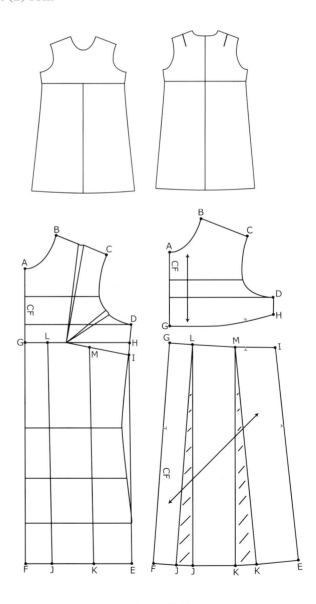

Figure 5.21

Back

1. Trace the back sloper, including the shoulder dart (exclude the waist dart), and extend the length as front. Utilize back contouring (see Back Contouring).
2. Mark **N**, **O**, **P**, **Q**, **R**, and **S** as shown (*Fig. 5.22*).
3. Draw a line on the back, level with **GH** on the front, through to the center back. Mark **T** and **U**.
4. Divide the **RS** line into two and a half parts. Mark **V** and **W**.
5. Divide **TU** into two and a half parts. Mark **X** and **Y**.
6. Connect **V-X** and connect **W-Y**.
7. Cut along the **TU** line.
8. Cut from **V**, hinging at **X**. Cut from **W**, hinging at **Y**. Insert equally as desired (example: 4" [10.2cm] each insertion).
9. True the front and back patterns at the shoulders and sides. Check that the connections at the high-neck/shoulder point, end of shoulder, underarm, and base at side are smooth.

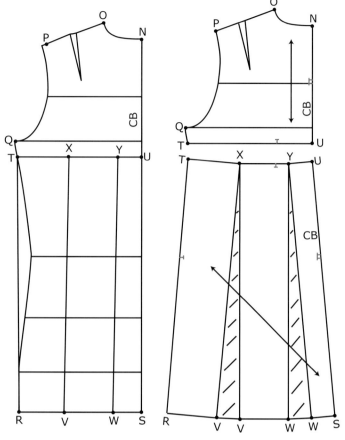

Figure 5.22

Drafting Tip:
Back insertions are often slightly wider than front insertions to give the garment more volume in the back.

10. Top Back Pattern: **N-O-P-Q-T-U-N**
11. Arbitrarily notch along **UT**. Double notch the cross back at center back. Draw a length grainline. Add ½" (1.3cm) seam allowances. Drag the notches to the perimeter. Cut (2) self.
12. Back Base Pattern: **U-T-R-S-U**
13. Notch along the **TU** line corresponding to the notch on the top pattern.
14. Notch the waist at side. Double notch the center back. Draw a bias grainline. Add 1" (2.5cm) seam allowances at sides and center back, ½" (1.3cm) everywhere else, and a 1" (2.5cm) hem. Drag the notches to the perimeter. Cut (2) self.

TRAPEZE DRESS

A swing silhouette is fitted from the shoulder to the cross front and cross back, and flares from there. Waist shaping is not needed because of the fullness. Because the silhouette should have volume and not hug the body, the pattern is cut on the length grain rather than bias.

Front

1. Trace the front sloper, including the shoulder, armhole, and side darts (exclude the waist dart). Extend the length from the low hip as desired. Manipulate the shoulder and armhole darts into the side dart. Mark **A**, **B**, **C**, **D**, **E**, and **F** as shown (*Fig. 5.23*).
2. Mark **G** and **H** on the cross-front guideline as shown.
3. Divide the **FE** base into two and a half parts. Mark **I** and **J**.
4. Divide **GH** into two and a half parts. Mark **K** and **L** 1" (2.5cm) below the **GH** line.
5. Connect **I-K**.
6. Connect **J-L**.
7. Cut from **I** to **K** to **H**, hinging at **H**, and insert as desired (example: 2"–3" [5.1–7.6cm]).
8. Cut from **J** to **L** to **H**, hinging at **H**, and insert as the **IKH** insertion.
9. Connect **D-E** in a straight line.
10. Blend the base in a smooth line.
11. Back the side dart off to the **LJ** line. True the dart legs.
12. Front Pattern: **A-B-C-D-E-J-I-F-A**, including the side dart
13. Notch the waist at the center front and side. Draw a length grainline parallel to the center front. Add ½" (1.3cm) seam allowances and a 1" (2.5cm) hem. Drag the notches to the perimeter. Cut (2) self.

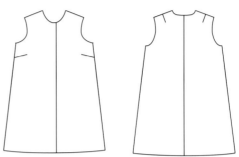

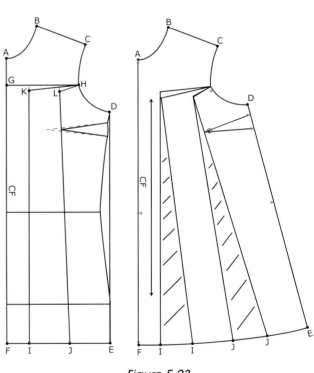

Figure 5.23

Drafting Tip:

Because this pattern does not have a seamline at the top of the insertions, the insertions need to angle toward the perimeter of the pattern. By dropping the insertion lines 1" (2.5cm) below the line, the insertions lines will not cross, and the pattern can be kept in one piece when cutting insertions.

Back

1. Trace the back sloper, including shoulder dart. Extend the length as front. Utilize back contouring (see Back Contouring). Mark **M, N, O, P, Q**, and **R** as shown (*Fig. 5.24*).
2. Mark **S** and **T** on the cross-back guideline as shown.
3. Divide the **QR** base into two and a half parts. Mark **U** and **V**.
4. Divide **ST** into two and a half parts. Mark **W** and **X** 1" (2.5cm) below the **ST** line.
5. Connect **U-W**.
6. Connect **V-X**.
7. Cut from **U** to **W** to **S**, hinging at **S**, and insert as desired (example: 3"–4" [7.6–10.2cm]). The back insertion amount can be more than the front insertion amount.
8. Cut from **V** to **X** to **S**, hinging at **S**, and insert as the **UWS** insertion.
9. Connect **P-Q** in a straight line.
10. Blend the base in a smooth line.
11. True the front and back patterns at the shoulders and sides. Check that the connections at the high-neck/shoulder point, end of shoulder, underarm, and base at side are smooth.
12. Back Pattern: **M-N-O-P-Q-U-V-R-M**
13. Notch the waist at the side. Double notch the center back at the cross back and the waist. Draw a length grainline parallel to the center back. Add ½" (1.3cm) seam allowances and a 1" (2.5cm) hem. Drag the notches to the perimeter. Cut (2) self.

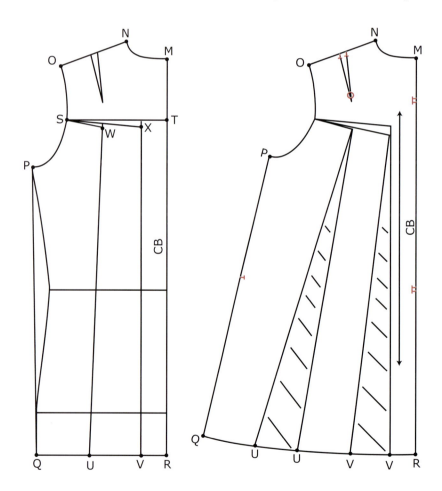

Figure 5.24

Design Tip:

To add to the drama of a trapeze silhouette, drop the center-back base 1" (2.5cm), or more; drop the side seams ½" (1.3cm), or half the adjustment at the center back; and blend to zero midway along the front base. Most garments are level around the base. Try this adjustment to see if it adds refinement or elegance.

 Test Your Knowledge

1. Describe a dart-equivalent seam line and a nondart-equivalent seam line.

2. List the five rules for drafting princess seams.

3. Why would waist shaping be taken at the neck and shoulder?

4. Do flare insertion amounts on the front and back need to match?

5. Describe how to draft the center-back base longer than the center front. What is the reason for this adjustment?

This chapter offers instruction on how to build a flattering neckline that will not gape or fall off the shoulder. Exercises include boat neckline, V-neckline, scoop, sweetheart, strapless, funnel, and surplice necklines.

OBJECTIVES

Upon completion of this chapter, you will be able to

- Draft necklines so they do not slip off the shoulders or gape at the neckline
- Understand the differences between neckline shapes and styles
- Pattern for a clean finish on sleeveless garments

CHAPTER 6
Necklines

Rules for Well-Fitting Necklines and Bodices

HIGH-NECK/SHOULDER POINT ADJUSTMENT

For a neckline to fit without gaping, the width of the back neckline should be wider than the front neckline from center back to the start of the shoulder strap. The inside placement of the shoulder strap is called the **high-neck/shoulder point**.

If the start of the shoulder strap (high-neck/shoulder point) is close-fitting at the neck, the back neckline should be ⅜" (1cm) wider. If the high-neck/shoulder point is moved toward the middle of the shoulder, the back neckline should be wider by ⅝" (1.6cm) at the start of the shoulder strap. With a high-neck/shoulder point moved out toward the end of shoulder, the back neckline should be ⅞" (2.2cm) wider. It is important to note that the front and back shoulder straps are the same width, but the width from center back to the start of the back shoulder strap is wider than the front by ⅜", ⅝", or ⅞" (1, 1.6, or 2.2cm).

Let's break this rule into steps.

1

Draw a line that's the measurement of the front shoulder on the sloper, excluding the shoulder dart (*Fig. 6.1*). Let's use 4½" (11.4cm) as an example. Above the line, write zero at the start of the line. At the end of the line, write the shoulder length measurement (4½" [11.4cm]). In the middle of the line, write half the shoulder measurement (2¼" [5.7cm]). Below the zero, write ⅜" (1cm). Below the halfway mark, write ⅝" (1.6cm). Below the full shoulder measurement, write ⅞" (2.2cm).

Option: To be more precise, divide the shoulder into four equal parts above the line: 0, 1⅛" (2.9cm), 2¼" (5.7cm), 3⅜" (8.6cm), and 4½" (11.4cm). Write below the line: ⅜" (1cm), ½" (1.3cm), ⅝" (1.6cm), ¾" (1.9cm), and ⅞" (2.2cm).

Figure 6.1

2

Measure the exposed shoulder on the front neckline. The exposed shoulder is found by measuring how far the sloper high-neck/shoulder point was moved to the start the shoulder strap. Where the shoulder strap starts is the new high-neck/shoulder point. See **AB** on *Fig. 6.2*. Bring the measurement of **AB** to the line drawn in Step 1 to figure out how much wider the back neckline needs to be. For example, if **AB** is 2¼" (5.7cm), find 2¼" (5.7cm) on the top of the line, note the amount under 2¼" (5.7cm), and record that the back must be wider by ⅝" (1.6cm). If **AB** does not line up exactly with the top numbers, then round to the nearest or further divide the line to be more precise.

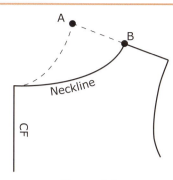

Figure 6.2

3

Square up from the center-front neckline until level with the high-neck/shoulder point (**C**) (*Fig. 6.3*). Square a line over from **C** to the new high-neck/shoulder point and mark **D**. Measure **CD**.

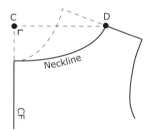

Figure 6.3

4

Add the **CD** measurement to the fraction found in Step 2 for the width of the back neckline. With our example: **CD** + ⅝" (1.6cm) = **EF** (neckline width in back). Note that this measurement is straight across, not curved. It is not the measurement of the back neckline; it is a phantom line. Once you find **F**, the neckline can be shaped as desired.

5

If the shoulder dart ends up in the neckline, which happens with wide necklines like boat necklines, then the dart will need to be added to the neckline, and point **F** will need to be moved out the width of the dart. Do not consider Step 5 unless the shoulder dart falls in the drawn neckline shape (*Fig. 6.4*).

This neckline rule is complicated and involves a lot of steps. There will be plenty of opportunities to practice the rule with the exercises ahead.

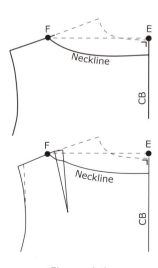

Figure 6.4

BACK CONTOURING

If using a center-back seam, utilize back contouring by coming in ⅜" (1cm) at the center-back waist and blending to zero at the cross-back guideline (*Fig. 6.5*). Back contouring allows the garment to fit closer to the body along the center back. Use it whenever a garment has a center-back seam.

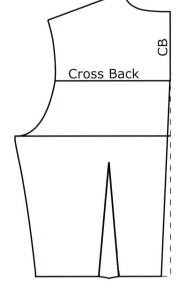

Fitting Tip:
There is the option of reducing the back waist dart ⅜" (1cm) to account for what is removed with back contouring. However, most necklines require a more fitted bodice, so it is recommended to maintain the original back waist dart for a more fitted silhouette.

Figure 6.5

LOWERED NECKLINES

If drafting a V-neckline or low neckline on the front or back, drop the high-neck/shoulder point ⅛" (3.2mm) and blend to zero at the end of shoulder. Do this to counter any bias stretch that is likely to happen in the neckline (*Fig. 6.6*).

At what depth is a neckline considered low? In front, it is any neckline that ends at or lower than the upper breast tissue. In back, a neckline is considered low if it is lower than the cross-back guideline.

On the front, use a **front neckline dart** to prevent a neckline from gaping when the base of the neckline is 1" (2.5cm) or more below the breast tissue. It helps to draw a radius around the high figure point to figure out if a neckline dart is needed. Measure from the center of the breast to the base of the breast tissue (or where the underwire of a bra might sit). After finding that measurement, use a compass to draw a radius around the high figure point using that measurement. When a neckline depth is lower than 1" (2.5cm) below the radius, a neckline dart will be needed to prevent gaping (*Fig. 6.7*).

How wide the neckline dart should be is determined by cup size (see Neckline Dart Chart). Further widening of the neckline dart width could be needed after the first fitting.

Neckline Dart Chart

- Use a ½" (1.3cm) dart for an A cup
- Use a ⅝" (1.6cm) dart for a B cup
- Use a ¾" (1.9cm) dart for a C cup
- Use a ⅞" (2.2cm) dart for a D cup

Add ⅛" (3.2mm) to the ⅞" (2.2cm) dart for every size larger than a D cup. See Chapter 3 measuring and calculating for cup size.

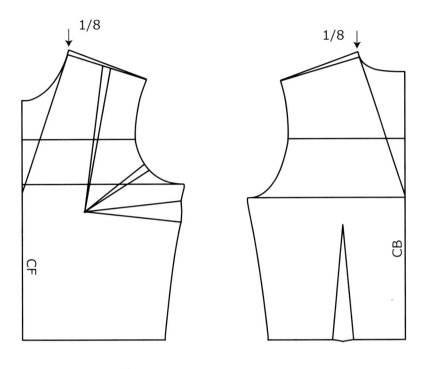

Figure 6.6

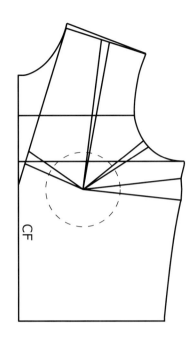

Figure 6.7

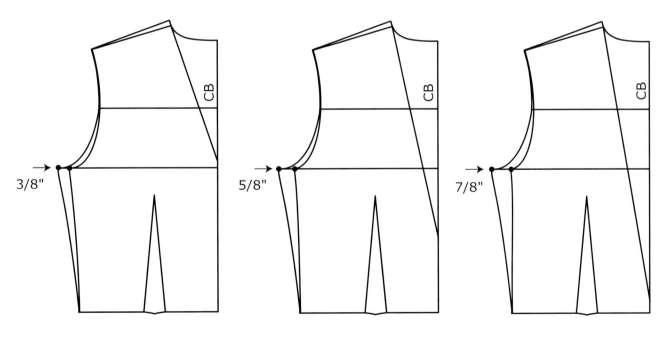

Figure 6.8

The neckline dart will be manipulated with the other darts rather than sewn into a garment. The top leg of the dart should be placed on the neckline level with the top of the radius. The second leg is below that and the pivotal point is either the high or low figure point depending on the dart manipulation.

Do not use a neckline dart on lowered back drafts. A neckline dart in back will form a breast cup, which is not needed. With a low back neckline, come in ⅜" (1cm) at the top of the side seam/underarm and blend to the waist at side (*Fig. 6.8*). This will bring the back into negative ease which is needed for the fabric to hug the back and not gape. With back necklines below the base of the armhole, come in ⅝" (1.6cm). With a back neckline depth to the waist, come in ⅞" (2.2cm).

SHAPING THE FRONT WAIST DART

For a garment to fit snug through the rib cage, bow the legs of the waist dart out ¼"–⅜" (0.6–1cm) on each leg (*Fig. 6.9*).

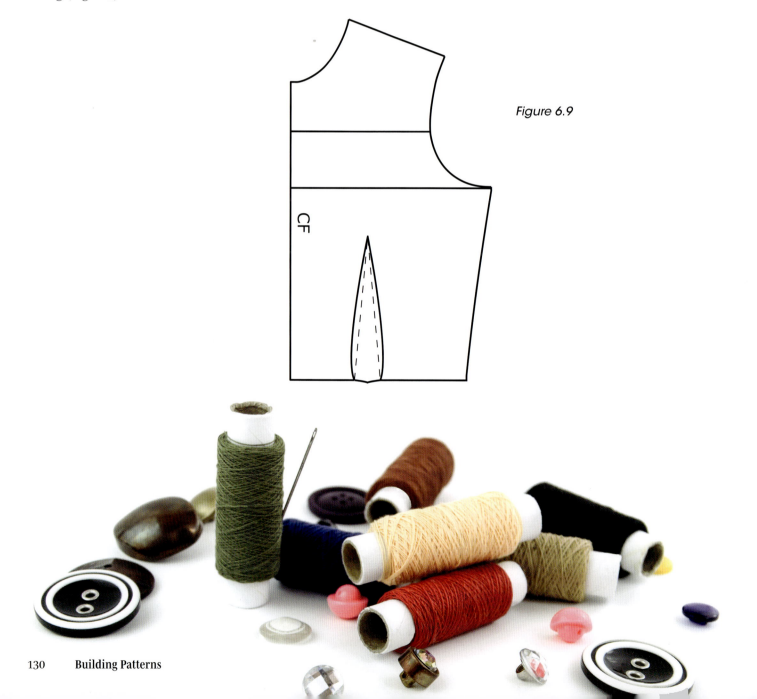

Figure 6.9

FACINGS

Facings add support and structure to necklines and armholes to prevent stretching. **All-in-one facings** are used when a garment is sleeveless and does not have a collar attached. All-in-one facings encompass both the neckline and armhole openings. Facings are traced off the finished front and back pattern pieces. Facings extend down from the center-front and center-back neck by about 2"–3" (5.1–7.6cm), and they extend down from the underarm along the side seam about 2" (5.1cm). Facings have the same notches, markings, and grainline as the shell of the garment.

If a dart ends up in a facing, sew the dart. Facings are interfaced. Interfacing is cut on the same grainline as the facing itself. The base of a facing is often sewn to lining fabric. Lining pattern pieces can be traced from the pattern below the facing line.

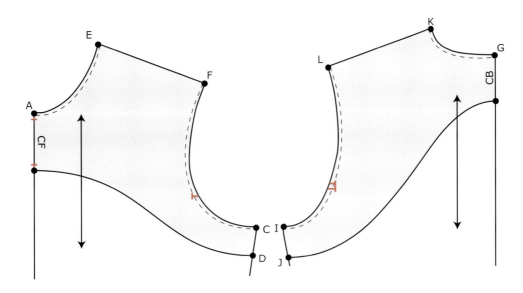

Figure 6.10

Front (trace the sloper for practice)

1. **AB** = 1"–3" (2.5–7.6cm) down from the center-front neck
2. **CD** = 1"–2" (2.5–5.1cm) down from the underarm/bust point at the side
3. Connect **B-D** in a shallow curve.
4. Mark the shoulder **E** and **F** as shown (*Fig. 6.10*).
5. Trace **A-E-F-C-D-B-A** for the facing. Trim 1/16" (1.6mm) off the neckline and the armhole openings. This will allow the seam to tuck under slightly and not show on the outside.
6. Notch in the armhole 3½" (8.9cm) up from the underarm. This is standard front-armhole-notch placement. Draw the grainline as on the garment. Add seam allowance. Drag notches to the perimeter. Cut (1) self on fold. Cut (1) interfacing on fold.

Drafting Tip:
When a pattern piece is shaded, it means the piece should be interfaced for added support and structure.

- - - - - - -

Notching Tip:
When a garment has an armhole facing or has sleeves, always include notches so the sewer can keep track of the front and back of a garment. Standards vary per company, but a common standard notching system is to single notch the front at 3½" (8.9cm) up from the underarm along the armhole curve. Double notch the back at 3" (7.6cm) and 3¼" (8.3cm) up from the underarm along the armhole curve. Single notches denote front, and double notches denote back.

Back
1. **GH** = 1"–3" (2.5–7.6cm) down from the center-back neck
2. **IJ** = as **CD** on the front. **IJ** must match **CD** on the front because these seams will be sewn together. Make sure the front and back blend smoothly.
3. Connect **H-J** in a shallow curve.
4. Mark the shoulder **K** and **L** as shown (*Fig. 6.10*).
5. Trace **G-K L-I-J-H-G** for the facing. Trim ¹⁄₁₆" (1.6cm) off the neckline and the armhole openings. This will allow the seam to tuck under slightly and not show on the outside.
6. Notch in the armhole 3" (7.6cm) and 3¼" (8.3cm) up from the underarm. This is standard back armhole notch placement.
7. Draw the grainline as on the garment. Drag notches to the perimeter. Cut (2) self. Cut (2) interfacing.

No need to cut and sew this exercise. This is just practice for the exercises ahead.

Seam Allowance Tip:
Seam allowances on all-in-one facings and the shell of the garments are usually ¼" (6.4mm) at the neckline and the armholes and ½"–¾" (1.3–1.9cm) at the shoulder seams, sides, and center back. Many center fronts are cut on fold. Enclosed seam allowances like those with all-in-one facings are generally smaller because ½"–¾" (1.3–1.9cm) seam allowance would be too bulky around curves and would have to be trimmed to ¼" (6.4mm) anyway.

Neckline Facing

When a garment has sleeves, a simpler **neckline facing** is required. Neckline facings are drafted about 1½"–2" (3.8–5.1cm) from the neckline edge. Just like all-in-one facings, 1/16" (1.6mm) should be trimmed from the neckline edge of the front and back facing pieces (*Fig. 6.11*). Neckline facings require the same grainline, notching, and seam allowance as the shell of the garment. Neckline facings are interfaced. Neckline facings can either hang free inside the garment or the outside edge can be sewn to lining fabric if the garment is lined.

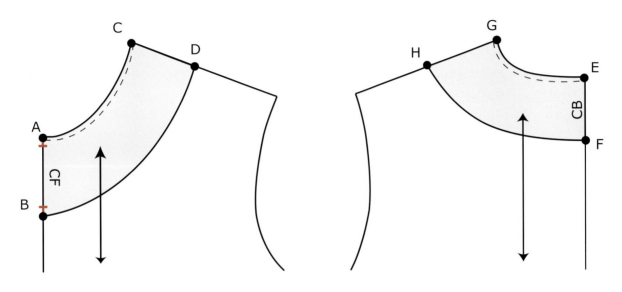

Figure 6.11

Alternate Seam Finishes:

If facings are not used to clean up armhole and/or neckline edges, bias tape can be used. Or lining can be brought all the way to the armhole and neckline edges. If that is the case, stabilize the armhole and neckline edges with a strip of bias-cut interfacing or twill tape. This will help prevent stretching of the armholes and neckline.

Exercises

BOAT NECKLINE

A boat neckline is a high, wide neckline. The shape resembles the shallow shape at the bottom of a boat.

Front

1. Trace the front sloper to the waist, including the darts. Mark **A**, **B**, **C**, **D**, **E**, and **F** as shown (*Fig. 6.12*).
2. Choose a pivotal point for the dart manipulation. The example shows a dart manipulation into the waist dart. Therefore, the low figure pivotal point will be used. Bring the dart points to the pivotal point.
3. Manipulate the shoulder, armhole, and side darts into the waist dart. This will allow for a clearer path to draw the neckline. For a tighter fit, bow out the waist dart legs (see Shaping the Front Waist Dart).
4. **CG** = the desired width of the shoulder seam (example: 1¾" [4.4cm])

Designer Tip:
The neckline exercises ahead will show the darts manipulated into the waist dart.
But, as the designer, you can choose any dart manipulation.

5. Connect **A-G** in a shallow curve. Be sure to square off at **A** for ¾" (1.9cm) so the center-front neckline is flat.
6. Front Pattern: **A-G-C-D-E-F-A**, including the final dart manipulation
7. Notch the center-front neckline (**A**), notch along the neckline, and 3½" (8.9cm) up from the underarm to match with the facing. Notch the dart legs and awl-punch ½" (1.3cm) down from the dart point. Draw a length grainline. Add ¼" (6.4mm) seam allowance at the neckline and armhole. Add ½" (1.3cm) seam allowance everywhere else (except the center front, which is cut on a fold). Drag the notches to the perimeter. Cut (1) self on fold at center front.
8. Draw a **front facing** and trace it out as a separate pattern piece (see Facings, page 131). Include matching notches and grainline. Include ¼" (6.4mm) seam allowance at the neckline and armhole, and ½" (1.3cm) everywhere else (except the center front, which is cut on fold). Drag the notches to the perimeter. Cut (1) self on fold at center front. Cut (1) interfacing on fold at center front.
9. Before moving onto the back, figure out the high-neck/shoulder point adjustment (see High-Neck/Shoulder Point Adjustment).

- Step 1: Note the measurement of the front exposed shoulder _____ (**BG**).
- Step 2: Consult the chart for the needed amount to extend the back high-neck/shoulder point (⅜", ⅝", or ⅞" [1, 1.6, or 2.2cm]) _____.
- Step 3: Note the measurement of the width of the front neckline _____ (**HG**).
- Step 4: Add the chart width to the **HG** measurement in Step 3 = _____.
- Keep the result from Step 4 on hand for drafting the back.

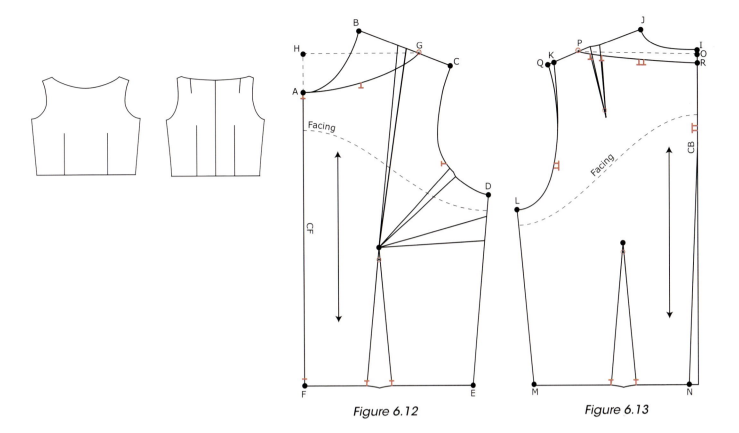

Figure 6.12 Figure 6.13

Back

1. Trace the back sloper to the waist, including the darts. Utilize back contouring if the garment will have a center-back seam (see Back Contouring). Mark **I**, **J**, **K**, **L**, **M**, and **N** as shown (*Fig. 6.13*).
2. **OP** = Step 4 measurement _____ + the width of the shoulder dart = _____. For example, if the Step 4 measurement is 5½" (14cm) and the shoulder dart width is ½" (1.3cm), then **OP** = 6" (15.2cm).
3. **PQ** = shoulder width as front (example: 1¾" [4.4cm]). It is okay if **Q** is further out than **K**.
4. **IR** = center back depth of neckline (example: 1" [2.5cm])
5. **RP** = back neckline shape. Be sure to square off at **R** for ¾" (1.9cm) for a flat center back shape.
6. The shoulder dart should end up in the neckline. Make sure the second leg of the dart is at least ½" (1.3cm) away from **P**. Move the entire shoulder dart in as needed, so the second leg is at least ½" (1.3cm) inside the high-neck/shoulder point. There would be too much bulk if the second leg and **P** collided. True the dart legs by folding the dart bulk toward the end of shoulder. Make sure the dart legs are the same length. Part of the dart length and width will have been cut off when drawing the neckline. Keep the shorter dart length, but widen the dart to its original width.
7. Back Pattern: **R-P-Q-L-M-N-R**, including the darts
8. True the front and back patterns at the shoulder, underarm/side, and base at side. True notches, seams, and dart legs.
9. Double notch the cross back at center back. Double notch the neckline and double notch the armhole 3" (7.6cm) and 3¼" (8.3cm) up from the underarm to match with the facing. Notch the dart legs and awl-punch ½" (1.3cm) down from the dart point. Draw a length grainline. Add ¼" (6.4mm) seam allowance at the neckline and armhole. Add ½" (1.3cm) everywhere else. Drag the notches to the perimeter. Cut (2) self.
10. Draw a **back facing** (see Facings, page 131) and trace it out as a separate pattern piece. Include matching notches and grainline. Include ¼" (6.4mm) seam allowance at the neckline and armhole and ½" (1.3cm) everywhere else. Drag the notches to the perimeter. Cut (2) self. Cut (2) interfacing.

V-NECKLINE

A V-neckline can be drafted in the front or back of a garment and can be designed at any depth.

Structural Tip:
Avoid both a very low back and a very low front. Without the support of either a high front or back, it can be hard to keep the shoulder straps up.

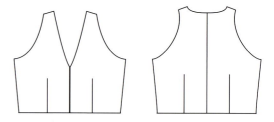

Front

1. Trace the front sloper to the waist, including the darts. Mark **A**, **B**, **C**, **D**, **E**, and **F** as shown (*Fig. 6.14*).
2. Choose a pivotal point for the dart manipulation. The example shows a dart manipulation into the waist dart. Bring the dart points to the pivotal point.
3. Manipulate the shoulder, armhole, and side darts into the waist dart.
4. **BG** = lower the high-neck/shoulder point ⅛" (3.2mm) to counter bias stretch in the neckline (see Lowered Necklines). **G** will be the start of the shoulder strap.
5. **AHG** = draw a right angle and note the measurement of **HG**
6. Draw a radius around the high figure point (see Lowered Necklines).
7. **I** = desired depth of the neckline at center front (mark **I** more than 1" [2.5cm] lower than the top of the radius to practice using a neckline dart).

Design Tip:
A straight line will look harder to the eye.
A curved line will expose more skin and look softer.

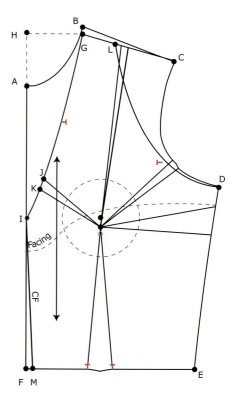

Figure 6.14

Drafting Tip:
When an armhole is lowered more than 3" (7.6cm), the armhole may gape. An additional dart might be needed in the lowered armhole in the fitting stage. It is similarly sized to the neckline dart based on cup size. It can be sewn or manipulated out.

---

8. Connect **G-I** for the neckline. The line can be straight or curved.

9. **JK** = neckline dart (see the Neckline Dart Chart). Draw the dart to the pivotal point. Fold the neckline dart into the waist dart (or the designer's choice of dart manipulation). Smooth the neckline where the dart was folded out.

10. **GL** = desired width of the shoulder strap (example: 2" [5.1cm]). Start experimenting with different shoulder strap widths and placement.

11. Connect **L-D** for the armhole shape. Option: Lower the armhole.

12. **FM** = ½" (1.3cm) in at the center-front waist

13. Connect **I-M** for the new center front. This adjustment will force a center-front seam.

14. Front Pattern: **G-L-D-E-M-I-G**, including the final dart manipulation

15. Notch arbitrarily along the neckline to match later with the facing, and notch 3½" (8.9cm) up from the underarm to match with the facing. Notch the dart legs and awl-punch ½" (1.3cm) down from the dart point. Draw a length grainline. Add ¼" (6.4mm) seam allowance at the neckline and armhole. Add ½" (1.3cm) seam allowance everywhere else. Drag the notches to the perimeter. Cut (2) self.

16. Draw a **front facing** and trace it out as a separate pattern piece. Include matching notches and grainline. Include ¼" (6.4mm) seam allowance at the neckline and armhole and ½" (1.3cm) everywhere else. Drag the notches to the perimeter. Cut (2) self. Cut (2) interfacing.

17. Before moving onto the back, figure out the high-neck/shoulder point adjustment (see High-Neck/Shoulder Point Adjustment).

- Step 1: Note the measurement of the front exposed shoulder _____. (In this case, zero because the shoulder was not moved out.)
- Step 2: Consult the chart for the needed amount to extend the back high-neck/shoulder point (⅜", ⅝", or ⅞" [1, 1.6, or 2.2cm]) _____. (Since the shoulder was not moved out, use ⅜" [1cm].)
- Step 3: Note the measurement of the width of the front neckline _____ (**HG**).
- Step 4: Add the chart width to the **HG** measurement in Step 3 = _____.
- Keep the result from Step 4 on hand for drafting the back.

Drafting Tip:
When a garment has a low V-neckline in front, forcing a neckline dart, the center-front waist wants to kick out. Anticipate this by coming in ½" (1.3cm) at the center-front waist and blend to zero at the base of the neckline. The waist dart can by reduced by ½" (1.3cm) to accommodate this adjustment or leave the width of the front waist dart for a tighter fit.

Fitting Tip:

Adding a neckline dart or lowered armhole dart to a dart manipulation can tip the final dart into a width that is too wide for the dart leg length. Look critically at the sewn dart during the fitting stage. If after careful marking, sewing, and pressing, the dart puckers at the point, the dart is too wide. In that case, go back to the draft and split the dart into two darts (a waist dart and a French dart) using both the high figure point (for the French dart) and low figure point (for the waist dart). Back off each ½"–¾" (1.3–1.9cm) so there is a separation between the two darts. Or turn the draft into a princess seam.

Back

1. Trace the back sloper to the waist, including the darts. Utilize back contouring if the garment will have a center-back seam (see Back Contouring). Mark **N**, **O**, **P**, **Q**, **R**, and **S** as shown (*Fig. 6.15*).
2. **TU** = Step 4 measurement from the high-neck/shoulder point adjustment
3. **UV** = shoulder width as front (example: 2" [5.1cm])
4. Connect **N-U** for the back neckline. Be sure to square over for ¾" (1.9cm) at **N** for a flat shape at the center back.
5. Connect **V-Q** for the back armhole (lower the armhole if lowered in front).
6. Back Pattern: **N-U-V-Q-R-S-N**, including the waist dart

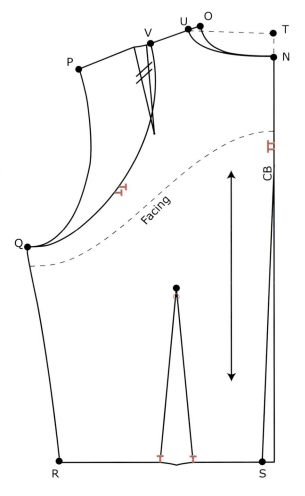

Drafting Tip:

When the shoulder is cut in significantly, the back shoulder dart should be ignored. A good rule of thumb is to ignore the back shoulder dart if any part of the dart is cut off with the shape of a cut in armhole.

Figure 6.15

7. True the front and back patterns at the shoulder, underarm/side, and base at side. True notches, seams, and dart legs.
8. Double notch the cross back at center back. Double notch the armhole 3" (7.6cm) and 3¼" (8.3cm) up from the underarm to match with the facing. Notch the dart legs and awl-punch ½" (1.3cm) down from the dart point. Draw a length grainline. Add ¼" (6.4mm) seam allowance at the neckline and armhole, add ½" (1.3cm) everywhere else. Drag the notches to the perimeter. Cut (2) self.
9. Draw a **back facing** and trace it out as a separate pattern piece. Include matching notches and grainline. Include ¼" (6.4mm) seam allowance at the neckline and armhole and ½" (1.3cm) everywhere else. Drag the notches to the perimeter. Cut (2) self. Cut (2) interfacing.

Additional Practice:
Draft a neckline with a low V in the back and a high, round neckline in front. Remember to review Lowered Necklines (page 128) for the back, and come in at the underarm/bust for negative ease.

SCOOP NECKLINE
Front
1. Trace the front sloper to the waist, including the darts. Mark **A**, **B**, **C**, **D**, **E**, and **F** as shown (*Fig. 6.16*).
2. Choose a pivotal point for the dart manipulation. The example shows a dart manipulation into the waist dart. Bring the dart points to the pivotal point.
3. Manipulate the shoulder, armhole, and side darts into the waist dart.
4. **BG** = lower the high-neck/shoulder point ⅛" (3.2mm) to counter bias stretch in the neckline (see Lowered Necklines)
5. **H** = high-neck/shoulder point placement for the start of the shoulder strap
6. **AIH** = draw a right angle and note the measurement of **IH**
7. Draw a radius around the high figure point (see Lowered Necklines).
8. **J** = desired depth of the neckline at center front. If **J** is more than 1" (2.5cm) lower than the top of the radius, include a neckline dart.
9. Connect **H-J** in a scoop shape for the neckline. Square for about ¾" (1.9cm) at **J** to flatten the base of the neckline so it appears as a scoop rather than a V-neckline.
10. **KL** = neckline dart (see Lowered Necklines). Draw the dart to the pivotal point. Fold the neckline dart into the waist dart (or the designer's choice of dart manipulation). Smooth the neckline where the dart was folded out.
11. **GM** = desired width of the shoulder strap. Start experimenting with different widths and different placement of the shoulder strap.
12. Connect **M-D** for the armhole shape.
13. Front Pattern: **H-M-D-E-F-J-H**, including the final dart manipulation

14. Notch arbitrarily along the neckline to match later with the facing, and notch 3½" (8.9cm) up from the underarm to match with the facing. Notch the dart legs and awl-punch ½" (1.3cm) down from the dart point. Draw a length grainline. Add ¼" (6.4mm) seam allowance at the neckline and armhole. Add ½" (1.3cm) seam allowance everywhere else. Drag the notches to the perimeter. Cut (1) self on fold at center front.

15. Draw a **front facing** and trace it out as a separate pattern piece. Include matching notches and grainline. Include ¼" (6.4mm) seam allowance at the neckline and armhole and ½" (1.3cm) everywhere else. Drag the notches to the perimeter. Cut (1) self on fold at center front. Cut (1) interfacing on fold at center front.

16. Before moving onto the back, figure out the high-neck/shoulder point adjustment (see High-Neck/Shoulder Point Adjustment).

- Step 1: Note the measurement of the front exposed shoulder _____ (**GH**)
- Step 2: Consult the chart for the needed amount to extend the back high-neck/shoulder point (⅜", ⅝", or ⅞" [1, 1.6, or 2.2cm]) _____.
- Step 3: Note the measurement of the width of the front neckline _____ (**IH**).
- Step 4: Add the chart width to the **IH** measurement in Step 3 = _____.
- Keep the result from Step 4 on hand for drafting the back.

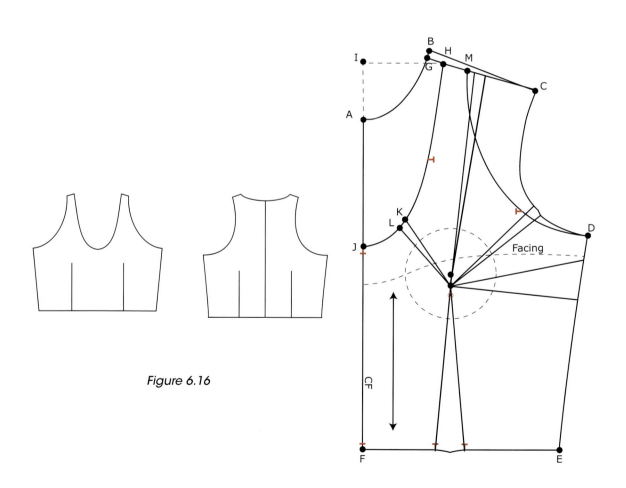

Figure 6.16

Back

1. Trace the back sloper to the waist, including the darts. Utilize back contouring if the garment will have a center-back seam (see Back Contouring). Mark **N**, **O**, **P**, **Q**, **R**, and **S** as shown (*Fig. 6.17*).
2. **TU** = Step 4 measurement from the high-neck/shoulder point adjustment
3. **UV** = shoulder width as front
4. Connect **N-U** for the back neckline. Be sure to square over for ¾" (1.9cm) at **N** for a flat shape at the center back.
5. Connect **V-Q** for the back armhole. Do not include the back shoulder dart if any part of the dart was cut off with **VQ**.
6. Back Pattern: **N-U-V-Q-R-S-N**, including the waist dart
7. True the front and back patterns at the shoulder, underarm/side and base at side. True notches, seams, and dart legs.
8. Double notch the cross back at center back. Double notch the armhole 3" (7.6cm) and 3¾" (9.5cm) up from the underarm to match with the facing. Notch the dart legs and awl-punch ½" (1.3cm) down from the dart point. Draw a length grainline. Add ¼" (6.4mm) seam allowance at the neckline and armhole, and ½" (1.3cm) everywhere else. Drag the notches to the perimeter. Cut (2) self.
9. Draw a **back facing** and trace it out as a separate pattern piece. Include matching notches and grainline. Include ¼" (6.4mm) seam allowance at the neckline and armhole and ½" (1.3cm) everywhere else. Drag the notches to the perimeter. Cut (2) self. Cut (2) interfacing.

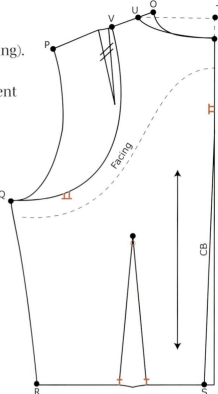

Figure 6.17

SWEETHEART NECKLINE

Front

1. Trace the front sloper to the waist, including the darts. Mark **A**, **B**, **C**, **D**, **E**, and **F** as shown (*Fig. 6.18*).
2. Choose a pivotal point for the dart manipulation. The example shows a dart manipulation into the waist dart. Bring the dart points to the pivotal point.
3. Manipulate the shoulder, armhole, and side darts into the waist dart.
4. **BG** = lower the high-neck/shoulder point ⅛" (3.2mm) to counter bias stretch in the neckline (see Lowered Necklines)
5. **H** = high-neck/shoulder point (placement as desired) and the start of the shoulder strap
6. **AIH** = draw a right angle and note the measurement of **IH**
7. Draw a radius around the high figure point (see Lowered Necklines).
8. **J** = desired depth of the neckline at center front. If **J** is more than 1" (2.5cm) lower than the top of the radius, include a neckline dart. The diagram shows a higher neckline without the dart but include the dart if the neckline is low.
9. **K** = desired placement for neckline shape (often on or near the cross-front guideline).

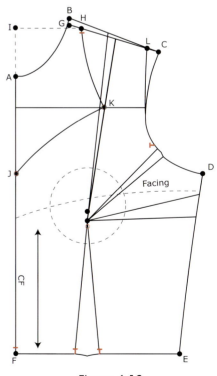

Figure 6.18

10. Connect **J-K-H** for the neckline shape. **J** and **K** do not have to come to points. **J** can be flattened for a less traditional shape at the center front and **K** can be softened.
11. **HL** = shoulder width as desired
12. Connect **L-D** for the armhole shape.
13. Front Pattern: **H-L-D-E-F-J-K-H**, including the final dart manipulation
14. Awl-punch **J** and **K**, and notch 3½" (8.9cm) up from the underarm to match with the facing. Notch the dart legs and awl-punch ½" (1.3cm) down from the dart point. Draw a length grainline. Add ¼" (6.4mm) seam allowance at the neckline and armhole. Add ½" (1.3cm) seam allowance everywhere else. Drag the notches to the perimeter. Cut (1) self on fold at center front.
15. Draw a **front facing** and trace it out as a separate pattern piece. Include matching drill holes, notches, and grainline. Include ¼" (6.4mm) seam allowance at the neckline and armhole and ½" (1.3cm) everywhere else. Drag the notches to the perimeter. Cut (1) self on fold at center front. Cut (1) interfacing on fold at center front.
16. Before moving onto the back, figure out the high-neck/shoulder point adjustment (see High-Neck/Shoulder Point Adjustment).

- Step 1: Note the measurement of the front exposed shoulder _____ (**GH**).
- Step 2: Consult the chart for the needed amount to extend the back high-neck/shoulder point (⅜", ⅝", or ⅞" [1, 1.6, or 2.2cm]) _____.
- Step 3: Note the measurement of the width of the front neckline _____ (**IH**).
- Step 4: Add the chart width to the **IH** measurement in Step 3 = _____.

Back

1. Trace the back sloper to the waist, including the darts. Utilize back contouring if the garment will have a center-back seam (see Back Contouring). Mark **M**, **N**, **O**, **P**, **Q**, and **R** as shown (*Fig. 6.19*).
2. **ST** = Step 4 measurement from the high-neck/shoulder point adjustment
3. **TU** = shoulder width as front, plus shoulder dart (if the full dart ends up in the shoulder line)
4. Connect **M-T** for the back neckline. Be sure to square over for ¾" (1.9cm) at **M** for a flat shape at the center back.
5. Connect **U-P** for the back armhole.
6. Back Pattern: **M-T-U-P-Q-R-M**, including the waist dart
7. True the front and back patterns at the shoulder, underarm/side, and base at side. True notches, seams, and dart legs.
8. Double notch the cross back at center back. Double notch the armhole 3" (7.6cm) and 3¼" (8.3cm) up from the underarm to match with the facing. Notch the dart legs and awl-punch ½" (1.3cm) down from the dart point. Draw the grainline. Add ¼" (6.4mm) seam allowance at the neckline and armhole. Add ½" (1.3cm) everywhere else. Drag the notches to the perimeter. Cut (2) self.
9. Draw a **back facing** and trace it out as a separate pattern piece. Include matching notches and grainline. Include ¼" (6.4mm) seam allowance at the neckline and armhole and ½" (1.3cm) everywhere else. Drag the notches to the perimeter. Cut (2) self. Cut (2) interfacing.

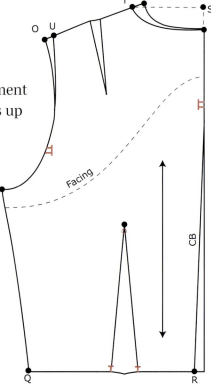

Figure 6.19

STRAPLESS NECKLINE
Front

1. Trace the front sloper, including each dart. Remove ¼" (6.4mm) ease down the side for a tighter fit. Mark **A**, **B**, **C**, **D**, **E**, and **F** as shown (*Fig. 6.20*).
2. Use the high figure point (**G**) as the pivotal point for the shoulder, armhole, and side darts. Manipulate the shoulder dart and the armhole dart into the side dart to clear a path to draw the neckline.
3. Draw a radius around the high figure point (see Lowered Necklines).
4. **H** = desired depth of the neckline at center front
5. **I** = desired depth of the side seam under the arm
6. Connect **H-I** for the neckline shape as desired. The radius will show how much of the bustline will be exposed.
7. Draw a ¾" (1.9cm) dart centered over the manipulated shoulder dart line on the **HI** neckline. Mark ⅜" (1cm) on either side of the manipulated shoulder dart line. Label **J** and **K** as shown. Draw the dart to the pivotal point (**G**). True the dart legs **KG** and **JG**.
8. **L** = mark the low figure point (top of the waist dart)
9. Connect **G-L**.
10. Mark the base of the waist dart **M** and **N** as shown. Bow the legs of the dart out ⅜" (1cm) (see Shaping the Front Waist Dart).
11. Cut along **MLGJ**. Cut along **NLGK**. Cut the waist dart and the bust dart away. Fold the side dart out. Smooth the perimeter of the pattern pieces.
12. Center Front Pattern: **H-J-G-L-M-F-H**
13. Notch the center front top (**H**) and base (**F**). Notch arbitrarily along **LM** to help align the pieces when sewing. Draw a length grainline. Add ½" (1.3cm) seam allowance everywhere except at the center front, which will be cut on fold. Drag the notches to the perimeter. Cut (1) self on fold at center front.

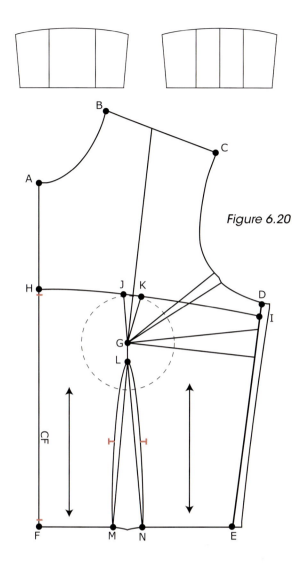

Figure 6.20

14. Use the same center front pattern piece for the **front facing**. Interface the entire facing. Cut (1) self on fold. Cut (1) interfacing on fold.
15. Side-Front Pattern: **K-I-E-N-L-G-K**
16. Mark a corresponding notch along **LN** to match to the notch along **LM**.
17. Draw a length grainline perpendicular to the waistline. Add ½" (1.3cm) seam allowance. Drag the notches to the perimeter. Cut (2) self.
18. Use the same side-front piece for the **front facing**. Interface the entire facing. Cut (2) self. Cut (2) interfacing.

Back

1. Trace the back sloper, including the darts. Adjust the ease at the side seam as front. Utilize back contouring if the garment will have a center-back seam (see Back Contouring). Mark **O**, **P**, **Q**, **R**, **S**, and **T** as shown (*Fig. 6.21*).
2. **RU** = depth of the side seam under the arm (as **DI** on front)
3. **V** = desired depth of the neckline at center back
4. Tape the front side panel to the back aligning the side seams, and then connect **U-V** for the back neckline shape as desired. Separate the pieces after the **UV** line is drawn.
5. Extend the line from the top of the waist dart to the neckline (**VU**). Mark **W** as shown. (If the neckline is below the dart point, mark **W** on each side of the dart opening.)
6. Mark the base of the waist dart **X** and **Y** as shown.

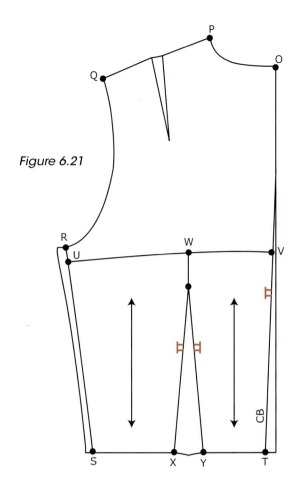

Figure 6.21

Drafting Tip:
It helps to temporarily tape front and back pieces together at the side seam to draw a smooth transition between the front and back. If the two are not attached before drawing the connection, a peak or a valley could form at the seam.

---

7. Cut along **YW**. Cut along **XW**. Cut the waist dart away. Smooth the perimeter of the pattern pieces.
8. Center Back Pattern: **V-W-Y-T-V**
9. Double notch arbitrarily along **WY** to help align the pieces when sewing. Draw a length grainline perpendicular to the waistline. Add ½" (1.3cm) seam allowance. Drag the notches to the perimeter. Cut (2) self.
10. Use the same center back pattern piece for the **back facing**. Interface the entire facing. Cut (2) self. Cut (2) interfacing.
11. Side-Back Pattern: **W-X-S-U-W**
12. Mark a corresponding double notch along **WX** to match to the double notch along **WY**. Draw a length grainline perpendicular to the waistline. Add ½" (1.3cm) seam allowance. Drag the notches to the perimeter. Cut (2) self.
13. Use the same side-back piece for the **back facing**. Interface the entire facing. Cut (2) self. Cut (2) interfacing.
14. True the pattern pieces, notches, and connections.

Building Patterns

FUNNEL NECKLINE

A funnel neckline is a high, round neckline that sits away from the neck stem. Darts are added in the neckline for a closer fit through the curve of the neck. For something different, the center back will be on a fold and the center front will have a seam.

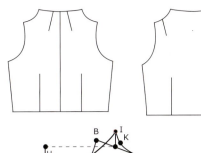

Note that the instructions cycle through the alphabet twice: first with uppercase letters, then with lowercase letters.

Front

1. Trace the front sloper to the waist, including the darts. Mark **A**, **B**, **C**, **D**, **E**, and **F** as shown (*Fig. 6.22*).
2. Choose a pivotal point for the dart manipulation. The example shows a dart manipulation into the waist dart. Bring the dart points to the pivotal point.
3. Manipulate the shoulder, armhole, and side darts into the waist dart.
4. **BG** = extend out 1" (2.5cm) along the shoulder slope for the high-neck/shoulder point
5. **AHG** = draw a right angle and note the measurement of **HG**
6. **GI** = square a line up from **G** for 1" (2.5cm) (this will be the height of the funnel neckline)
7. **AJ** = 1" (2.5cm) height at center front
8. Connect **J-I** in a shallow curve. Square off at **J** for ½" (1.3cm) for a flatter center front shape.

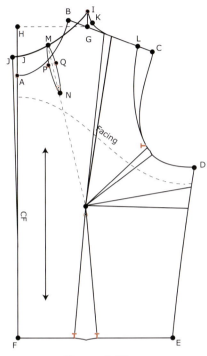

Figure 6.22

9. **GK** = ½" (1.3cm) at a 45-degree angle from **G**
10. **GL** = shoulder width as desired (example: 3" [7.6cm])
11. Connect **I-K-L** for the new shoulder. Blend into the existing shoulder quickly so the shoulder line is not raised.
12. Connect **L-D** for the armhole.
13. **JM** = 1½" (3.8cm) along **JI**
14. Connect **M** to the high figure point in a dotted line.
15. **MN** = 4" (10.2cm) along the dotted line
16. **O** = half **MN**
17. **OP** = ¼" (6.4mm) to shape the dart
18. **OQ** = ¼" (6.4mm) to shape the dart
19. 1 Connect **M-P-N-Q-M** for the neckline dart.
20. Move **J** out ¼" (6.4mm) at the center front for more room in the neckline. Re-mark **J** and blend to the waist.
21. Front Pattern: **J-M-I-K-L-D-E-F-J**, including the darts
22. Notch 3½" (8.9cm) up from the underarm to match with the facing. Notch the waist dart legs and **M** on the neck dart. Awl-punch ½" (1.3cm) down from the waist dart point and ½" (1.3cm) up from **N**. Awl-punch **I**. Draw a length grainline. Add ¼" (6.4mm) seam allowance at the neckline and armhole. Add ½" (1.3cm) seam allowance everywhere else. Drag the notches to the perimeter. Cut (2) self.

Design Tip:

Connect the base of the neckline dart with the top of the waist dart to create a princess seamline. Princess seams offer another seamline in which to refine the fit of a garment.

23. Draw a **front facing** and trace it out as a separate pattern piece. Include matching awl-punches, notches, and grainline. Keep the neckline dart in the facing. Include ¼" (6.4mm) seam allowance at the neckline and armhole and ½" (1.3cm) everywhere else. Drag the notches to the perimeter. Cut (2) self. Cut (2) interfacing.

24. Before moving onto the back, figure out the high-neck/shoulder point adjustment (see High-Neck/Shoulder Point Adjustment).

- Step 1: Note the measurement of the front exposed shoulder _____ (**GH**).
- Step 2: Consult the chart for the needed amount to extend the back high-neck/shoulder point (⅜", ⅝", or ⅞" [1, 1.6, or 2.2cm]) _____.
- Step 3: Note the measurement of the width of the front neckline _____ (**IH**).
- Step 4: Add the chart width to the **IH** measurement in Step 3 = _____.

Back

1. Trace the back sloper to the waist, including the darts. Utilize back contouring if the garment will have a center-back seam (see Back Contouring). Or keep the center back straight for a cut on fold as shown (*Fig. 6.23*). Mark **R**, **S**, **T**, **U**, **V**, and **W**.
2. **XY** = Step 4 measurement from the high-neck/shoulder point adjustment
3. **YZ** = square a line up from **Y** for 1" (2.5cm)
4. **Ra** = additional height of 1" (2.5cm) at the center-back neck
5. Connect **Z-a** in a shallow curve. Remember to square off at a for a flat center back.
6. **b** = ½" (1.3cm) at a 45-degree angle from **Y**
7. **Yc** = shoulder width as front (**GL**), plus the width of the shoulder dart
8. Connect **Z-b-c** for the new shoulder. True the back shoulder to the front shoulder, considering the width of the back dart.
9. Connect **c-U** for the armhole.
10. Back Pattern: **a-Z-b-c-U-V-W-a**, including the darts
11. True the front and back patterns at the shoulder, underarm/side, and base at side. True seams and dart legs.
12. Double notch the armhole 3" (7.6cm) and 3¼" (8.3cm) up from the underarm to match with the facing. Notch the dart legs and awl-punch ½" (1.3cm) from the dart points. Awl-punch **Z**. Draw a length grainline. Add ¼" (6.4mm) seam allowance at the neckline and armhole. Add ½" (1.3cm) everywhere else except at the center back because it will be cut on a fold. Drag the notches to the perimeter. Cut (1) self on center-back fold.
13. Draw a **back facing** and trace it out as a separate pattern piece. Include the shoulder dart. Include matching notches, drill holes, and grainline. Include ¼" (6.4mm) seam allowance at the neckline and armhole and ½" (1.3cm) everywhere else. Drag the notches to the perimeter. Cut (1) self on center-back fold. Cut (1) interfacing on center-back fold.

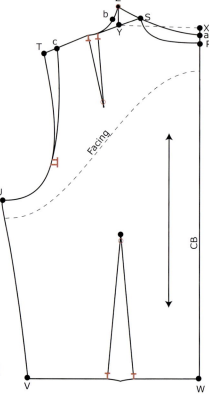

Figure 6.23

SURPLICE NECKLINE

A surplice neckline is used on wrap dresses and shirts. The back of a surplice dress is usually simple and cut on fold.

Front

1. Trace the right and left side of the front sloper to the waist as shown. Mark **right** and **left** side **as worn**. On the right side, include the shoulder, armhole, side, and waist darts. On the left side, just include the waist dart. Mark **A**, **B**, **C**, **D**, **E**, **F**, **G**, **H**, and **I** as shown (*Fig. 6.24*).

Vocabulary Tip:
"**As worn**" refers to the pattern as it is placed on the body with correct side out.

---

2. Choose the high figure point for the bust darts (shoulder, armhole, and side). Choose the low figure point for the waist dart.
3. Manipulate the shoulder and armhole darts into the side dart on the right side.
4. **IJ** = lower the high-neck/shoulder point ⅛" (3.2mm) (see Lowered Necklines).
5. Draw a radius around the high figure points on the right and left sides (see Lowered Necklines).
6. Connect **J-K** for the neckline. Keep the neckline under the bust radius on the left side.
7. **A⌐J** = draw a right angle and note the measurement of **LJ**
8. Include a neckline dart (see Lowered Necklines). Bring the dart point to the high figure point.
9. Manipulate the neckline dart into the side dart. Smooth the neckline. Since the neckline is low, the neckline dart might need to be widened at the first fitting if there is additional gaping.
10. Fold out the dart on the left side and smooth the neckline. The right-side waist and side darts will be sewn. Side darts can be manipulated into French darts.
11. Adjust the end of shoulder in if a narrower shoulder width as desired.
12. Front Pattern: **J-K-E-F-G-H-J**, including the darts.

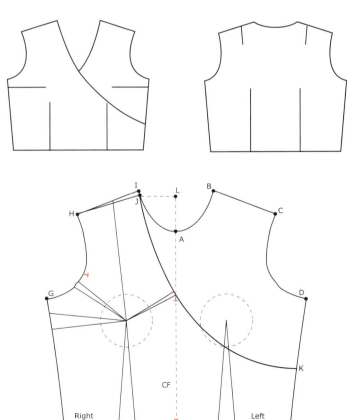

Figure 6.24

13. Notch 3½" (8.9cm) up from the underarm to match with the facing. Notch the waist dart legs and the side dart legs. Awl-punch ½" (1.3cm) away from the dart points on the side and waist darts. Arbitrarily notch in the neckline to help match with the facing. Draw a length grainline on the center front guideline. Add ¼" (6.4mm) seam allowance at the neckline and armhole. Add ½" (1.3cm) seam allowance everywhere else. Drag the notches to the perimeter. Cut (2) self.

14. Because so much of this pattern piece will need to be faced, face the entire piece with lightweight fabric or lining. Include matching drill holes, notches, and grainline. Sew the side and waist darts in the facing as well. Include ¼" (6.4mm) seam allowance at the neckline and armhole and ½" (1.3cm) everywhere else. Drag the notches to the perimeter. Cut (2) self. Interface around the armholes and along the neckline for stability.

15. Before moving onto the back, figure out the high-neck/shoulder point adjustment (see High-Neck/Shoulder Point Adjustment).
- Step 1: Note the measurement of the front exposed shoulder (zero).
- Step 2: Consult the chart for the needed amount to extend the back high-neck/shoulder point (⅜" [1cm]).
- Step 3: Note the measurement of the width of the front neckline ____ (**LJ**).
- Step 4: Add the chart width to the **LJ** measurement in Step 3 = _____.

Back

1. Trace the back sloper to the waist, including the darts. Mark **M**, **N**, **O**, **P**, **Q**, and **R** as shown (*Fig. 6.25*).
2. **ST** = Step 4 measurement from the high-neck/shoulder point adjustment
3. Connect **M-T** for the back neckline. Square at **M** for ¾" (1.9cm) for flat center-back neckline.
4. **O** = adjust **O** in or out, so the front and back shoulders match in length. Do not include the back shoulder dart width in the measurement because that will be sewn out. Blend the end of shoulder to **P**.
5. Back Pattern: **M-T-O-P-Q-R-M**, including the darts
6. True the front and back patterns at the shoulder, underarm/side and base at side. True notches, seams, and dart legs.
7. Double notch the armhole 3" (7.6cm) and 3¼" (8.3cm) up from the underarm to match with the facing. Notch the dart legs and awl-punch ½" (1.3cm) from the dart points. Draw a length grainline. Add ¼" (6.4mm) seam allowance at the neckline and armhole. Add ½" (1.3cm) everywhere else except at the center back because it will b cut on a fold. Drag the notches to the perimeter. Cut (1) self on cente back fold.
8. Like the front, face the entire back with lightweight fabric or lining. Include the shoulder and waist darts in the facing. Include matching notches, drill holes, and grainline. Include ¼" (6.4mm) seam allowance at the neckline and armhole and ½" (1.3cm) everywhere else. Drag the notches to the perimeter. Cut (1) self on center-back fold. Interface around the armholes and along the neckline for stability.

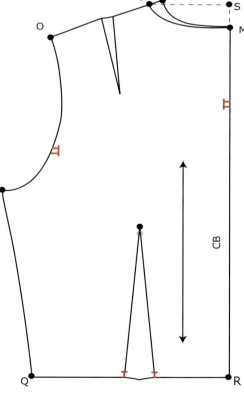

Figure 6.25

Test Your Knowledge

1. Explain why a high-neck/shoulder point adjustment is important to the fit of a neckline.

2. How does utilizing back contouring affect the fit in the back?

3. What is the importance of drawing a radius around the high figure point? How is the measurement of the radius determined?

4. Why is a neckline dart important in low front necklines. How is the size of the neckline dart determined?

5. Seam allowance at the neck and armholes are reduced to ¼" (6.4mm) from the usual ½" (1.3cm). Why?

Chapter 7 includes instructions on how to draft a collar with band, shawl collar, trench coat collar, roll collar, notched collar, hoods, as well as information on drafting button plackets and facings.

OBJECTIVES

Upon completion of this chapter, you will be able to

- Identify the components of a collar and define the vocabulary
- Pattern both simple and complicated collar patterns
- Understand button plackets and button placement

CHAPTER 7
Collars

Rules for Drafting Collars

STAND, ROLL LINE, HEIGHT, AND FALL

The **stand** is the distance on a collar from the neckline edge up to the roll line. The **roll line** is where the collar peaks in height. The roll line height at the center back is the collar **height**. The distance from the height back down toward the neckline to the outer-collar edge is the **fall**. The fall shows on the outside of a garment, and the stand is against the neck and is covered by the fall. The fall should be long enough to cover the neckline seam. The **turn of the cloth** is where a fabric switches direction at the roll line of a collar or on a lapel.

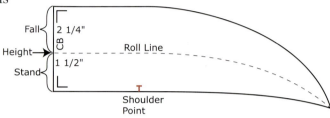

To find the stand, roll line, height, and fall on a collar, divide the collar measurement at the center back into two and a half parts. For example: A collar measurement of 3¾" (9.5cm) will yield two whole parts of 1½" (3.8cm) and a half part of ¾" (1½" [3.8cm] + 1½" [3.8cm] + ¾" [1.9cm] = 3¾" [9.5cm]). Many center-back collars measure 3¾" (9.5cm) because it looks proportional and divides neatly.

Mark 1½" (3.8cm) up from the neckline edge for the **stand**. The top of the stand is the **height** of the collar, which is also the start of the **roll line**. To figure out the **fall**, add one full portion to the half portion (1½" [3.8cm] + ¾" [1.9cm] = 2¼" [5.7cm]). This measurement of 2¼" (5.7cm) allows the collar to cover the stand, accounts for turn of the cloth, and covers the neckline seam.

It is important to find the roll line on a collar because the area of the stand up to the **roll line** is often built up with interfacing, underlining, or a machine- or hand-stitched pattern that keeps the collar **stand** stiff and supportive of the **height** and the collar **fall**. The roll line will happen whether it is drawn in or not. It's only mandatory to draw a roll line on a pattern if the roll line will be supported by interfacing, underlining, or a stitch pattern (*Fig. 7.1*).

Figure 7.1

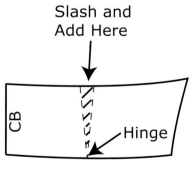

Figure 7.2

COLLAR FALL ADJUSTMENT

If the collar fall is not covering the neckline edge of a garment, slash the muslin mock-up from the outer-collar edge to the neckline at the **high-neck/shoulder point** on both right and left sides to see how much the collar wants to open at the outer edge to allow the collar to relax down and cover the seam. Let that opening dictate how much to insert at the outer-collar edge (usually ⅜"–¾" [1–1.9cm]). Conversely, if a collar is too relaxed and the desired height of the stand is not met, slash the collar from the outer-collar edge to the high-neck/shoulder points and close out fullness until the desired collar height and fall are met (*Fig. 7.2*).

TURN OF THE CLOTH

Collars and lapels appear to lose width when they change direction or turn at the roll line. Add ⅜" (1cm) in width to a collar or lapel to account for turn of the cloth.

SEAM STRETCH

Because collars are often cut on bias and bias tends to stretch, the neckline edge of a collar should be cut slightly smaller than the neckline on the garment. Collar measurements are broken up from center back to the high-neck/shoulder point, and then from the high-neck/shoulder point to the center front or through the extension (*Fig. 7.3*). With a measurement of up to 5" (12.7cm), the collar should be reduced by ¹⁄₁₆" (1.6mm) at the neckline edge. With a measurement between 5" (12.7cm) and 10" (25.4cm), reduce by ⅛" (3.2mm). From 10"–15" (25.4–38.1cm), reduce by ³⁄₁₆" (4.8mm).

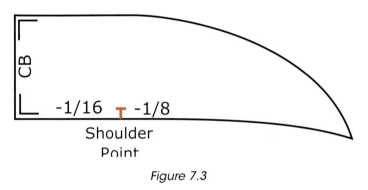

Figure 7.3

TRIMMING THE UNDERCOLLAR

To avoid showing the seam attaching the upper and undercollar at the outer-collar edge, trim the undercollar pattern ¹⁄₁₆" (1.6mm) at the outer-collar edge and blend to zero at any collar points. Or experiment with trimming the neckline edge ¹⁄₁₆" (1.6mm) instead (*Fig. 7.4*).

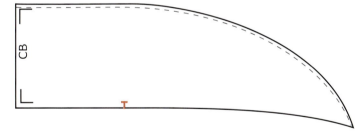

Figure 7.4

BREAK POINT

The break point is where the base of the lapel meets the bodice (see arrow in *Fig. 7.5*).

Figure 7.5

BUTTONS, BUTTONHOLES, AND EXTENSIONS

Since many garments with collars also have buttons, it is helpful learn more about button closures before moving onto the collar exercises.

Buttons

Button size needs to be considered before drafting bodices. The size of the button will determine the width of the extension. Buttons are ordered by metric **ligne** (**L**) size.

> ## Ligne Size
>
> - 12L is a ¼" (6.4mm) button used for button-down collars.
> - 15L is a ⅜" (1cm) button used down the front of blouses and shirts.
> - 20L is a ½" (1.3cm) button used down the front of blouses and shirts.
> - 24L is a ⅝" (1.6cm) button that could be used on sleeve vents on coats and jackets.
> - 30L is a ¾" (1.9cm) button that could be used on coats and jackets.
> - 36L is a ⅞" (2.2cm) button that could be used on double-breasted coats and jackets.
> - 40L is a 1" (2.5cm) button that could be used on coats and overcoats.
>
> There are more sizes, but these are the most used in apparel.

Buttons are either two- or four-hole **sew-through buttons** or **shank buttons**. Mark button placement on a pattern before marking buttonhole placement. Buttons are placed along the center guideline (center front, center back, or the center of a style line). The placement should denote the center of the button. Button placement should be marked with a drill hole (*Fig. 7.6*).

With snug-fitting blouses, dresses, or jackets, place a button level with the high figure point. Buttons are generally evenly spaced with the edge of the top button, sitting ¼"–½" (0.6–1.3cm) down from the finished edge of a garment. On a shirt, place the bottom button at or near the high-hip guideline. On a jacket, the last button is often placed level with the high-hip guideline and the placement of the last button on a coat is often level with the low-hip guideline. These are general guidelines. Button placement varies greatly. Experiment.

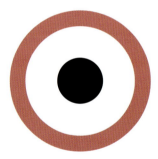

Figure 7.6

Buttonholes

Make sure buttonhole placement is level with button placement. Buttonholes should be ⅛" (3.2mm) wider than the diameter of the button, or ¼" (6.4mm) wider for thicker fabrics or buttons over 1" (2.5cm) in diameter.

Buttonholes can be horizontal, vertical, or slanted. With buttonholes over ¾" (1.9cm), horizontal buttonholes tend to be more stable and will gape less than vertical buttonholes. For stability, keep vertical buttonholes at a length of ¾" (1.9cm) or less.

Horizontal and slanted buttonholes begin ⅛" (3.2mm) over the center guideline in the extension. From there, a buttonhole is drawn back in toward the body of the garment. After buttoning, the center of the button will slide toward and sit on the center-front line. Vertical buttonholes are placed along the center guideline with the center of the button in line with the center of the buttonhole.

Buttonhole placement and size are marked with a line, showing the finished length of the buttonhole and a ⅛" (3.2mm) bar across each end.

Extensions

Button extensions correlate to the size of the button and extend out from the center front (or center back or side depending on button placement). For example, if a garment is using a ¾" (1.9cm) diameter button, the extension should be ¾" (1.9cm) from the center front guideline (Fig. 7.7).

Extensions have a second layer of fabric behind them called an **extension facing**. The facing is interfaced and supports the weight of the button and the cut of the buttonhole.

Vertical and horizontal buttonholes have different facing widths. Vertical button/buttonhole facings should be twice the width of the extension. For example, if the extension measures ¾" (1.9cm), the facing should be 1½" (3.8cm) (¾" [1.9cm] + ¾" [1.9cm] = 1½" [3.8cm]). With horizontal buttonholes, the width of the facing should be twice the width of the extension plus ¼" (6.4mm). For example, if the extension measures ¾" (1.9cm), the facing should be ¾" (1.9cm) x 2" (5.1cm) + ¼" (6.4mm) = 1¾" (4.4cm). The additional ¼" (6.4mm) keeps a horizontal buttonhole from ending too close to the edge of an extension, which will cause the buttonhole to lose support.

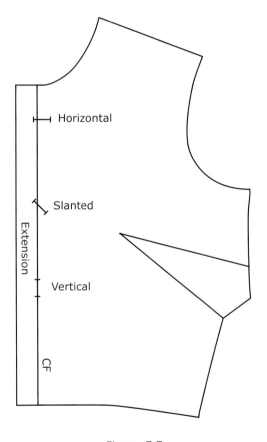

Figure 7.7

Exercises

The following exercises are shown on short bodices to the waist with the darts manipulated into a French dart. Experiment with lengths and dart manipulations.

STANDARD BUTTON PLACKET
Front Bodice (Right and Left Sides)

1. Trace the front sloper, including the dart, and mark **A**, **B**, **C**, **D**, **E**, and **F** as shown (*Fig. 7.8*).
2. Decide button diameter (example: ½" [1.3cm]). That will determine the width of the button extension.
3. **AG** = button extension as button diameter
4. **FH** = **AG**
5. Connect **G-H**.
6. **GI** = width of the button-extension facing (use horizontal buttonholes), **AG** x 2" (5.1cm) + ¼" (6.4mm). (Example: ½" [1.3cm] x 2" [5.1cm] = 1" [2.5cm] + ¼" [6.4mm] = 1¼" [3.2cm]).
7. **HJ** = **GI**
8. Connect **I-J**.
9. Fold back on the **GH** line and trace the garment shape over **GI** and **HJ**. Unfold the pattern. Draw in the traced shapes. Mark **GH** as a fold line. Mark the placement of the buttons and buttonholes on the pattern (see Buttons, Buttonholes, and Extensions).
10. Pattern: **I-G-A-B-C-D-E-F-H-J-I**, including the dart
11. Notch the center-front neck (**A**) and base (**F**). Notch the fold line (**G** and **H**).
12. Notch and awl-punch the dart. Draw a length grainline parallel to the center front. Add ¼" (6.4mm) seam allowance along the facing edge and around the neckline. Add ½" (1.3cm) seam allowance everywhere else. Drag the notches to the perimeter. Cut (2) self. Interface the facing: **I-G-H-J-I**.

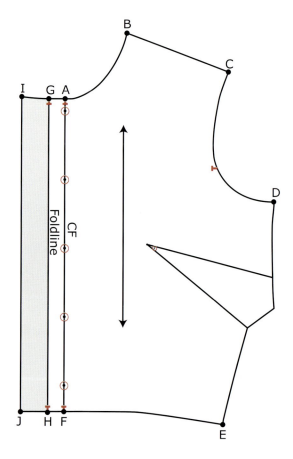

Figure 7.8

Tips:

- **Design Tip:** Often, women's garments lap right over left. Men's garments lap left over right.
- **Grainline Tip:** Garments with button closures should be cut on the length grainline to stabilize buttonholes.
- **Seam Allowance Tip:** Seam allowance along the edge of a button/buttonhole facing should be limited to ¼" (6.4mm). Any more and the seam allowance will end up under the buttonhole, resulting in poor stitch quality.

Back Bodice

1. Trace the back sloper, including the darts, and mark **K**, **L**, **M**, **N**, **O**, and **P** as shown (*Fig. 7.9*).
2. Pattern: **K-L-M-N-O-P-K**, including the darts
3. True the pattern. Notch the center-back neck (**K**) and base (**P**). Notch and awl-punch the darts. Draw a length grainline parallel to the center back. Add ¼" (6.4mm) seam allowance at the neckline and ½" (1.3cm) everywhere else. Drag the notches to the perimeter. Cut (1) self on fold at center back.

Marking Tip:

It is a good practice to start applying standard notching in the front and back bodice armholes. Front notching is 3½" (8.9cm) up from the base of the armhole. Back double notching is a 3" (7.6cm) and 3¼" (8.3cm) up from the base of the armhole. Notching helps line up armhole facings or sleeves in a garment.

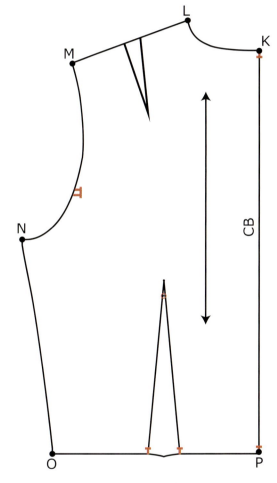

Figure 7.9

HIDDEN-BUTTON PLACKET

The instructions below are for a right-over-left style hidden-button placket. Switch the right and left sides for a left-over-right orientation. Draft separate right and left sides.

Front Bodice—Left Side (as worn)

1. Trace the front sloper, including the dart, and mark **A**, **B**, **C**, **D**, **E**, and **F** as shown (*Fig. 7.10*).
2. Decide button diameter (example: ½" [1.3cm]). That will determine the width of the button extension.
3. **AG** = button extension as determined above
4. **FH** = as **AG**
5. Connect **G-H**.
6. **GI** = width of the button-extension facing (use vertical buttonholes). For vertical buttonholes, the facing should be the width of the button extension, **AG** x 2 (example: ½" [1.3cm] x 2" [5.1cm] = 1" [2.5cm]).
7. **HJ** = **GI**
8. Connect **I-J**.
9. Fold back on the **GH** line, and trace the neckline shape over **GI** and the base shape over **HJ**. Unfold the pattern. Draw the traced shapes.
10. Mark the placement of the buttons on the pattern.
11. Pattern: **I-G-A-B-C-D E-F-H-J-I**, including the dart
12. Notch the center-front neck (**A**) and base (**F**). Notch the fold line (**G** and **H**). Notch and awl-punch the dart. Draw a length grainline parallel to the center front. Indicate left side as worn. Add ¼" (6.4mm) seam allowance along the facing edge and around the neckline. Add ½" (1.3cm) seam allowance everywhere else. Drag the notches to the perimeter. Cut (1) self. Interface the facing: **I-G-H-J-I**.

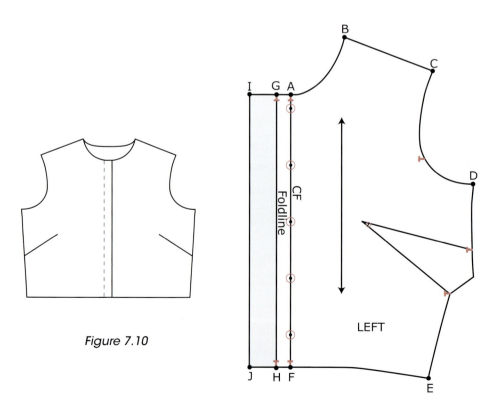

Figure 7.10

Front Bodice—Right Side (as worn)

1. Flip and trace the left front bodice and mark **K**, **L**, **M**, **N**, **O**, **P**, **Q**, **R**, **S**, and **T** as shown (*Fig. 7.11*). Mark **LS** as a fold line. Mark **KT** as a fold line.
2. **KU** = **KL** less ⅛" (3.2mm), so it will tuck under the outside flap
3. **TV** = **KU**
4. Connect **U-V**.
5. **UW** = **KU**
6. **VX** = **UW**
7. Connect **W-X**.
8. Fold under at the **LS** fold line, then bring the **LS** fold line to within ⅛" (3.2mm) of the **UV** line. Then, fold at **UV** so **WX** sits under **KT**. Trace the garment shape along **L-M-N**. Unfold the pattern. Draw the traced shape. Mark **UV** as a fold line.
9. Mark the placement of the vertical buttonholes on the pattern.
10. Pattern: **W-U-K-L-M-N-O-P-Q-R-S-T-V-X-W**, including the dart
11. Notch the center-front neck (**M**) and base (**R**). Notch the fold lines (**L** and **S**, **K** and **T**, and **U** and **V**). Notch and awl-punch the dart. Draw a length grainline parallel to the center front. Indicate right side as worn. Add ¼" (6.4mm) seam allowance along the facing edge and around the neckline. Add ½" (1.3cm) seam allowance everywhere else. Drag the notches to the perimeter. Cut (1) self. Interface the facing: **L-K-U-W-X-V-T-S-L**.

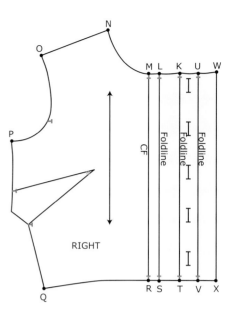

Figure 7.11

Back Pattern

Use the Standard Button Placket—Back Bodice pattern (page 157) for this exercise. True the pattern.

CAMP COLLAR

The upper and undercollar form one piece for a camp collar (*Fig. 7.12*). Use the Standard Button Placket—Front Bodice (page 156) and Back Bodice (page 157) for this exercise. The lettered instructions start where the Standard Button Placket exercise left off.

1. **QR** = front neckline measurement (**AB**) plus back neckline measurement (**KL**), less ¼" (6.4mm)
2. **QS** = down ⅛" (3.2mm)
3. **ST** = center-back collar width as desired (example: 3¾" [9.5cm])
4. **RU** = **QT**
5. **RV** = 1" (2.5cm) to build a bias curve into the neckline edge.

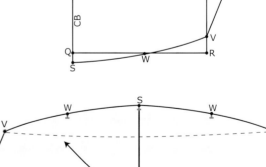

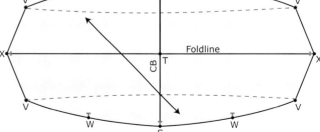

Figure 7.12

> **Drafting Tip:**
> The neckline edge of a collar needs to be curved for the collar to hug the neck.
> If a neckline edge is straight, a collar will stand straight rather than contour.

6. Connect **S-V** in a shallow curve for the neckline edge of the collar. Square off at **S** for ¾" (1.9cm).
7. **SW** = the back neckline measurement less the amount needed for seam stretch (see Seam Stretch).
8. **WV** = the front neckline measurement (not through the extension, as this collar meets at the center front guideline) less the amount needed for seam stretch (see Seam Stretch). Adjust at **V** as necessary.
9. Connect **T-U**.
10. **UX** = ¾"–1½" (1.9–3.8cm) to form the collar point (use 1½" [3.8cm] for collar points that are closer together and ¾" [1.9cm] for collar points further apart)
11. Connect **V-X**.
12. Pattern: **S-Q-T-U-X-V-W-S**
13. Create an all-in-one upper- and undercollar pattern by tracing the pattern on a folded piece of pattern paper with **SQT** on the fold. Open the pattern and mark as the upper collar.
14. Fold the pattern again along the **XUTUX** line, trace the full upper-collar pattern, and mark as the undercollar. This pattern piece includes the upper and undercollar with the fold line representing the outer-collar edge, and **V-W-S-W-V** representing the neckline edge.
15. Final Pattern (starting at the lower center back): **S-W-V-X-V-W-S-W-V-X-V-W-S**
16. Draw the roll line (see Stand, Roll Line, Height, and Fall).
17. True the pattern. Notch the center back (**S**), the high-neck point (**W**), and the fold line (**X**). Awl-punch **V**. Draw a bias grainline off the center back. Add ¼" (6.4mm) seam allowance around the collar pattern. Drag the notches to the perimeter. Cut (1) self. Cut (1) interfacing.

> **Drafting Tip:**
> Always square for about ¾" (1.9cm) off the center-back guideline of a collar.
> Squaring will prevent the center-back collar from forming a dip or a peak.

COLLAR WITH BAND

Use the Standard Button Placket—Front Bodice (page 156) and Back Bodice (page 157) for this exercise. While the camp collar met at the center front guideline, the band on this collar is drafted through the extension. The lettered instructions start where the Standard Button Placket exercise left off.

Note that the instructions cycle through the alphabet twice: first with uppercase letters, then with lowercase letters.

Band

1. **QR** = front neckline measurement, including the extension (**GAB**) plus back neckline measurement (**KL**), less ¼" (6.4mm) (*Fig. 7.13*)
2. **QS** = down ⅛" (3.2mm)
3. **ST** = center back band width as desired (example: 1" [2.5cm])
4. **RU** = square a line up from **R**, equal in length to **ST**
5. **RV** = 1" (2.5cm) to build a bias curve into the neckline edge. It is okay if **U** and **V** end up at the same point.
6. Connect **S-V** in a shallow curve for the band edge. Square off at **S** for ¾" (1.9cm).
7. **SW** = the back neckline measurement less the amount needed for seam stretch (see Seam Stretch).
8. **WV** = the front neckline measurement through the extension less the amount needed for seam stretch (see Seam Stretch). Adjust at **V** as needed.
9. **VX** = square a line off **WV** the desired width of the band at front (example: ⅞" [2.2cm]). Square off as close as possible given that **WV** is slightly curved. The front and back widths of the band do not have to be the same.
10. Connect **T-X** for the top of the band. Square off at **T** for ¾" (1.9cm). The curve should mimic the **SWV** line.
11. **XY** = mark in the amount of the button extension (**GA**)
12. **VZ** = as **XY**. Connect **Y-Z** for center front.
13. Curve the top of the band at **X** for ⅛" (3.2mm) as shown (*Fig. 7.13*). Re-mark **X**.
14. Pattern: **S-Q-T-Y-X-V-Z-W-S**
15. Notch the center back (**S** and **T**) and the center front (**Y** and **Z**). Notch the high-neck/shoulder point (**W**). Draw a length grainline parallel to the center back of the pattern. Add ¼" (6.4mm) seam allowance around the piece. Drag the notches to the perimeter. Cut (2) self on fold at center back. Interfacing both bands.

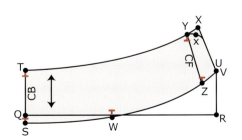
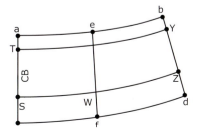
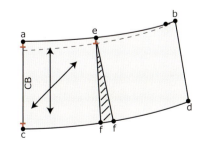

Figure 7.13

Design Tip:
The band pattern can also stand alone as a band collar.

Collar

1. Trace the band without the extension, and mark **S**, **T**, **Y**, **Z**, and **W** as shown (*Fig. 7.13*).
2. **Ta** = ½" (1.3cm)
3. **Yb** = ½" (1.3cm)
4. Connect **a-b**. Square off at **a** for ¾" (1.9cm).
5. **ac** = the width of the collar at center back (example: 2" [5.1cm])
6. The collar should cover the band with consideration taken for turn of the cloth and covering the neckline seam. A good rule of thumb is to double the band height.
7. **Zd** = extend the **bYZ** line to the desired collar point length (example: 2½" [6.4cm] total)
8. Connect **c-d** for the outer-collar edge. Square off at **c** for ¾" (1.9cm).
9. Square a line off **SW** at **W**, drawing out to each edge of the collar. Mark **e** and **f** as shown.
10. Slash from **f**, hinging at **e**, and insert ⅜" (1cm). Smooth the outer edge of the pattern.
11. Check that **ab** on the collar equals the measurement of **TY** on the band. It might be a bit off. Move **b** out as necessary. Connect **b-d** in a straight line (ignoring **Y** and **Z**).
12. Pattern: **c-a-e-b-d-c**
13. Draw the roll line ¼" (6.4mm) down from **a** and draw toward **b**. Since the band is the stand of the collar, the roll line is closer to the bottom edge of the collar.
14. Trace the pattern for an upper and undercollar, and trim the undercollar 1/16" (1.6mm) at the outer-collar edge (see Trimming the Undercollar).
15. True the pattern. Notch the center back (**a** and **c**). Add ¼" (6.4mm) seam allowance around the pieces. Drag the notches to the perimeter. Cut (1) self, upper collar on fold at center back on the length grainline. Cut (1) undercollar on a bias fold at center back. Interface the undercollar.

Grainline Tip:
Upper and undercollars should be cut separately and with different grainlines. Upper collars are cut with the length grain along the center back. Undercollars are cut on a bias grainline off the center back. The undercollar is interfaced. If the interfacing has a grainline, cut the interfacing on same grainline as the cut piece.

Why the two different grainlines? The upper-collar-length grainline allows the grainline/fabric pattern on the collar to match the grainline/fabric pattern on the garment at the center back while giving structure and support to the collar. The undercollar is cut on the bias grainline to help the collar curve around the neck smoothly. The two different grainlines are necessary for a collar to contour to the neckline (undercollar) while still maintaining some structure (upper collar).

PETER PAN COLLAR

A Peter Pan collar sits flat against the bodice and does not have a stand, height, or roll line. The collar meets at the center front. Use the Standard Button Placket—Front Bodice (page 156) and Back Bodice (page 157) for this exercise. The lettered instructions start where the Standard Button Placket exercise left off.

1. Attach the front and back Standard Button Placket patterns together at the shoulder (*Fig. 7.14*).
2. Draw the desired shape of the collar on top of the bodices. The collar should meet at the center front. A Peter Pan collar is often about 2"–2½" (5.1–6.4cm) wide all around. The front of the collar is traditionally rounded.
3. Arbitrarily mark **Q** along the rounded edge of the collar. Mark **R** at the center-back base of the collar.
4. Pattern: **A-Q-R-K-B/L-A**
5. Trace the pattern for an upper and undercollar, and trim the undercollar ¹⁄₁₆" (1.6mm) at the outer-collar edge (see Trimming the Undercollar).
6. True the pattern. Notch the center back (**K** and **R**). Add ¼" (6.4mm) seam allowance around the piece. Drag the notches to the perimeter. Add a length grainline at center back. Cut (2) self on fold at center back. No need for a bias grainline since this collar sits flat against the bodice. Cut (1) interfacing on fold at center back. Interfacing the undercollar can make this collar too stiff. Use a lightweight interfacing, since it does not need much structure.

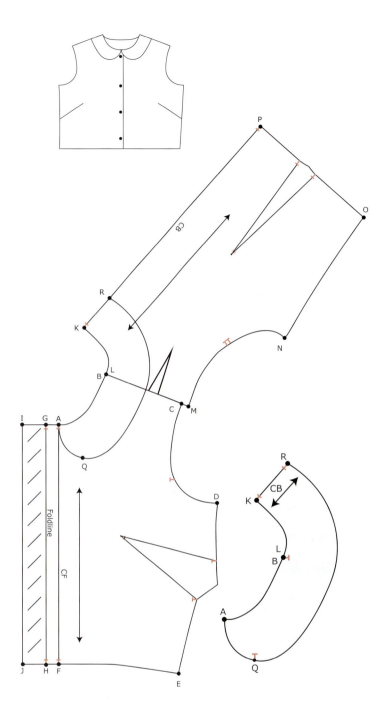

Figure 7.14

Fitting Tip:

If the Peter Pan collar is hovering above the bodice rather than resting on it, it could be that the interfacing is too stiff or the outer-collar edge needs more measurement. Cut from the outer-collar edge to the **B/L** line, and insert as needed to allow it to relax down (see Collar Fall Adjustment).

FACINGS

A shirt, dress, jacket, or coat has either a button placket or facings—never both. Choose one or the other based on the style of your garment. For example, a button-down or button-up shirt has a button placket. A jacket or coat usually has a facing.

Vocabulary Tip:
There is a difference between a button-down and a button-up shirt.
A **button-down shirt** has buttons along the center front and buttons holding the collar points down. A **button-up shirt** has buttons along the center front only.

Front Facing

1. Trace the front sloper, including the dart, and draft an extension as the button diameter. Mark **A, B, C, D, E, F, G,** and **H** as shown (*Fig. 7.15*). Mark the center front.
2. **CI** = width of the facing at shoulder (example: 2" [5.1cm])
3. **GJ** = width of the facing at base (example: 2" [5.1cm] from the center front)
4. Pattern: **A-B-C-I-J-G-H-A**. Note that the facing encompasses the extension as well.
5. Notch the center-front neck (**B**) and base (**G**). Draw a length grainline parallel to the center front. Add ¼" (6.4mm) seam allowance to the neckline and along the edge of the facing at **AH**. Add ½" (1.3cm) seam allowance everywhere else. Drag the notches to the perimeter. Cut (2) self. Cut (2) interfacing.

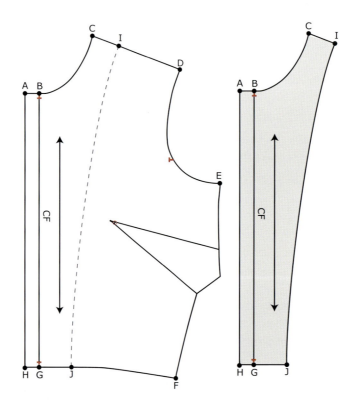

Figure 7.15

Back Facing

1. Trace the back sloper, including the darts, and mark **K**, **L**, **M**, **N**, **O**, and **P** as shown (*Fig. 7.16*).
2. **LQ** = as **CI** on the front facing
3. **KR** = depth of the back facing as desired (example: 2" [5.1cm])
4. Connect **Q-R** for the base of the facing. Square off at **R** for ½" (1.3cm).
5. Pattern: **K-L-Q-R-K**
6. True the pattern. Notch the center-back neck (**K**) and base (**R**). Draw a length grainline parallel to the center back. Add ¼" (6.4mm) seam allowance to the neckline and ½" (1.3cm) everywhere else. Drag the notches to the perimeter. Cut (1) self on fold at center back. Cut (1) interfacing on fold at center back.

Lining is usually attached to the edges of a facing. Use the remaining patterns as lining pieces.

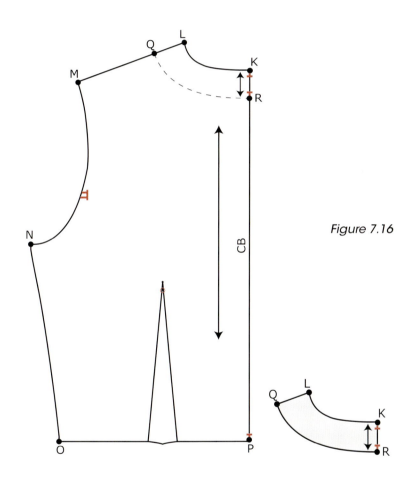

Figure 7.16

SHAWL COLLAR

A shawl collar is drafted on a bodice with a V-neckline and has a facing rather than a button placket.

Front Bodice

1. Trace the front sloper, including the dart, and mark **A**, **B**, **C**, **D**, **E**, and **F** as shown (*Fig. 7.17*).
2. **BG** = V-neckline depth and shape as desired (can be straight or curved)
3. **FH** = width of the button extension as the diameter of the button
4. Square a line up from **H** for the button extension
5. **GI** = continuation of the neckline shape (**BG**) through the button extension
6. Note the measurement of the front neckline (**BI**) for drafting the collar. This collar is drafted through the extension.
7. Pattern: **B-C-D-E-F-H-I-B**, including the dart
8. Notch the center-front base (**F**). Notch **I**. Notch and awl-punch the dart. Draw a length grainline parallel to the center front. Add ¼" (6.4mm) seam allowance to the neckline and along the **IH** edge. Add ½" (1.3cm) seam allowance everywhere else. Drag the notches to the perimeter. Cut (2) self.
9. Include a **front facing** using the facing instructions.

Back Bodice

1. Trace the back sloper, including the darts, and mark **J**, **K**, **L**, **M**, **N**, and **O** as shown (*Fig. 7.17*).
2. Note the measurement of the back neckline (**JK**).
3. Pattern: **J-K-L-M-N-O-J**, including the dart
4. Notch the center-back neck (**J**) and base (**O**). Notch and awl-punch the darts. Draw a length grainline parallel to the center back. Add ¼" (6.4mm) seam allowance to the neckline and ½" (1.3cm) everywhere else. Drag the notches to the perimeter. Cut (1) self on fold at center back.
5. Include a **back facing** using the facing instructions.

Collar

1. **PQ** = front neckline measurement (**BI**), plus back neckline measurement (**JK**), less ⅜" (1cm) (*Fig. 7.17*)
2. **PR** = 1½" (3.8cm) to build a bias curve into the neckline edge
3. Connect **R-Q** in a shallow curve for the neckline edge. Square off at **R** for ¾" (1.9cm).
4. Connect **T-Q** for the outer collar. Square off at **T** for ¾" (1.9cm).
5. **RS** = the back neckline measurement less the amount needed for seam stretch (see Seam Stretch)
6. **SQ** = the front neckline measurement through the extension less the amount needed for seam stretch (see Seam Stretch)
7. Adjust at **Q** as necessary.
8. **RT** = center back width of the collar (example: 3¾" [9.5cm])
9. Connect **T-Q** for the outer collar. Square off for ¾" (1.9cm).
10. The shape shown is traditional, but the outer collar can be scalloped, pointed, or any shape as desired.
11. Pattern: **R-T-Q-S-R**. Be sure to cut off the area below **RSQ**.
12. Draw the roll line (see Stand, Roll Line, Height, and Fall).
13. Trace the pattern for an upper and undercollar, and trim the undercollar at the outer-collar edge as needed (see Trimming the Undercollar).

14. True the pattern. Notch the center back (**R** and **T**), the high-neck point (**S**), and arbitrarily along the outer-collar edge. Trace an upper collar and add a length grainline at center back. Trace an undercollar and add a bias grainline off the center back. Add ¼" (6.4mm) seam allowance around the pieces. Drag the notches to the perimeter. Cut (1) self, upper collar on center-back fold. Cut (1) self, undercollar on a bias fold (or cut 2 pieces on bias with a center-back seam). Interface the undercollar.

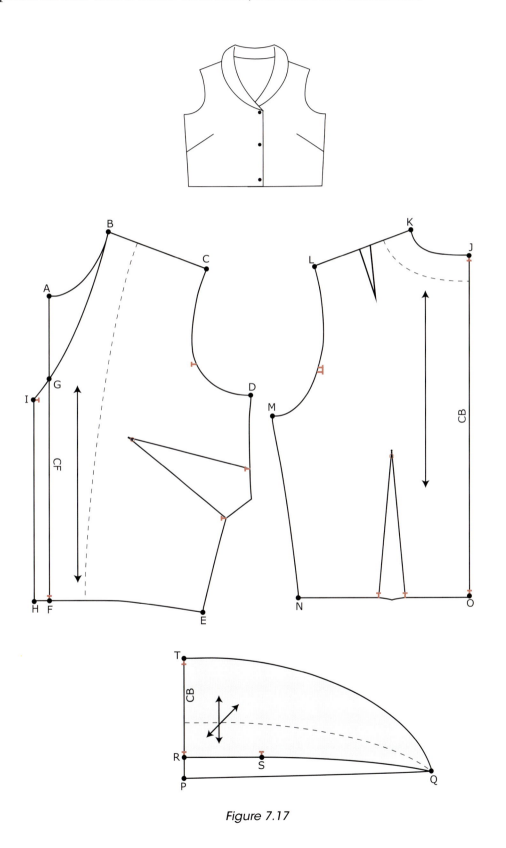

Figure 7.17

ROLL COLLAR ON A V-NECKLINE

Because the back neckline measurement is needed to draft the front, begin this draft with the back bodice. The upper collar is attached to the facing, so facings must be included with a roll collar on a V-neckline. The shawl collar and the roll collar on a V-neckline look similar. However, the shawl collar is a separate pattern piece, and the roll collar is attached as one to the bodice.

Back Bodice and Facing

1. Trace the back sloper, including the darts, and mark **A**, **B**, **C**, **D**, **E**, and **F** as shown (*Fig. 7.18*).
2. Note the measurement of the back neckline (**AB**).
3. Pattern: **A-B-C-D-E-F-A**, including the darts
4. Notch the center-back neck (**A**) and base (**F**). Notch and awl-punch the darts.
5. Draw a length grainline parallel to the center back. Add ¼" (6.4mm) seam allowance along the neckline and ½" (1.3cm) everywhere else. Drag the notches to the perimeter. Cut (1) self on fold at center back.
6. Include a back facing: **A-B-G-H-A**
7. Notch the center-back neck (**A**) and base (**H**). Draw a length grainline parallel to the center back. Add ¼" (6.4mm) seam allowance around the neckline and ½" (1.3cm) everywhere else. Drag the notches to the perimeter. Cut (1) self on fold at center back. Cut (1) interfacing on fold at center back.

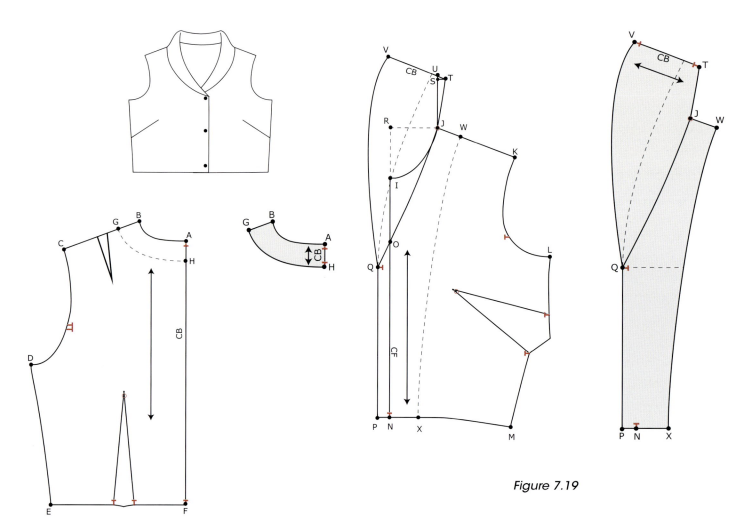

Figure 7.18

Figure 7.19

168 Building Patterns

Front Bodice and Undercollar

1. Trace the front sloper, including the dart, and mark **I**, **J**, **K**, **L**, **M**, and **N** as shown (*Fig. 7.19*).
2. **JO** = V-neckline depth as desired (the **JO** line needs to be straight for the collar to fold back)
3. **NP** = width of the button extension as the diameter of the button
4. Square a line up from **P** for the button extension.
5. Connect **J-O** and continue the line through the extension. Mark **Q**.
6. **IR** = extend the center front guideline up until it is level with the high-neck/shoulder point (**J**)
7. Square a dotted line over from **R** to **J**.
8. **JS** = the back neckline measurement (**AB**) less ³⁄₁₆" (4.8mm), squared off **RJ**
9. **ST** = 1" (2.5cm) squared off **JS**
10. **JT** = connect for the back neckline. **JT** should measure as the back neckline measurement less ¹⁄₁₆" (1.6mm). Adjust at **T** if necessary.
11. **SU** = ½" (1.3cm) as a continuation of the **JS** line.
12. Connect **T-U** and continue the line until it measures as the desired center-back collar width (example: 3¾" [9.5cm]). Mark **V**.
13. Connect **V-Q** in any shape desired. Be sure to square off at **V** for ¾" (1.9cm).
14. Square at **T** toward **J**, off the **TV** line for about ¼" (6.4mm) to make sure the center-back neckline does not dip or peak. This will cause a slight curve in the line.
15. Pattern: **P-Q-V-T-J-K-L-M-N-P**, including the dart
16. Trim the outer-collar edge ¹⁄₁₆" (1.6mm) (see Trimming the Outer Collar).
17. Draw the roll line (see Stand, Roll Line, Height, and Fall).
18. Notch the center-front base (**N**). Notch the break point (**Q**). Awl-punch the high-neck point (**J**). Notch and awl-punch the dart. Draw a length grainline parallel to the center front. Add ¼" (6.4mm) seam allowance along **P-Q-V-T-J**, and ½" (1.3cm) everywhere else. Drag the notches to the perimeter. Cut (2) self.

Front Facing and Upper Collar

1. **JW** = shoulder facing width (as **BG** on the back facing) (*Fig. 7.19*)
2. **NX** = facing width at base from center front (example: 2" [5.1cm])
3. Connect **W-X** in a shallow curve.
4. Trace the pattern: **P-Q-V-T-J-W-X-N-P**
5. True the pattern. Notch the center-front base (**N**). Notch the break point (**Q**). Notch the center-back collar width (**T** and **V**). Awl-punch the high-neck point (**J**). Draw a grainline parallel to **VT**. The center back (**VT**) is on a fold. Add ¼" (6.4mm) seam allowance along **P-Q-V-T-J**, and ½" (1.3cm) everywhere else. Drag the notches to the perimeter. Cut (1) self on fold at **VT**. Cut (1) interfacing on fold at **VT**.
6. Note the dotted line level with the break point (**Q**) on the facing pattern. Separate the pattern at the dotted line to put the lower part of the facing on the length grain, thereby stabilizing buttonholes or any other closure.

TRENCH COAT COLLAR

A trench coat collar is usually drafted on jackets and coats. It is a collar with an exaggerated band and lapel. The band stops short of the center front and the collar sits on top of the band, flush with the band edge.

Note that the instructions cycle through the alphabet twice: first with uppercase letters, then with lowercase letters.

Front Bodice and Facing

1. Trace the front sloper, including the dart, and mark **A**, **B**, **C**, **D**, **E**, and **F** as shown (*Fig. 7.20*).
2. **BG** = depth of the band along the neckline (example: 3" [7.6cm])
3. **H** = desired depth of the neckline at center front
4. Connect **G-H** in a straight line.
5. **FI** = width of the button extension as button diameter
6. Square a line up from **I** for the button extension.
7. **GHJ** = continuation of the neckline (**GH**) through the button extension in a straight line
8. **GKJ** = draw the desired shape of the lapel against the bodice. Take into consideration the turn of the cloth (see Turn of the Cloth).
9. Fold the pattern paper under on the **GJ** line and trace the lapel (**G-K-J-G**). Unfold the paper and draw in the traced shape. Mark **L** as shown at the tip of the lapel.
10. Note the measurement of the front neckline (**BG**) to draft the band.
11. Pattern: **B-C-D-E-F-I-J-L-G-B**, including the dart
12. Notch the center-front base (**F**). Notch the break point (**J**). Awl-punch the tip of the lapel (**L**) and the point where the band meets the lapel along the neckline (**G**). Notch and awl-punch the dart. Mark **GJ** as a roll line. Draw a length grainline parallel to the center front. Add ¼" (6.4mm) seam allowance along **I-J-L-G-B** and ½" (1.3cm) everywhere else. Drag the notches to the perimeter. Cut (2) self.
13. Include a front facing that will incorporate the extension and the lapel. Include notches, drill hole, and grainline. Add ¼" (6.4mm) seam allowance along **I-J-L-G-B** and ½" (1.3cm) everywhere else. Drag the notches to the perimeter. Cut (2) self. Cut (2) interfacing.

Back Bodice and Facing

1. Trace the back sloper, including the darts, and mark **M**, **N**, **O**, **P**, **Q**, and **R** as shown (*Fig. 7.21*).
2. Note the measurement of the back neckline (**MN**).
3. Pattern: **M-N-O-P-Q-R M**, including the dart
4. Notch the center-back neck (**M**) and base (**R**). Notch and awl-punch the darts.
5. Draw a length grainline parallel to the center back. Add ¼" (6.4mm) seam allowance at the neckline and ½" (1.3cm) everywhere else. Drag the notches to the perimeter. Cut (1) self on fold at center back.
6. Include a back facing. Include notches at the center back top and bottom. Draw a length grainline. Add ¼" (6.4mm) seam allowance along the neckline and ½" (1.3cm) everywhere else. Drag the notches to the perimeter. Cut (1) self on fold at center back. Cut (1) interfacing on fold at center back.

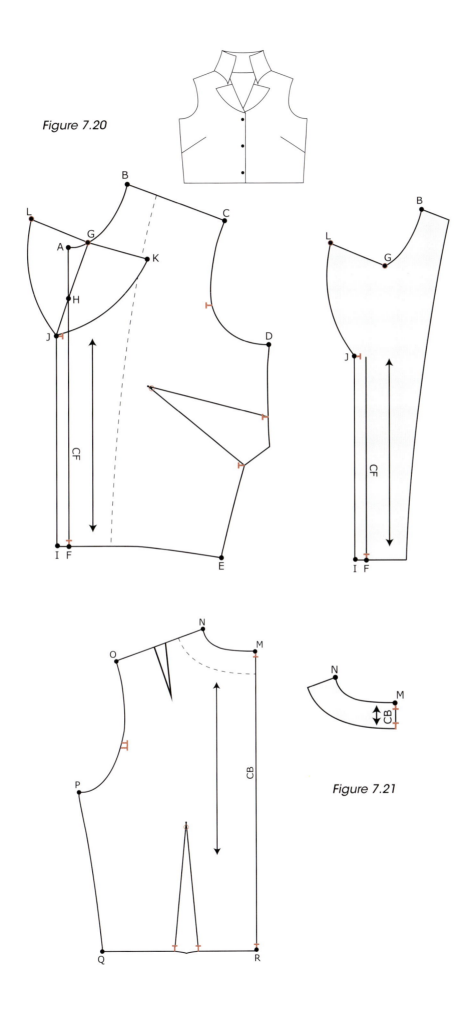

Figure 7.20

Figure 7.21

Band

1. **ST** = front neckline measurement (**BG**) plus back neckline measurement (**MN**), less ¼" (6.4mm) (*Fig. 7.22*)
2. **SU** = down ⅛" (3.2mm)
3. **UV** = center back band width as desired (example: 2" [5.1cm])
4. **TW** = **SV**
5. **TX** = 1" (2.5cm) to build a bias curve into the neckline edge
6. Connect **U-X** in a shallow curve for the band edge. Square off at **U** for ¾" (1.9cm).
7. **UY** = the back neckline measurement less the amount needed for seam stretch (see Seam Stretch)
8. **YX** = the front neckline measurement (**BG**) less the amount needed for seam stretch (see Seam Stretch). Adjust at **X** as necessary.
9. **XZ** = square a line off **YX** the desired width of the band at front (example: 2" [5.1cm]). Square off as closely as possible given that **YX** is slightly curved.
10. Connect **VZ** for the top of the band. Square off at **V** for ¾" (1.9cm). The curve should mimic the **UX** line.
11. Pattern: **U-S-V-Z-X-Y-U**
12. Notch the center back (**U** and **V**) and the high-neck point (**Y**). Draw a length grainline parallel to the center back. Add ¼" (6.4mm) seam allowance around the piece. Drag the notches to the perimeter. Cut (2) self on fold at center back. Cut (2) interfacing on fold at center back. Interface both bands.

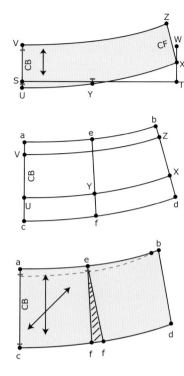

Figure 7.22

Collar

1. Trace the band and mark **U**, **V**, **Z**, **X**, and **Y** as shown (*Fig. 7.22*).
2. **Va** = ½" (1.3cm)
3. **Zb** = ½" (1.3cm)
4. Connect **a-b**. Square off at **a** for ¾" (1.9cm).
5. **ac** = the width of the collar at center back (example: 3" [7.6cm])
6. The collar should cover the band with consideration taken for turn of the cloth and for covering the neckline seam.
7. **bd** = extend the **bZXd** line to the desired collar point (example: 3" [7.6cm] total)
8. Connect **c-d** for the outer-collar edge. Square off at **c** for ¾" (1.9cm).
9. Square a line off **UY** at **Y**, drawing out to each edge of the collar. Mark **e** and **f** as shown.
10. Slash from **f**, hinging at **e**, and insert ⅜" (1cm). Smooth the outer edge of the pattern.
11. Check to make sure that **ab** on the collar equals the measurement of **VZ** on the band. Move **b** out as necessary.
12. Pattern: **c a-e-b-d-c**
13. Draw the roll line ¼" (6.4mm) down from **a** and draw toward **b**. Since the band is the stand of the collar, the roll line is closer to the bottom edge of the collar.
14. Trace the pattern for an upper (length grain) and under (bias) collar, and trim the undercollar at the outer-collar edge as needed (see Trimming the Undercollar).
15. True the pattern. Notch the center back (**a** and **c**). Be sure to note that the collar is flush with the band (**b** on the collar should meet **Z** on the band). Add ¼" (6.4mm) seam allowance around the pieces. Drag the notches to the perimeter. Cut (1) self, upper collar on fold at center back. Cut (1) self, undercollar on a bias fold (or cut 2 pieces on bias with a center-back seam). Interface the undercollar.

NOTCHED COLLAR

Drafting a notched collar is similar to drafting the Roll Collar on a V-Neckline, except that the collar portion is detached. Because the back neckline measurement is needed to draft the front, begin this draft with the back bodice.

Note that the instructions cycle through the alphabet twice: first with uppercase letters, then with lowercase letters.

Back Bodice and Facing

1. Trace the back sloper, including the darts. Move the high-neck point ⅛" (3.2mm) out and blend into the center-back neck. Mark **A**, **B**, **C**, **D**, **E**, and **F** as shown (*Fig. 7.23*).
2. Note the measurement of the back neckline (**AB**).
3. Pattern: **A-B-C-D-E-F-A**, including the darts
4. Notch the center-back neck (**A**) and base (**F**). Notch and awl-punch the darts.
5. Draw a length grainline parallel to the center back. Add ¼" (6.4mm) seam allowance along the neckline and ½" (1.3cm) everywhere else. Drag the notches to the perimeter. Cut (1) self on fold at center back.
6. Include a **back facing**.
7. Notch the center-back neck (**A**) and base. Draw a length grainline parallel to the center back. Add ¼" (6.4mm) seam allowance around the neckline and ½" (1.3cm) everywhere else. Drag the notches to the perimeter. Cut (1) self on fold at center back. Cut (1) interfacing on fold at center back.

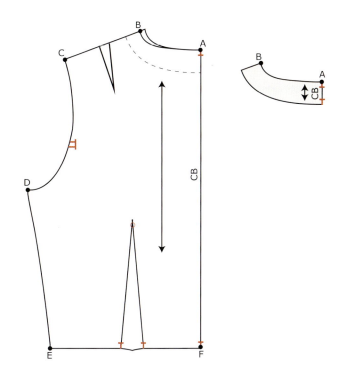

Figure 7.23

Patternmaking Tip:

Because a notched collar is usually used on a jacket or a coat, the high-neck/shoulder point is moved out ⅛"–¼" (3.2–6.4mm) on the front and back bodice to grade the neckline out to make room for a shirt or blouse collar to sit underneath.

Front Bodice and Facing

1. Trace the front sloper, including the dart. Move the high-neck point out ⅛"–¼" (3.2–6.4mm) as back and blend into the center-front neck. Mark **G, H, I, J, K,** and **L** as shown (*Fig. 7.24*).
2. **LM** = the width of the button extension as the diameter of the button. Square a line up from **M** for the extension.
3. **HN** = 1" (2.5cm) toward the center front continuing the slant of the shoulder
4. **O** = decide the depth at the center-front neckline
5. Connect **N-O** and continue the line until it reaches through the extension. Mark **P**.
6. **Q** = where the **NP** line intersects the **HG** line (or place **Q** anywhere on the **NP** line). **Q** is where the collar meets the lapel.
7. **QR** = width of the top of the lapel as desired considering turn of the cloth (example: 3" [7.6cm]) (see Turn of the Cloth)
8. Connect **R-P** in a convex shape.
9. **QS** = mark the **gorge point** where the collar splits off from the lapel (example: 1¼" [3.2cm])

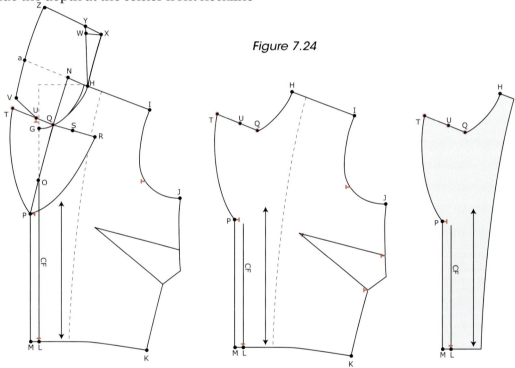

Figure 7.24

Design Tip:
If the edge of the lapel is a straight line rather than a convex line, the lapel can look bowed in. Bumping it out slightly can make it appear straighter.

10. Fold on **QP** and trace the lapel **Q-S-R-P-Q**. Unfold the paper and mark **U** and **T** as shown.
11. **TV** = decide the amount of the split between the collar and lapel (example: ¾" [1.9cm]), and mark it above **T**.
12. Connect **U-V**.
13. Square a dotted line up from the center front guideline until it is level with **H**.
14. Square a dotted line over to **H**.
15. **HW** = back neckline measurement (**AB**) less ³⁄₁₆" (4.8mm) squared off the dotted guideline
16. **WX** = 1" (2.5cm) squared off **HW**
17. Connect **H-X**. This is the back neckline.

Style Tip:
The shape of a lapel is a design choice. It will not affect the fit of a garment.
Experiment with the size, shape, and placement of a lapel.

---

18. **WY** = ½" (1.3cm) extension of the **HW** line.
19. Connect **X-Y** and continue the line until the center-back collar width is as desired (example: 3¾" [9.5cm]). Mark Z.
20. Connect **Z-V**. Square off at **Z** for ¾" (1.9cm).
21. Square at **X** toward **H**, off the **XZ** line for ¾" (1.9cm).
22. **a** = midway between **V** and **Z**
23. Connect **H-a** in a dotted line. The line may or may not cross **N**.
24. Trace the collar **X-Y-Z-a-V-U-Q-H-X**. Slash from **a** to **H** and insert ⅜" (1cm).
25. Trace the bodice pattern: **H-I-J-K-L-M-P-T-U-Q-H**, including the dart
26. On the bodice pattern, notch the center-front base (**L**) and the break point (**P**). Awl-punch the gorge point (**U**), the lapel tip (**T**), and the neckline where the collar and lapel meet (**Q**). Notch and awl-punch the dart. The lapel will roll back on the **QP** line. Draw the grainline parallel to the center front. Add ¼" (6.4mm) seam allowance along **M-P-T-U-Q-H** and ½" (1.3cm) everywhere else. Drag the notches to the perimeter. Cut (2) self.
27. Draft a **front facing** off the bodice and trace that out. The extension and lapel are included in the facing. Include notches, drill holes, and a length grainline. Add ¼" (6.4mm) seam allowance along **M-P-T-U-Q-H** and ½" (1.3cm) everywhere else. Drag the notches to the perimeter. Cut (2) self. Cut (2) interfacing.

Collar
1. Pattern: **X-Z-V-U-Q-H-X**
2. Make sure the center back is squared for ¾" (1.9cm) at **Z** and **X**. Smooth at **H** slightly. Include a roll line (*Fig. 7.25*).
3. Trace the pattern for an upper and undercollar, and trim the undercollar at the outer-collar edge (see Trimming the Undercollar).
4. True the pattern. Notch the center back (**X** and **Z**) and the high-neck point (**H**). Awl-punch **Q** and **U**. Draw a bias grainline on the undercollar and a length grainline on the upper collar. Add ¼" (6.4mm) seam allowance around the pieces. Drag the notches to the perimeter. Cut (1) self, upper collar on fold at center back. (Option: Interface the upper collar also for more structure.) Cut (2) undercollar pieces on bias with a center-back seam. Interface the undercollar pieces with bias-cut interfacing.

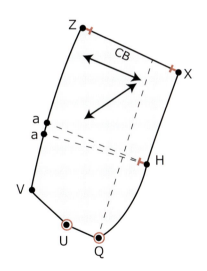

Figure 7.25

Patternmaking Tip:
On jackets and coats, the undercollar is cut in two pieces with a seam at the center back. This allows for better mirroring of the bias grainline, resulting the collar sitting evenly on the neckline.

HOOD

Draft a simple front and back bodice with a center-front zipper and facings.

1. **AB** = front + back neckline + ¼" (6.4mm) (*Fig. 7.26*)
2. **AC** = small: 12" (30.5cm), medium: 13" (33cm), or large: 14" (35.6cm) hoods. Subtract 1"–2" (2.5–5.1cm) for knit fabrics.
3. **BD** = **AC**
4. **AE** = 2½" (6.4cm)
5. Connect **E-B** getting to the **AB** line about midway.
6. **EF** = front neckline measurement less seam stretch (see Seam Stretch)
7. **BG** = back neckline measurement less seam stretch measured from **B** (see Seam Stretch)
8. **FG** = the gap in between the front and back measurements. This gap will be dart width.
9. **H** = the point of the dart centered between **F** and **G**, squared off the **AB** line. Use a dart length of 3¾" (9.5cm).
10. **F-H-G** = dart
11. The first leg of the dart (**F** is also the shoulder notch).
12. **DI** = 3" (7.6cm) at a 45-degree angle
13. Connect **C-I-B** for the top and center-back seam of the hood.
14. Notch the dart legs. Awl-punch the dart point. Draw a length grainline. Add a ½" (1.3cm) seam allowance. Drag the notches to the perimeter. Cut (2) self or (4) self if the hood will be faced.

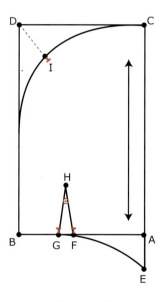

Figure 7.26

Design Tip:
C-A-E can be placed on a fold. Sew in ½" (1.3cm) from the fold to attach the two layers of fabric and create a casing for a drawstring. A buttonhole or grommet can be added near **E** to thread the drawstring through.

✓ Test Your Knowledge

1. Define the stand, roll line, height, and fall of a collar.

2. What is turn of the cloth?

3. Why is seam stretch a consideration when drafting a collar.

4. If the diameter of a button is ¾" (1.9cm), how wide is the button extension? How wide is the button-extension facing with vertical buttonholes? How about horizontal buttonholes?

5. Why are collars squared for about ¾" (1.9cm) at center back?

This chapter starts with building a basic sleeve sloper for womenswear or menswear. From the sloper, exercises are drafted, which include a two-piece sleeve with vent, short, cap, and three-quarter sleeves; sleeve plackets and cuffs; Juliet sleeves; bishop sleeves; sleeve gussets; and drop-shoulder bodices and sleeves. Instruction for drafting a knit sleeve sloper is included.

OBJECTIVES

Upon completion of this chapter, you will be able to

- Create a well-fitting sleeve sloper
- Use the sloper to design more intricate sleeve styles
- Accurately describe different sleeve styles

CHAPTER 8
Sleeves

Introduction to Sleeve Terms and Measuring

SLEEVE TERMS

- **Sleeve Cap:** The top area on a sleeve pattern between the front and back notches.
- **Cap Ease:** The difference between the sleeve measurement and the armhole (aka **armscye**) measurement. An additional amount is added to the sleeve for comfort and ease of movement. On blouses and dresses, add ½"–1" (1.3–2.5cm) ease to the sleeve. On jackets and coats, 1"–1½" (2.5–3.8cm) ease to the sleeve. If a garment is over-sized with a deep, wide armhole, no added ease is necessary.
- **Sleeve Ease:** Any ease allowance beyond the size and shape of the arm.
- **Biceps Level:** A guideline level with the biceps.
- **Elbow Level:** A guideline level with the elbow.
- **Wrist Level:** A guideline level with the wrist.
- **Sleeve Base:** The base of the sleeve regardless of length.
- **Quartering a Sleeve:** The sleeve sloper is divided into four parts using the guidelines drawn in the original sleeve draft. These lines are labeled quarter lines. Quarter lines are used as cut lines to add details like vents, plackets, or insertions for fullness.
- **Notches:** On the cap, one notch is used to indicate front, and two notches to indicate back. One notch at the top of the cap shows where the sleeve meets the shoulder seam. The elbow guideline is notched on either side (*Fig. 8.1*).

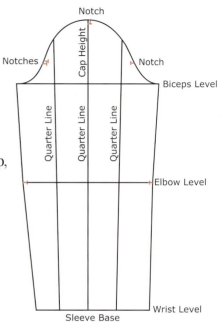

Figure 8.1

Vocabulary Tip:
The front and back armholes on a garment make up the **armscye**, or the armhole. Either word is appropriate.

WHAT AND HOW TO MEASURE FOR SLEEVES

Take the following measurements to draft a sleeve. Ask the model if they are right-or left-handed, and measure on their dominant side (*Fig. 8.2*).

- **Shoulder (1):** Measure the **front** shoulder length off a bodice sloper or pattern. Measure the pattern, not the body.
- **Elbow Length (2):** With the model's hand on their hip bone, measure from the end of the shoulder to the center of the elbow.

Building Patterns

- **Sleeve Length (3):** With the model's hand on their hip bone, measure from the end of the shoulder to the center of the elbow, then continue to the base of the wrist bone.
- **Elbow Breadth (4):** With the model's hand on their hip bone, measure around the bent elbow.
- **Biceps (5):** Have the model bring their fingertips to the end of shoulder. Measure around the flexed biceps.
- **Wrist (6):** Measure around the wrist using the wrist bones as a guide.
- **Hand (7):** Add 2" (5.1cm) to the wrist measurement to allow for the hand to pass comfortably through an opening at the base of a sleeve in a garment made from woven fabric.

Measuring Tip:
Measure on the model's dominant side because it is usually more muscular and defined. Having the model place their hand on their hip bone while measuring lengths adds a bit of length, so the sleeve do not appear to shorten when moving the arms.

Sleeve Measurements
Shoulder (1): _____
Elbow Length (2): _____
Sleeve Length (3): _____
Elbow Breadth (4): _____
Biceps (5): _____
Wrist (6): _____
Hand (7): _____

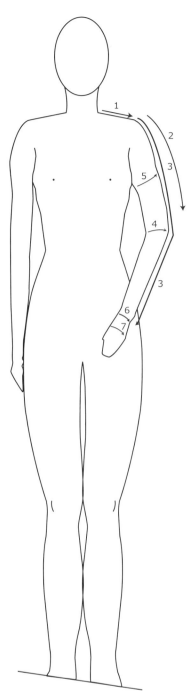

Figure 8.2

There are three back bodice considerations that will make the sleeve feel more comfortable by offering more mobility when moving the arms forward.
1. Include the back shoulder dart.
2. Add ¼"–⅜" (0.6–1cm) to the back end of shoulder and ease that amount back into the front shoulder when sewing. The sewn shoulder will measure as the front shoulder length; however, a pocket of fabric will be released below the back shoulder line.
3. Add ¼"–⅜" (0.6–1cm) at the cross back at center back, and blend to zero at the center-back neck and to zero about 6" (15.2cm) below the cross back (or blend into the back contouring). This will force a center-back seam, which also helps because the seam will have some give. The back shoulder dart already exists in the sloper, so experiment with adding to the back shoulder and the cross back.

Always have the armholes square off the end of shoulder for at least 1" (2.5cm) on the front and back bodice (womenswear), or square from the end of shoulder to the cross-front and cross-back guidelines (menswear). Squaring gives more room and will help the sleeve hang nicely without a peak at the shoulder seam.

Exercises

BASIC SLEEVE SLOPER

Measure the front and back armholes of the garment or a sloper. Decide how much ease will be added in the cap: ½"–1" (1.3–2.5cm) for dresses and blouses; 1"–1½" (2.5–3.8cm) for jackets and coats; zero for oversized armholes.

Find the square size for drafting the sleeve based on the sum. For example, 8¾" (22.2cm) front armhole + 9¼" (23.5cm) back armhole = 18" (45.7cm) + ¾" (1.9cm) ease = 18¾" (47.6cm). Find the appropriate **square size** on the Square Size Chart and begin the draft (*Fig. 8.3*). Round to the nearest number or round down if in between. In the example, find 18¾" (47.6cm) on the chart, and note that 18¾" (47.62cm) needs a square size of 3½" (8.9cm).

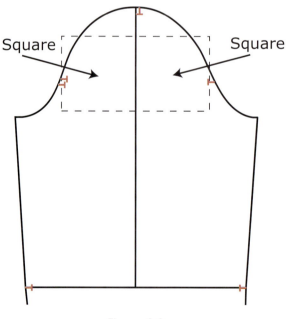

Figure 8.3

Square Size Chart

- 15 ¾" (40cm), use a 2 ¾" (7cm) square size
- 16 ¼" (41.3cm), use a 2 ⅞" (7.3cm) square size
- 16 ¾" (42.5cm), use a 3" (7.6cm) square size
- 17 ¼" (43.8cm), use a 3 ⅛" (7.9cm) square size
- 17 ¾" (45.1cm), use a 3 ¼" (8.3cm) square size
- 18 ¼" (46.4cm), use a 3 ⅜" (8.6cm) square size
- 18 ¾" (47.6cm), use a 3 ½" (8.9cm) square size
- 19 ¼" (48.9cm), use a 3 ⅝" (9.2cm) square size
- 19 ¾" (50.2cm), use a 3 ¾" (9.5cm) square size
- 20 ¼" (51.4cm), use a 3 ⅞" (9.8cm) square size
- 20 ¾" (52.7cm), use a 4" (10.2cm) square size
- 21 ¼" (54cm), use a 4 ⅛" (10.5cm) square size
- 21 ¾" (55.2cm), use a 4 ¼" (10.8cm) square size
- 22 ¼" (56.5cm), use a 4 ⅜" (11.1cm) square size
- 22 ¾" (57.8cm), use a 4 ½" (11.4cm) square size
- 23 ¼" (59.1cm), use a 4 ⅝" (11.7cm) square size
- 23 ¾" (60.3cm), use a 4 ¾" (12.1cm) square size
- 24 ¼" (61.6cm), use a 4 ⅞" (12.4cm) square size
- 24 ¾" (62.9cm), use a 5" (12.7cm) square size

Increase the square size ⅛" (3.2mm) for every ½" (1.3cm) over 24 ¾" (62.9cm).
Reduce the square size ⅛" (3.2mm) for every ½" (1.3cm) under 15 ¾" (40cm).

Drafting Tips:

- Some minor adjustments might be required, but starting with the appropriate square size will get the draft close to the measurement needed.
- If the front and back armhole measurements change with a newly drafted garment, a new sleeve needs to be drafted with the appropriate square size.
- Generally, menswear markets use a cap height of 1"–1 ¼" (2.5–3.2cm), resulting in a flatter, wider cap. Womenswear markets use a height of 1 ½"–1 ¾" (3.8–4.4cm), resulting in a higher, narrow cap. The more fitted the sleeve, the higher the cap.

Sleeve Sloper

Note that the instructions cycle through the alphabet twice: first with uppercase letters, then with lowercase letters.

1. **AB** = sleeve length as measured, less men's: 1¼" (3.2cm) or women's: 1¾" (4.4cm) for the cap height (*Fig. 8.4*). For example, if the sleeve length is 24" (61cm), **AB** (men's) = 22¾" (57.8cm) and **AB** (women's) = 22¼" (56.5cm).
2. **AC** = square size as determined by chart
3. **AD** = square size as determined by chart
4. **AE** = as **AC**
5. **EF** = **AC**
6. **EG** = **AD**
7. Connect **C-A-D-G-E-F-C**.
8. **BH** = as **AC**
9. **BI** = as **AD**
10. Connect **C-H**.
11. Connect **D-I**.
12. Connect **H-I**.
13. **AJ** = men's: 1¼" (3.2cm) or women's: 1¾" (4.4cm) for the cap height
14. **JK** = elbow length as measured
15. **CL** = half the **CF** measurement
16. **EM** = ⅝" (1.6cm)
17. **N** = half the **EG** measurement
18. **O** = one-third the **DG** measurement
19. Connect **L-M**.
20. **P** = half **LM**
21. **Q** = ½" (1.3cm) from **P**
22. Connect **J-O-N-M-Q-L-J**.
23. Square a line out from **K**, and mark **R** as it falls on the **CH** line.
24. Square a line out from **K**, and mark **S** as it falls on the **DI** line.
25. Decide the base width (example: hand measurement + ½" [1.3cm]). Divide that measurement in half.
26. **BT** = half the desired base width
27. **BU** = as **BT**
28. Connect **T-U**.
29. Fold on the **CH** line and trace **L-Q-M**. Open the draft and draw in the shape, marking **V** as shown. Smooth the pattern at **L**.
30. Fold on the **DI** line and trace **O-N-M**. Open the draft and draw in the shape, marking **W** as shown. Smooth the pattern at **O**.

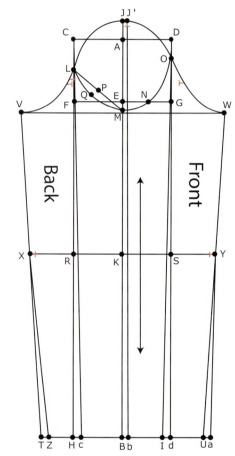

Figure 8.4

31. Adjust **J** toward the front the amount of the difference between the front and back armhole measurements. For example, if the front measures 8¾" (22.2cm) and the back measures 9¼" (23.5cm), move **J** toward the front ½" (1.3cm). Mark **J'**. The maximum **J'** can be moved is ¾" (1.9cm). Even if more measurement is needed, stop the adjustment at ¾" (1.9cm). After ¾" (1.9cm), the notch will be sliding down the front curve too much.
32. Redraw the top of the sleeve so **J'** is as high as **J**. Square for ⅛" (3.2mm) on each side of **J'**.
33. Measure **J'-O-W**. Adjust at **W** if necessary, so that **J'-O-W** equals the front armhole measurement plus ease. For example, if adding ¾" (1.9cm) ease to the entire sleeve cap, add ⅜" (1cm) to the front armhole measurement. If an adjustment is needed, keep **W** level with **M**.
34. Measure **J'-L-V**. Adjust at **V** if necessary, so that **J'-L-V** equals the back armhole measurement plus ease. For example, if adding ¾" (1.9cm) ease to the entire sleeve cap, add ⅜" (1cm) to the back armhole measurement. If an adjustment is needed, keep **V** level with **M**. Check that **V**, **M**, and **W** are on the same plane.
35. Lay the armhole of the front bodice on the **WO** line. The sleeve should closely mimic the shape of the bodice from the underarm (**W**) to about 3½" (8.9cm) up. It is okay to tilt the bodice slightly to align the curves. If the lines don't match, split the difference between the two lines.
36. Lay the armhole of the back bodice on the **VL** line. The sleeve should closely mimic the shape of the bodice from the underarm (**V**) to 3¼" (8.3cm) up. It is okay to tilt the bodice slightly to align the curves. If the lines don't match, split the difference between the two lines.
37. Connect **V-T**.
38. Connect **W-U**.
39. Measure **VT** and **WU**. Check the lengths of **VT** and **WU**. If there is a discrepancy, make sure **V** and **W** are on the same plane as **M**, then make a note on the sleeve to ease the longer seam into the shorter one.
40. Extend the elbow guideline (**R-K-S**) until it meets the **VT** line. Mark **X**.
41. Extend the elbow guideline (**R-K-S**) until it meets the **WU** line. Mark **Y**.
42. Make sure the elbow clearance on the sleeve is wider than the elbow breadth measurement. Adjust **X** and **Y** out equally if more room is needed and blend. For a slimmer sleeve, bring **X** and **Y** in equally as desired and blend. It is okay to have a concave or convex shape if the sleeve fits the elbow.
43. **TZ** = ¾" (1.9cm)
44. **Ua** = ¾" (1.9cm)
45. **Bb** should equal the same distance as **JJ'**.
46. Connect **X-Z**.
47. Connect **Y-a**.
48. **c** = half **Zb**
49. **d** = half **ba**
50. Connect **L-c**, **J'-b**, and **O-d** for the quarter lines.
51. Fold the sleeve and make sure **WY** to **VX** align. Turn the sleeve into a tube and make sure there is a smooth transition between **V** and **W**.
52. Pattern: **J'-O-W-Y-a-d-b-c-Z-X-V-L-J'**
53. Mark one front notch at 3½" (8.9cm) from **W**. Mark two back notches at 3" (7.6cm) and 3¼" (8.3cm) up from **V** as shown. These notches should align with notches on the front and back bodices. Notch the center of the sleeve cap at **J'**. Notch the elbow guideline at **X** and **Y**. Draw a grainline on the **J'-b** line. Add ½" (1.3cm) seam allowance and a 1½" (3.8cm) hem allowance. Drag the notches to the perimeter. Cut (2) self.

Truing Tip:
True the hem allowance on any pattern piece by folding the hem allowance up and under the pattern (*Fig. 8.5*) and tracing the side shapes over the hem allowance underneath. Unfold to mark the shape at sides. Notch the sides at the base where the hem will fold up. Many hem allowances are interfaced for added structure.

TRANSFERRING THE SLEEVE SLOPER TO TAG
Once the basic sleeve has been fitted and adjusted, trace it onto tag as a sleeve sloper (*Fig. 8.6*). Square the edges at the base and the biceps line for ¼" (6.4mm). Include quarter lines, biceps and elbow guidelines, grainline, notches, mark for the front and back of the sleeve (single notch shows front; double notch shows back), name, date, and measurements. It can help to awl-punch the quarter lines as they fall on the elbow and biceps lines. This makes it easier to mark those lines when tracing. Do not include seam and hem allowances on a sloper.

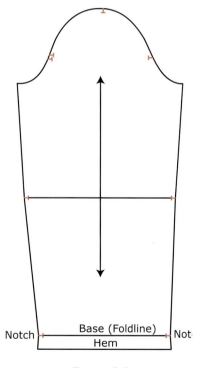

Figure 8.5

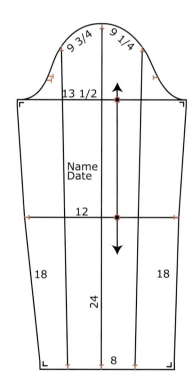

Figure 8.6

Knit Sleeve Sloper
When drafting a knit sleeve sloper, measure the front and back armhole on the knit garment. Find the square size without ease. Measure the arm, but do not add additional ease at the cap, biceps, elbow, or base. The knit sleeve sloper should have a snug fit.

TAILOR SLEEVE

A tailor sleeve has a dart at the back elbow. The dart allows flexibility to bend the elbow when a fitted sleeve is desired.

1. Trace the basic sleeve sloper. Mark **A** through **H** as shown (*Fig. 8.7*).
2. **FI** = ½" (1.3cm) below the elbow guideline at back
3. Connect **F-H-I** for the elbow dart. Fold the dart and true the legs and the dart bulk.
4. **EJ** = drop the back base ½" (1.3cm) to make up for the drop at **FI**
5. Connect **J-D** for the base of the sleeve.
6. Pattern: **A-B-C-D-J-I-F-G-A**, including the dart
7. Notch the cap at **A**. Notch the dart legs **F** and **I**. Awl-punch the dart point ½" (1.3cm) in from **H**. Notch the front elbow at **Y**. Single notch the front of the sleeve and double notch the back of the sleeve in the cap. Include a length grainline on the middle quarter line. Add ½" (1.3cm) seam allowance and 1½" (3.8cm) hem allowance. Drag the notches to the perimeter. Cut (2) self.

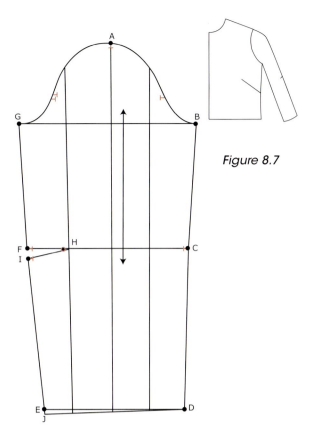

Figure 8.7

Design Tip:

Get creative with the elbow dart. Try adding three ¼"–⅜" (0.6–1cm) wide elbow darts, 1" (2.5cm) above 1" (2.5cm) and below the original elbow dart. Experiment with adding matching darts on the front seam. If adding additional darts, remember to adjust the length at the base as needed.

TWO-PIECE SLEEVE WITH VENT

Two-piece sleeves with vents are found on jacket and coat sleeves. The vent is drafted onto the back quarter line of a sleeve. Buttons on sleeve vents are usually ⅝" (1.6cm) in diameter. Buttonholes are horizontal.

1. Trace the basic sleeve sloper. Mark **A** through **L** as shown (*Fig. 8.8*).
2. Cut the sleeve apart on the front (**BF**) and back (**LH**) quarter lines.
3. Attach the **KJ** line to the **CD** line to form one piece or the under sleeve. Straighten the base from **F** to **H**. Smooth at **CK**. Often **CK** must drop by about ⅛" (3.2mm) to smooth it out.
4. Under sleeve: **B-C/K-L-G-F-B**
5. Upper sleeve: **A-B-F-G-H-L-A**
6. **HM** = 5" (12.7cm), or as desired, for the height of the vent marked on both the upper and the under sleeve on the back quarter line
7. Working on the upper sleeve, mark out 1½" (3.8cm) for the buttonhole facing. Mark **MN**. Facings for horizontal buttons are button diameter x 2 + ¼" (6.4mm). For example, ⅝" (1.6cm) + ⅝" (1.6cm) = 1¼" (3.2cm) + ¼" (6.4mm) = 1½" (3.8cm).
8. Fold at **MH** and trace the base shape over **HO** to true it.
9. **PQ** = draw a line ⅝" (1.6cm) from the **MH** line as a guideline for the buttonhole placement (⅝" [1.6cm] because the button diameter is ⅝" [1.6cm])

10. Mark buttonhole placement, starting ⅛" (3.2mm) over the **PQ** line as shown. Buttonholes should be ⅛" (3.2mm) longer than button diameter (⅝" [1.6cm] button + ⅛" [3.2mm] = ¾" [1.9cm] buttonhole). Square buttonholes off the **PH** line or the base. Hem allowance on sleeves is generally 1½" (3.8cm).

11. Working on the **under sleeve**, mark 1½" (3.8cm) (or as **MN** on the upper sleeve) out from the **MH** line for the button extension. Mark **R** and **S**.

12. **TU** = additional 1½" (3.8cm) out for the button facing

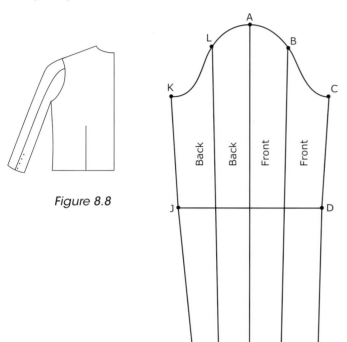

Figure 8.8

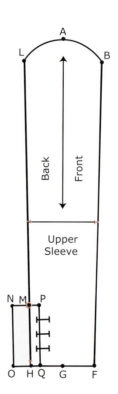

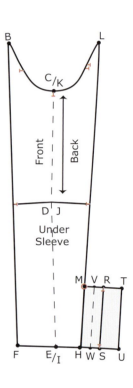

Construction Tip:
With a functional sleeve vent, keep the last button/buttonhole above the hem to reduce bulk.

---

13. Fold back on the **RS** line, and true the top and bottom of the button facing as it sits behind **MRSH**.
14. **VW** = draw a line ⅝" (1.6cm) from the **HM** line as a guideline for button placement
15. Place the **PQ** line on the upper sleeve over the **VW** line on the undersleeve and mark for button placement to correspond with buttonhole placement.
16. Upper Sleeve: **L-A-B-F-G-H-O-N-M-L**
17. Interface **M-H-O-N-M**. Notch the fold line at **MH**. Notch **A**. Notch the elbow guideline.

Awl-punch **M**. Notch **H**. Mark the grainline along the **AG** line. Mark the buttonholes. Add ½" (1.3cm) seam allowance and 1½" (3.8cm) hem allowance. Drag the notches to the perimeter. Cut (2) self.

18. Under Sleeve: **B-C/K-L-M-R-T-U-S-H-I/E-F-B**
19. Interface **M-R-T-U-S-H**. Notch the fold line at **RS**. Notch the elbow guideline. Notch **C/K**. Awl-punch **M**. Mark button placement. Mark a grainline along the **C/K** and **E/I** line. Add ½" (1.3cm) seam allowance and 1½" (3.8cm) hem allowance. Drag the notches to the perimeter. Cut (2) self.

SLEEVE WITH PLACKET, PLEATS, AND CUFF

A sleeve with a placket, pleat, and cuff are found on button-up or -down shirts. There are two 1" (2.5cm) pleats, which help give more room around the forearm. The placket is generally 5" (12.7cm) high and is placed near or on the back quarter line. The placket usually has two or three ½" (1.3cm) buttons and corresponding vertical buttonholes. The cuff height is usually 2" (5.1cm). The cuff has one or two ½" (1.3cm) buttons with corresponding ⅝" (1.6cm) horizontal or vertical buttonholes.

Note that the instructions cycle through the alphabet twice: first with uppercase letters, then with lowercase letters.

1. Trace the basic sleeve sloper. Cut 2" (5.1cm) off the base for the cuff height. Most cuffs have a height of 2" (5.1cm). Mark **A**, **B**, **C**, **D**, and **E** (*Fig. 8.9, Sleeve*).
2. Measure the arm 2" (5.1cm) up from the wrist and decide whether to adjust the **CD** measurement narrower for a tighter sleeve base and cuff. Because the sleeve has a cuff and a placket, both of which have buttons/buttonholes, the base can be narrowed. Re-mark **C** and **D** if the base was narrowed.
3. **CF** = 1" (2.5cm) to accommodate a pleat
4. **DG** = 1" (2.5cm) to accommodate a pleat
5. Connect **B-F**.
6. Connect **E-G**.
7. Divide **GF** into four equal parts.
8. **GH** = one-quarter **GF**
9. **HI** = ¼" (6.4mm) down. **HI** is lowered ¼" (6.4mm). When the arm bends, it tends to pull the placket up. This ¼" (6.4mm) adjustment keeps it level.
10. **IJ** = length of the placket opening (example: 5" [12.7cm])
11. Connect **G-I-F** in a shallow curve for the sleeve base.
12. **IK** = distance from placket line to first pleat (example: 1¼" [3.2cm])
13. **KL** = 1" (2.5cm) pleat width

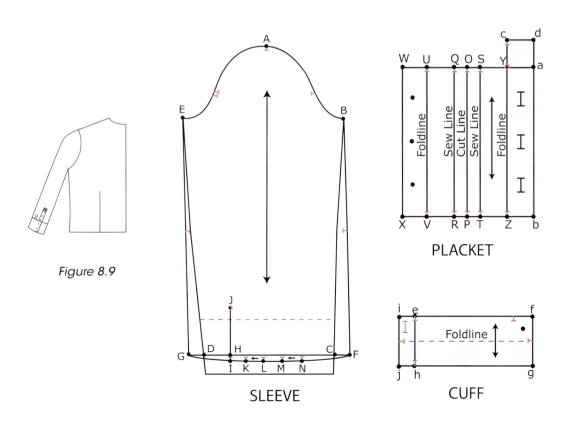

Figure 8.9

SLEEVE

PLACKET

CUFF

14. **LM** = 1" (2.5cm) distance between the pleats
15. **MN** = 1" (2.5cm) pleat width
16. Fold the pleats with the bulk away from the placket line and trace the base shape over the pleat bulk.
17. Sleeve: **A-B-F N-M-L-K-I-G-E A**
18. Notch the front and back of the sleeve. Notch the top of the sleeve (**A**). Notch the base of the placket (**I**) and notch the pleats (**KL** and **MN**). Awl-punch the top of the placket line (**J**). Notch the elbow. Draw a length grainline. Add ½" (1.3cm) seam allowance and drag the notches to the perimeter. Cut (2) self. Fold the pleats with the bulk away from the placket line and trace the base shape over the pleat bulk.
19. Sleeve: **A-B-F N-M-L-K-I-G-E A**
20. Notch the front and back of the sleeve. Notch the top of the sleeve (**A**). Notch the base of the placket (**I**) and notch the pleats (**KL** and **MN**). Awl-punch the top of the placket line (**J**). Notch the elbow. Draw a length grainline. Add ½" (1.3cm) seam allowance and drag the notches to the perimeter. Cut (2) self.

Placket

A standard finished-placket width is 1" (2.5cm) with the under placket measuring ¾" (1.9cm). The under placket is always ¼" (6.4mm) narrower than the top. That allows the top of the placket to fully cover the under placket. The upper placket has vertical buttonholes, and the under placket holds the buttons.

1. **OP** = as **IJ** on the sleeve (length of the placket line, example: 5" [12.7cm])
2. Mark **OP** as a cut line (*Fig. 8.9*, Placket).
3. **OQ** = ⅜" (1cm)
4. **PR** = ⅜" (1cm)
5. Connect **Q-R** and mark as a sew line.
6. **OS** = ⅜" (1cm)
7. **PT** = ⅜" (1cm)
8. Connect **S-T** and mark as a sew line.
9. **QS** should equal ¾" (1.9cm).
10. **RT** should equal ¾" (1.9cm).
11. **QU** = ¾" (1.9cm)
12. **RV** = ¾" (1.9cm)
13. Connect **U-V** and mark as a fold line.
14. **UW** = ¾" (1.9cm)
15. **VX** = ¾" (1.9cm)
16. Connect **W-X**.
17. **SY** = 1" (2.5cm) (**SQ** + ¼" [6.4mm])
18. **TZ** = 1" (2.5cm)
19. Connect **Y-Z** and mark as a fold line.
20. **Ya** = 1" (2.5cm) as **SY**
21. **Zb** = 1" (2.5cm)
22. Connect **a-b**.
23. Connect **W-a**.
24. Connect **X-b**.
25. **Yc** = 1" (2.5cm)
26. **ad** = 1" (2.5cm) as **Yc**
27. Connect **Y-c-d-a** for the box on top of the placket. This box hides the seam allowances at the top of the placket.
28. Mark button and corresponding vertical buttonhole placement in the areas shown. Use ½" (1.3cm) buttons and ⅝" (1.6cm) buttonholes.
29. Placket: **W-U-Q-O-S-Y-c-d-a-b-Z-T-P-R-V-X W**
30. Notch or awl-punch the sew lines and fold lines. Awl-punch the corner at **Y**. Add a length grainline. Add ½" (1.3cm) seam allowance. Drag the notches to the perimeter. Cut (2) self. Cut (2) interfacing.

Design Tip:

Experiment with placket height. A 5" (12.7cm) height is average, but it can go as high as the elbow or even the cap.

Cuff

1. Draw a line equal to **DC** on the sleeve pattern (sleeve base, less the pleat amounts) (*Fig. 8.9*, Cuff). Mark **e** and **f**.
2. **fg** = double the finished width of the cuff (example: 4" [10.2cm] for a 2" [5.1cm] finished cuff)
3. **eh** = **fg**
4. **ei** = 1" (2.5cm) extension, as the extension on the placket
5. **hj** = as **ei**
6. Mark a fold line in the center of the pattern.
7. Mark button and horizontal buttonhole placement.
8. Cuff: **i-e-f-g-h-j-i**
9. Notch at **e** and **h**. Notch the fold line. Draw a length grainline. Add ½" (1.3cm) seam allowance around the piece. Drag the notches to the perimeter. Cut (2) self. Cut (2) interfacing.

CAP, SHORT, AND THREE-QUARTER SLEEVES

Trace the basic sleeve sloper. Mark off lengths for a cap sleeve, a short sleeve, and a three-quarter sleeve (*Fig. 8.10*).

- A **cap sleeve** length is any length above the biceps line. A common cap sleeve length is about 3"–4" (7.6–10.2cm) from the shoulder notch. Cap sleeves do not have an underarm seam. The base of a cap sleeve can be straight or curved. If the front and back armhole notches are cut off, move the notches up into the pattern. Change the notches on the bodice so they correspond. Ease does not need to be added to a cap sleeve.
- A **short sleeve** is any length between the biceps line and the elbow. Short sleeves do have an underarm seam. The base of a short sleeve is generally straight.
- A **three-quarter sleeve** length is found by taking three-quarters of the full length of the sleeve, then subtracting 1" (2.5cm). For example, 24" (61cm) x ¾ = 18" (45.7cm) − 1 = 17" (43.2cm) for the length from the cap. Subtracting 1" (2.5cm) gives the arm a more elongated look.

On these sleeves, include the notches and draw a length grainline. Add ½" (1.3cm) seam allowance and a ½"–1" (1.3–2.5cm) hem allowance (shorter hem allowance on shorter sleeves). Drag the notches to the perimeter. Cut (2) self of each.

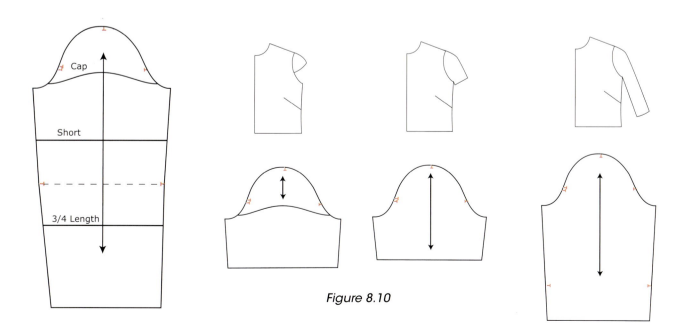

Figure 8.10

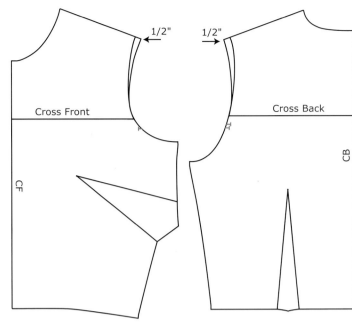

Design Tip:
Cut the shoulder of the bodice in ½" (1.3cm) and blend to the cross front and cross back, so the puff will sit on top of the shoulder. Make this adjustment to any bodice that has a sleeve with gathers, darts, pleats, or other kinds of volume at the cap (*Fig. 8.11*).

Figure 8.11

PUFF SLEEVE

1. Trace the basic sleeve sloper, including the quarter lines, and adjust the length as desired. Mark **A** through **J** as shown (*Fig. 8.12*).
2. Number the pattern 1 through 4 as shown. Separate the pattern at **J-G**, **A-F**, and **B-E**.
3. Decide the insertion amount (example: 3" [7.6cm] per insertion).
4. Draw a horizontal guideline on a piece of pattern paper.
5. Tape Piece 1 down with the base (**H-G**) flush with the horizontal guideline. Add the insertion amount (example: 3" [7.6cm]) on the horizontal guideline. Because the quarter lines are often slanted, the insertion amount might be slightly different at the base and the cap.
6. Tape Piece 2 down with the base (**G-F**) flush with the horizontal guideline. Add the insertion amount at the base.
7. Tape Piece 3 down with the base (**F-E**) flush with the horizontal guideline. Add the insertion amount at the base.
8. Tape Piece 4 down with the base (**E-D**) flush with the horizontal guideline.
9. Smooth the top of the pattern between the front and back notches. Re-mark **A** as the shoulder notch at the center of the middle insertion as shown.
10. Sleeve: **A-C-D-E-F-G-H-I-A**
11. Notch the front and back of the sleeve. Notch the top of the sleeve (**A**). Put a notch directly under **A** on the sleeve base. Draw a length or cross grainline (a cross grainline offers more volume). Add ½" (1.3cm) seam allowance. Drag the notches to the perimeter. Cut (2) self.

Drafting Tip:
Insertions should not be added below the front and back notches.
Adding insertions under the arm is too bulky and uncomfortable.

Band

1. **KL** = band measurement (measurement around arm—not the sleeve—at the desired length of the sleeve, plus ½" [1.3cm] ease).
2. **KN** = double the desired finished width of the band (example: 2" [5.1cm] for a 1" [5.1cm] finished band).
3. **NM = KL**
4. **LM = KN**
5. Connect for a rectangle. Draw a fold line in the center of the pattern piece.
6. Band: **K-L-M-N-K**
7. Notch the fold line and notch the center of the band at the top and bottom. Draw a length grainline. Add ½" (1.3cm) seam allowance. Drag the notches to the perimeter. Cut (2) self. Cut (2) interfacing. Include a sleeve head.

Construction Tip:

A **sleeve head** is a gathered piece of fabric that fills out the sleeve cap and prevents puffs, gathers, pleats, or darts from collapsing at the cap. Cut a 18" x 5" (45.7 x 12.7cm) piece of cross-grain fabric (tulle, organza, or cotton). Fold the long side in half. Gather the 18" (45.7cm) cut edge to 6" (15.2cm) using a basting stitch. Sew the gathered sleeve head to the armhole/sleeve seam allowance, centering it over the shoulder notch (3" [7.6cm] on either side of the shoulder notch).

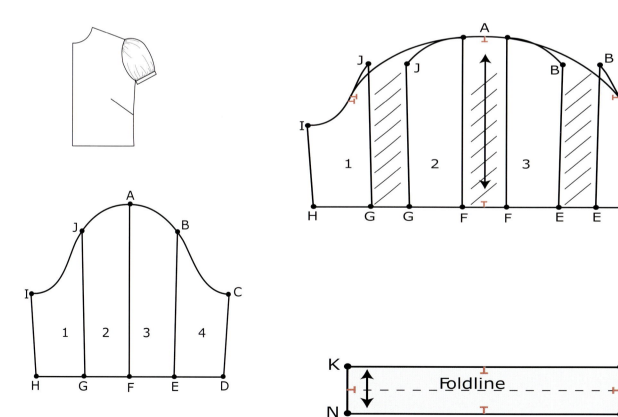

Figure 8.12

JULIET SLEEVE

A Juliet sleeve is a two-part sleeve. The upper piece is a Puff Sleeve (page 192) that is sewn to a tight-fitting lower piece, called the **glove**. Cut the end of shoulder on the front and back bodice in ½" (1.3cm), so the fullness sits on top of the shoulder. A Juliet sleeve will hold its shape better if a sleeve head is included.

1. Trace the basic sleeve sloper, including the quarter lines and elbow guideline. Adjust the elbow ease so it is elbow breadth plus ¾" (1.9cm). Adjust the base ease, so it is wrist plus ¾" (1.9cm). Mark **A**, **B**, **C**, **D**, and **E** as shown (*Fig. 8.13*).
2. **BF** = 1" (2.5cm)
3. **EG** = 1" (2.5cm)
4. Connect **G-F**.
5. Cut at **G-F**.
6. Add 1½" (3.8cm) below the **GF** line. Adding 1½" (3.8cm) will help the sleeve blouse over the glove.
7. Draft a puff sleeve on the upper piece, using the quarter lines as insertion areas.
8. Upper Sleeve: **A-B-H-I-E-A**
9. Notch the front and back of the sleeve. Notch the top of the sleeve (**A**). Put a notch directly under **A** on the sleeve base. Draw a length or cross grainline (a cross grainline offers more volume). Add ½" (1.3cm) seam allowance. Drag the notches to the perimeter. Cut (2) self. Include a sleeve head.
10. Glove: **G-F-C-D-G**
11. Notch the elbow. Draw a length grainline (or a bias grainline if the glove feels too tight). Add ½" (1.3cm) seam allowance and a 1½" (3.8cm) hem allowance. Drag the notches to the perimeter. Cut (2) self.

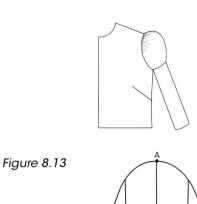

Figure 8.13

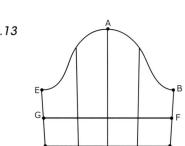

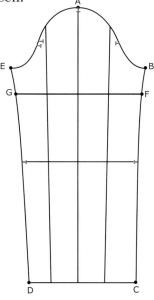

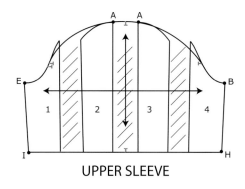

UPPER SLEEVE

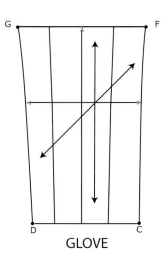

GLOVE

BISHOP SLEEVE

A bishop sleeve is a bell-shaped sleeve gathered into a cuff at the base. The sleeve blouses over the cuff. The cuff is commonly 3" (7.6cm) in height and has a button closure on the back quarter line.

Sleeve

1. Trace the basic sleeve sloper, including the quarter lines. Mark **A** through **J** as shown (*Fig. 8.14*).
2. Slash **GA**, hinging at **A**, and insert as desired (example: 3" [7.6cm]).
3. Slash **FB**, hinging at **B** and insert. Insertions can be consistent or can graduate to bigger insertions toward the back.
4. Slash **HL**, hinging at **L** and insert.
5. Smooth the base from **H** to **D**. The base will be curved.
6. Straighten the underarm seams **I** to **H** and **C** to **D**.
7. Sleeve: **A-B-C-D-H-I-J-A**
8. Notch from **H**, one-quarter of **HD** (the cuff will open at this notch). Notch the front and back of the sleeve. Notch the top of the sleeve (**A**). Notch the elbow. Draw a length or cross grainline (a cross grainline offers more volume). Add ½" (1.3cm) seam allowance. Drag the notches to the perimeter. Cut (2) self.

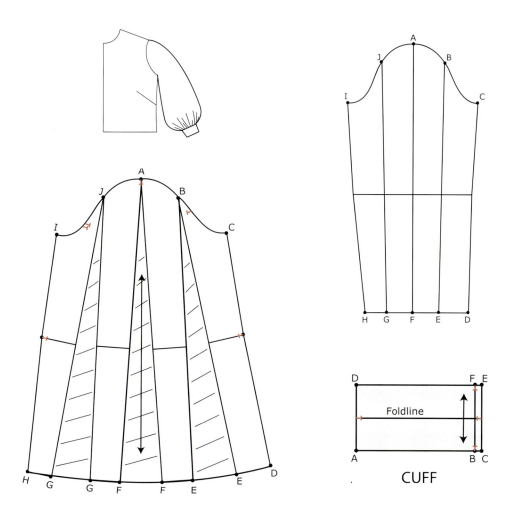

Figure 8.14

Cuff

1. **AB** = measure around the forearm at 3" (7.6cm) up from the wrist and add ½" (1.3cm) ease (*Fig. 8.14*, Cuff)
2. **BC** = ½" (1.3cm) extension (for buttons/buttonholes)
3. **AD** = 6" (15.2cm)
4. **CE** = 6" (15.2cm)
5. **F** = square up from **B** to complete the extension line
6. Mark for button and buttonhole placement. Use three ½" (1.3cm) buttons with corresponding ⅝" (1.6cm) horizontal buttonholes. Mark the first button ½" (1.3cm) up from the fold line, then space the other buttons 1" (2.5cm) apart. The cuff will open at the notch on the back quarter.
7. Cuff: **A-D-F-E-C-B-A**
8. Notch at **B** and **F**. Mark and notch the fold line at the center. Draw a length grainline. Add ½" (1.3cm) seam allowance around the piece. Drag the notches to the perimeter. Cut (2) self. Cut (2) interfacing.

Design Tip:
Skip the cuff instructions on the bishop sleeve for a bell sleeve. Keep it slightly shorter in length because there is so much volume at the base, which can get in the way when wearing.

GIGOT SLEEVE

A gigot sleeve has fullness at the cap created by fabric gathers or pleats, then reduces in size to a slim fit down the arm. Cut the end of shoulder on the front and back bodice in ½" (1.3cm) so the fullness sits on top of the shoulder. A gigot sleeve will hold its shape better if a sleeve head is included. This version will have pleats at the cap.

1. Trace the basic sleeve sloper. Adjust the elbow ease to elbow breadth plus ¾" (1.9cm). Mark **A, B, C, D**, and **E** as shown (*Fig. 8.15*).
2. **AF** = 2" (5.1cm) extension from the shoulder notch
3. **FG** = 1" (2.5cm)
4. Connect **A-G**. Adjust at **G** as needed so **AG** equals 2" (5.1cm).
5. **FH** = 1" (2.5cm)
6. Connect **A-H**. Adjust at **H** as needed so **AH** equals 2" (5.1cm).
7. **HI** = distance as desired between the pleats (example: 1¼" [3.2cm])
8. **IJ** = 2" (5.1cm) as **GH**

Variation Tip:
Sew the pleats as darts. Pleats and gathers give a soft look. Sewing darts into the cap gives an edgier look. Use the same pattern, just mark for darts rather than pleats

9. **K** = centered under **IJ**, ⅛" (3.2mm) below the original sleeve shape of **AB** Connect **K-I** and connect **K-J**. Adjust at **I** and **J** so each leg of the pleat equals 2" (5.1cm).
10. **GL** = distance as **HI** between the pleats (example: 1¼" [3.2cm])
11. **LM** = 2" (5.1cm)
12. **N** = centered under **LM**, ⅛" (3.2mm) below the original sleeve shape of **AE**
13. Connect **N-L** and connect **N-M**. Adjust at **L** and **M** so each leg of the pleat equals 2" (5.1cm). Make sure the inside of each pleat equals 2" (5.1cm).
14. Connect **E-M-L-G-F-H-I-J-B**.
15. Fold **M** to **L**, **G** to **F**, **H** to **F**, and **J** to **I**. Trace the sleeve shape to the pleat bulk underneath.
16. Measure the back of the sleeve (**G** to **L** plus **M** to **E**). Extend **E** as needed to get the back armhole measurement (without ease). Mark **O**. Be sure to extend **O** on the same plane as **E** and blend. Adjust the back notches to 3" (7.6cm) and 3¼" (8.3cm) from **O**.
17. Measure the front of the sleeve (**H** to **I** plus **J** to **B**). Extend **B** as needed to get the front armhole measurement (without ease). Mark **P**. Be sure to extend **P** on the same plane as **B** and blend. Adjust the front notch to 3½" (8.9cm) from **P**.
18. Blend **O** and **P** to the elbow guideline.
19. Sleeve: **O-M-L-G-F-H-I-J-P-C-D-O**
20. Notch the pleats (**M-L**, **G-F-H**, and **I-J**). Notch the front and back of the sleeve. Notch the elbow. Draw a length grainline. Add ½" (1.3cm) seam allowance and a 1¼" (3.2cm) hem allowance. Drag the notches to the perimeter. Cut (2) self. Include a sleeve head.

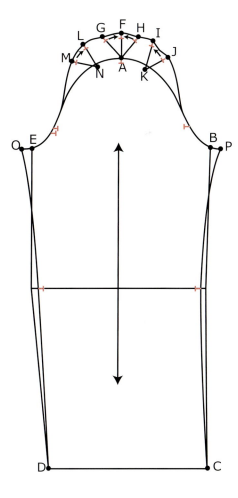

Figure 8.15

Design Tip:

A gigot sleeve and a Juliet sleeve have a similar look, but there are differences. A gigot sleeve is in one piece. A Juliet sleeve is in two pieces. A gigot sleeve can have pleats, darts, or gathers at the cap. A Juliet sleeve has a gathered puff at the cap. A Juliet sleeve tends to be tighter than a gigot at the glove. A gigot sleeve is sometimes referred to as a mutton leg sleeve.

LINING A SLEEVE

Self-Fabric Sleeve

1. Trace the basic sleeve sloper and add a 1½" (3.8cm) hem. Add ½" (1.3cm) seam allowance all around, including along the hem edge (to sew the top of the hem to the base of the lining).
2. Include the notches and a grainline. Cut (2) self.

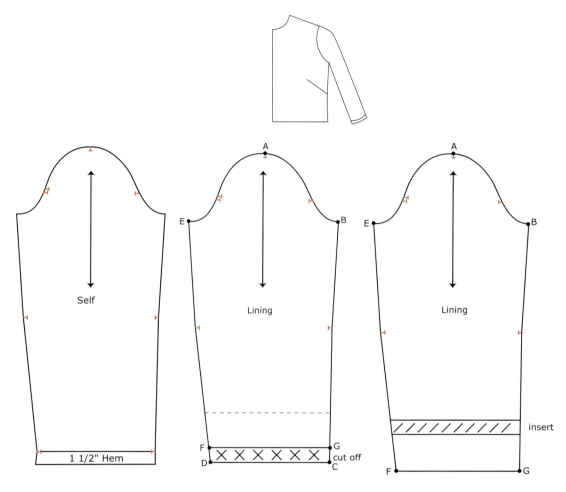

Figure 8.16

Sleeve Lining

1. Trace the self-fabric sleeve without the seam and hem allowance. Mark **A**, **B**, **C**, **D**, and **E** as shown (*Fig. 8.16*).
2. Cut the amount of the hem allowance up from the base of the sleeve and mark **F** and **G**.
3. Draw a line 3" (7.6cm) up from the **FG** line and cut the pattern apart on this line.
4. Insert 1" (2.5cm) at the slashed line. This will allow for a **jump pleat** and a **bagged lining**.
5. Smooth the pattern at the sides.
6. Pattern: **A-B-G-G-E-A**
7. Notch the front and back of the sleeve. Notch the top of the sleeve (**A**). Notch the elbow. Transfer the grainline from the self-fabric pattern. Add ½" (1.3cm) seam allowance around the entire piece. Drag the notches to the perimeter. Cut (2) lining.

GUSSET

Add a gusset under the arm for more mobility with tight-fitting sleeves. A gusset is a separate pattern piece sewn between the sleeve and bodice underarm seams.

1. Draw a vertical line measuring 3" (7.6cm). Mark **A** and **B** (*Fig. 8.17*).
2. Bisect that line with a horizontal line measuring 5" (12.7cm) with 2½" (6.4cm) on either side of the **AB** line. Mark **C** and **D**.
3. Connect the points.
4. Smooth points **A** and **B** slightly for easier sewing.
5. Pattern: **A-D-B-C-A**
6. Notch **A** and **B**. Awl-punch **C** and **D**. Draw a length grainline. Add ½" (1.3cm) seam allowance. Drag the notches to the perimeter. Cut (2) self.

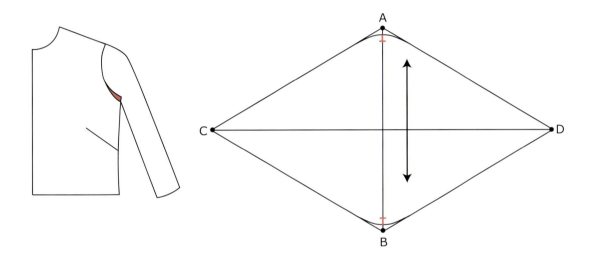

Figure 8.17

Fitting Tip:

The gusset pattern piece can also be used in the crotch seam of pants if more mobility is needed there.

DROP-SHOULDER BODICE AND SLEEVE

Front Bodice

1. Trace the front bodice sloper and mark **A**, **B**, **C**, **D**, **E**, and **F** as shown (*Fig. 8.18*).
2. **CG** = extend the shoulder as desired (example: 1" [2.5cm])
3. **GH** = raise the end of shoulder ⅛" (3.2mm) for every 1" (2.5cm) out. This step is optional. Do this if more wearing ease is needed in the armhole.
4. **DI** = lower the base of the armhole the amount the shoulder was extended
5. **IJ** = extend the bust at least half the amount the shoulder was extended, though it can be more (example: ½" [1.3cm]). There is the option of extending the waist (and hips) that same amount.
6. Connect **H-J** for the new armhole. Be sure to square off the shoulder at **H** for at least 1" (2.5cm).
7. Adjust the notch in the armhole to 3½" (8.9cm) from **J**.
8. Note the measurement of the new front armhole.
9. Connect **J-E** for the new side shape, including the dart. Depending on how much the side was lowered, the side dart will most likely need to be manipulated into a French dart.
10. Front Pattern: **A-B-H-J-E-F-A**
11. Notch and awl-punch the dart. Notch the armhole. Draw a length grainline. Add ½" (1.3cm) seam allowance. Drag the notches to the perimeter. Cut (2) self.

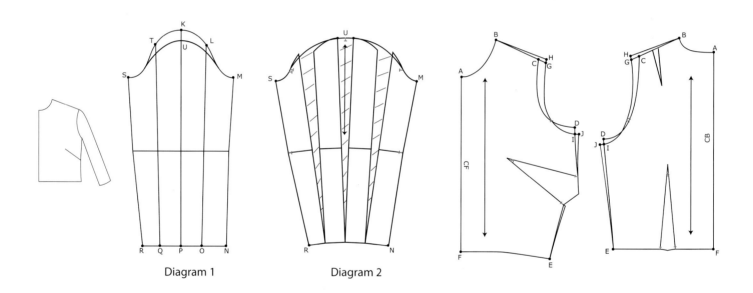

Diagram 1   Diagram 2

Figure 8.18

Drafting Tip:

The more the shoulder is extended, the flatter the armhole will look. Once the shoulder is extended 3" (7.6cm) or more, the armhole could start to become a straighter line.

Back Bodice

1. Follow the front bodice instructions for the back. Note the measurement of the new back armhole (*Fig. 8.18*).
2. Back Pattern: **A-B-H-J-E-F-A**
3. Notch and awl-punch the darts. Double notch the armhole at 3" (7.6cm) and 3¼" (8.3cm) from **J**. Draw a length grainline. Add ½" (1.3cm) seam allowance. Drag the notches to the perimeter. Cut (1) self on fold.

Sleeve

1. Trace the basic sleeve sloper, including the quarter lines. Mark **K** through **T** as shown (*Fig. 8.18*, Diagram 1).
2. **KU** = lower the sleeve cap the amount the shoulder was extended (**CG**)
3. Connect **S-U-M**, flattening the cap.
4. Measure **U-M** and **U-S** and compare the sleeve measurement to the new front and back armhole measurements and note the difference. Because this is a loose garment, ease is not needed in the sleeve. **UM** minus the front armhole (**HJ**) = _____. **US** minus the back armhole (**HJ**) = _____.
5. Cut on the quarter lines and add in the difference (*Fig. 8.18*, Diagram 2). For example, if the front of the sleeve needs an additional 1" (2.5cm), add ½" (1.3cm) in the middle quarter line, and ½" (1.3cm) in the front quarter line. If the back needs an additional ⅞" (2.2cm), add ½" (1.3cm) in the middle quarter line and ⅜" (1cm) in the back quarter line. The middle quarter line will have the largest insertion amount. Keep the front and back middle quarter line insertion amounts equal.
6. Smooth the cap (**SUM**).
7. Straighten the base (**RN**).
8. Sleeve: **U-M-N-R-S-U**
9. Adjust the notch on the front to 3½" (8.9cm) from **M**. Adjust the notches on the back to 3" (7.6cm) and 3¼" (8.3cm) from **S**. Adjust the shoulder notch to the center of the middle insertion. Notch the elbow. Draw a length grainline. Add ½" (1.3cm) seam allowance and a 1½" (3.8cm) hem allowance. Drag the notches to the perimeter. Cut (2).

 Test Your Knowledge

1. Why is it important to include quarter lines on a sleeve sloper?

2. What is the correct positioning of the front, back, and shoulder notches on a sleeve pattern?

3. What is a sleeve head? How is it drafted, constructed, and sewn in?

4. Describe the difference in length between cap, short, and three-quarter sleeves.

5. Describe the difference between Juliet, bishop, and gigot sleeves.

This chapter involves working through three basic pants foundations: slacks, trousers, and jeans. Using these foundations, students learn to draft flares, pleated pants, a jumpsuit, drawstring pants, and knit leggings. Drafting instructions are included for design details like a button fly, zipper fly, contoured waistband, back yoke, and belt loops.

OBJECTIVES

Upon completion of this chapter, you will be able to

- Draft a pants sloper
- Use that sloper to create varied pants looks
- Add finishing details like zipper or button flies, a back yoke, and belt loops to a pattern

CHAPTER 9
Pants

Introduction to Pants Drafting

PANTS TERMS

- **Waist Guideline:** Marks the placement of the waistline.
- **High-Hip Guideline:** Marks the placement of the high hip.
- **Low-Hip Guideline:** Marks the placement of the low hip.
- **Crotch:** The base of the torso between the legs.
- **Crotch Depth (Rise):** The measurement from waist to crotch.
- **Crotch Length:** The measurement from the center-front to center-back waist between the legs.
- **Crotch Level:** The horizontal width of pants from the front crotch to back crotch extension.
- **Crotch Extension:** The extension to the crotch point from the pants block.
- **Crotch Point:** The tip of the inseam at the end of the crotch extension.
- **Side Seam (Out Seam):** The seam running from the waist to the base along the side.
- **Inseam:** The seam running from the crotch point to the base of the pants between the legs.
- **Knee Guideline:** Shows the depth at side from waist to mid-knee.
- **Thigh Guideline:** Marks the placement of the thigh.
- **Calf Guideline:** Marks the placement of the calf.
- **Base:** The base of pants regardless of length.
- **Pants Foundation:** The fit of pants above the crotch level line (*Fig. 9.1*).

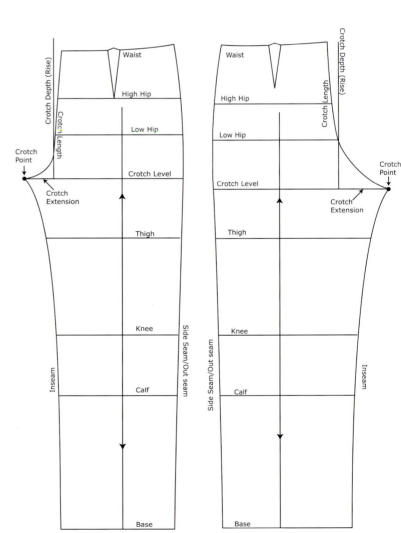

Figure 9.1

204   Building Patterns

MEASURING FOR PANTS

Refer to the instructions and the corresponding diagram (*Fig. 9.2*). Model should stand without shoes, feet about 4" (10.2cm) apart. They should retain their natural posture throughout the measuring process while looking straight ahead. If the arms need to be moved out of the way, have the model hold their arms out with the elbows at shoulder level.

Start the measuring process by having the model tie a ¼" (6.4mm) width elastic around the natural waistline. Have the client bend side-to-side to find where the body creases to find the natural waistline. Good positioning of the waist elastic for womenswear is about ½"–1" (1.3–2.5cm) above the top of the navel. *Placement of the elastic for menswear should be where the model likes the waistline of their pants to sit.* Check the position of the elastic frequently while measuring and readjust it if it is rolling up. The elastic is used as a measuring guide. Dress forms have twill tape pinned around the natural waistline, so an elastic is not needed. Take snug measurements, not tight or loose. Ease will be added later.

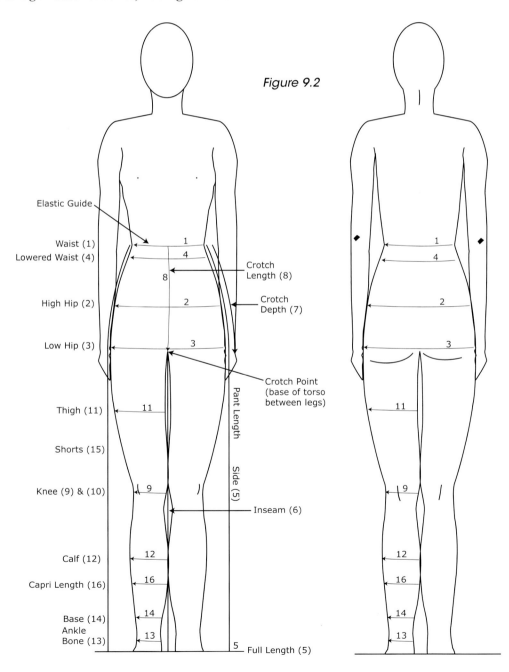

Figure 9.2

- **Waist (1):** Measure the waist around the elastic.
- **High Hip (2):** Measure 4½" (11.4cm) down from the bottom of the waist elastic at the sides. Use adhesive dots to mark the depth of the high hip. Once the side depth is marked, measure the circumference of the high hip. Note both depth and circumference measurements. *Skip the high-hip measurement on men's pants.*
- **Low Hip (3):** Measure 8½" (21.6cm) down from the base of the waist elastic at the sides. If the hips are wider at lower than 8½" (21.6cm), use that lower depth and circumference measurement. The hips are at the widest point where the rear end protrudes the most. Measure around the body, keeping the tape measure level. If the high-hip measurement is larger than the low-hip measurement, use the high-hip measurement for the low hip, so the fabric skims the low hip. Note both depth and circumference measurements.
- **Lowered Waistline (4):** Determine the desired depth at side from the base of the waist elastic (example: 2" [5.1cm]). Mark the depth. Measure around the body at the lowered-waistline depth. Note the depth and circumference measurements. *Skip this measurement on menswear pants because the waist is already lowered.*
- **Side Seam (5):** Measure both sides of the body from the base of the waist elastic to the floor. Note right- and left-side measurements. It is not uncommon to have one side longer because of a higher hip or longer leg. If one side is longer, record the measurement of the longer side.
- **Inseam (6):** Have the model hold the end of the tape measure at the base of their torso inside and against the leg (the longer leg if one is longer). Make sure the model is standing up straight. Note the measurement from the base of the torso to the floor along the inside of the leg.
- **Crotch Depth (7):** Subtract the inseam measurement from the side measurement. The difference is the crotch depth measurement.
- **Crotch Length (8):** Have the model hold the tape measure at the base of the center-front waist elastic. Bring the tape measure between the model's legs to the base of the waist elastic at the center back. The tape measure should be snug against the body. Note the measurement.
- **Knee (9 and 10):** Note the depth measurement from the base of the waist elastic at side to the middle of the knee (**9**). Then, take a circumference measurement around the knee (**10**).
- **Thigh (11):** Measure 8" (20.3cm) up from mid-knee (**9**) at the side. It is not unusual to have one thigh larger than the other, so take a circumference measurement around both thighs and record the larger measurement.
- **Calf (12):** Measure 5" (12.7cm) down from mid-knee, then take a circumference measurement around the calf. It is not unusual to have one calf larger than the other, so take a circumference measurement around both and record the larger measurement.

- **Ankle (13):** Measure around the ankle. The depth is 3" (7.6cm) shorter than the full-length measurement. Recording the circumference and the depth (3" [7.6cm] shorter than full length at side).
- **Base (14):** For a slacks pants sloper the base is 15"–17" (38.1–43.2cm). Choose a base width in that range or, with a low-hip measurement below 40" (101.6cm), use a 15" (38.1cm) base. With a low-hip measurement of 40"–50" (101.6–127cm), use a 16" (40.6cm) base. With a low-hip measurement of 50" (127cm) or more, use an 17" (43.2cm) base.
- **Pants Lengths (15, 16, 5):** Take three pants length measurements. For a short pants, take a measurement at the side from the base of the waist elastic to the model's desired height above the knee (**15**). Measure for capri-style pants from the base of the waist elastic at side to 1" (2.5cm) above the top of the ankle bone or as high as 2" or 3" (5.1 or 7.6cm) below the knee (**16**). Finally, note the full-length measurement taken from the base of the waist elastic at side to the floor (**5**).

Record of Measurements

NAME: _____

DATE: _____

Waist (1): _____

High Hip (2): _____ @ a depth of: _____ (skip in menswear)

Low Hip (3): _____ @ a depth of: _____

Lowered Waist (4): _____ @ a depth of: _____ (skip in menswear)

Side Seam (5): _____ (longer of the right and left sides)

Inseam (6): _____

Crotch Depth (7): _____ (subtract inseam from side seam)

Crotch Length (8): _____

Knee Depth (9): _____

Knee Circumference (10): _____

Thigh Circumference (11): _____ @ a height of 8" (20.3cm) from knee

Calf Circumference (12): _____ @ a depth of 5" (12.7cm) from knee

Ankle Circumference (13): _____ @ 3" (7.6cm) higher than full length _____

Base Circumference (14): _____

Above Knee Length (15): _____

Capri Length (16): _____

Full Length (5): _____ (the longer of the right and left sides)

Practice

Use these sample measurements (fits most Women's size 8 dress forms).

Waist: 26" (66cm)

High Hip: 34" (86.4cm)
  @ a depth of: 4½" (11.4cm)

Low Hip: 37" (94cm)
  @ a depth of: 8½" (21.6cm)

Lowered Waist: 30" (76.2cm)
  @ a depth of: 2" (5.1cm)

Side Seam: 40" (101.6cm)

Inseam: 30" (76.2cm)

Crotch Depth: 10" (25.4cm)

Crotch Length: 25" (63.5cm)

Knee: 13½" (34.3cm)
  @ a depth of: 24" (61cm)

Thigh: 18½" (47cm)
  @ 8" (20.3cm) above mid-knee

Calf: 12½" (31.8cm)
  @ 5" (12.7cm) below mid-knee

Ankle: 9½" (24.1cm)
  @ 3" (7.6cm) above full length measurement

Base: 15" (38.1cm)

Above Knee Length: 22" (55.9cm)

Capri Length: 30" (76.2cm)

Longer of Right/Left Side: 40" (101.6cm)

CALCULATING THE MEASUREMENTS

The **waist**, **high hip**, **low hip**, and **lowered-waist** circumference measurements plus ease are divided by four, because half the front (one-quarter of the entire pants) and half the back (one-quarter of the entire pants) are drafted. After dividing by four, ¼" (6.4mm) is added to the quotient for the front and ¼" (6.4mm) is subtracted from the quotient for the back. This redistribution allows for a flattering position of the side seam. There is more body mass in the front than the back (except at the low hip), so this calculation allows the front draft to be wider than the back draft. Of course, the low-hip area has more body mass in back, but to keep the side seam straight and consistent, and for a more flattering position of the side seam, continue with adding to the front and subtracting from the back on the low hip as well.

The **crotch** depth measurement for womenswear has ½"–¾" (1.3–1.9cm) added. The crotch depth for menswear has 1"–2" (2.5–5.1cm) added. This can be adjusted later but is a good place to start.

The **knee**, **thigh**, and **calf** measurements plus ease on the leg are divided by two. Because the back of the leg tends to be bigger than the front, ½" (1.3cm) is subtracted from the front and ½" (1.3cm) is added to the back. This redistribution allows for a more flattering position of the side seam. No ease is added to the **base** circumference, but the calculation is the same.

All other measurements are used as measured.

Ease Chart

Ease is added to circumference measurements (and to crotch depth).

Waist: ½" (1.3cm)

High Hip: 1" (2.5cm)

Low Hip: 1½" (3.8cm)

Lowered Waist: 0

Side Seam: as measured

Inseam: as measured

Crotch Depth: ½"–¾" (1.3–1.9cm) (*1"–2"* [2.5-5.1cm] *for menswear*)

Crotch Length: as measured

Knee: 1" (2.5cm)

Thigh: 1" (2.5cm)

Calf: 1" (2.5cm)

Ankle: 1" (2.5cm)

Pants Calculation Worksheet

Waist: _____ + ½" (1.3cm) ease = _____ ÷ 4 = _____
    Front: _____ + ¼" (6.4mm) = _____
    Back: _____ − ¼" (6.4mm) = _____

High Hip: _____ + 1" (2.5cm) ease = _____ ÷ 4 = _____
    Front: _____ + ¼" (6.4mm) = _____
    Back: _____ − ¼" (6.4mm) = _____
    (@ a depth of _____)

Low Hip: _____ + 1½" (3.8cm) ease = _____ ÷ 4 = _____
    Front: _____ + ¼" (6.4mm) = _____
    Back: _____ − ¼" (6.4mm) = _____
    (@ a depth of _____)

Lowered Waist: _____ + 0 ease = _____ ÷ 4 = _____
    Front: _____ + ¼" (6.4mm) = _____
    Back: _____ − ¼" (6.4mm) = _____
    (@ a depth of _____)

Side Seam: _____ (full length)

Inseam: _____

Crotch Depth: _____ + ½" or ¾" (1.9cm) = _____ (+ *1"–2"* [2.5–5.1cm] *menswear*)

Crotch Length: _____

Knee: _____ + 1" (2.5cm) ease = _____ ÷ 2 = _____
    Front: _____ − ½" (1.3cm) = _____
    Back: _____ + ½" (1.3cm) = _____
    (@ a depth of _____)

Thigh: _____ + 1" (2.5cm) ease = _____ ÷ 2 = _____
    Front: _____ − ½" (1.3cm) = _____
    Back: _____ + ½" (1.3cm) = _____
    (@ a height of 8" [20.3cm] from mid-knee)

Calf: _____ + 1" (2.5cm) ease = _____ ÷ 2 = _____
    Front: _____ − ½" (1.3cm) = _____
    Back: _____ + ½" (1.3cm) = _____
    (@ a depth of 5" [12.7cm] from mid-knee)

Ankle: _____ + 1" (2.5cm) ease = _____ ÷ 2 = _____
    Front: _____ − ½" (1.3cm) = _____
    Back: _____ + ½" (1.3cm) = _____
    (@ a height of 3" [7.6cm] above full length)

Base: _____ + 0 ease = _____ ÷ 2 = _____
    Front: _____ − ½" (1.3cm) = _____
    Back: _____ + ½" (1.3cm) = _____

Above Knee: _____

Capri Length: _____

Sample Pants Calculation Worksheet

Waist: 26" (66cm) + ½" (1.3cm) ease = 26 ½" (67.3cm) ÷ 4 = 6 ⅝" (16.8cm)
  Front: 6 ⅝" (16.8cm) + ¼" (6.4mm) = 6 ⅞" (17.5cm)
  Back: 6 ⅝" (16.8cm) − ¼" (6.4mm) = 6 ⅜" (16.2cm)

High Hip: 34" (86.4cm) + 1" (2.5cm) ease = 35" (88.9cm) ÷ 4 = 8 ¾" (22.2cm)
  Front: 8 ¾" (22.2cm) + ¼" (6.4mm) = 9" (22.9cm)
  Back: 8 ¾" (22.2cm) − ¼" (6.4mm) = 8 ½" (21.6cm)
  (@ a depth of 4½" [11.4cm])

Low Hip: 37" (94cm) + 1 ½" (3.8cm) ease = 38 ½" (72.4cm) ÷ 4 = 9 ⅝" (24.4cm)
  Front: 9 ⅝" (24.4cm) + ¼" (6.4mm) = 9 ⅞" (25.1cm)
  Back: 9 ⅝" (24.4cm) − ¼" (6.4mm) = 9 ⅜" (23.8cm)
  (@ a depth of 8½" [21.6cm])

Lowered Waist: 30" (76.2cm) + 0 ease = 30" (76.2cm) ÷ 4 = 7 ½" (19.1cm)
  Front: 7 ½" (19.1cm) + ¼" (6.4mm) = 7 ¾" (19.7cm)
  Back: 7 ½" (19.1cm) − ¼" (6.4mm) = 7 ¼" (18.4cm)
  (@ a depth of 2" [5.1cm])

Side Seam: 40" (101.6cm) _____ (full length)
Inseam: 30" (76.2cm)
Crotch Depth: 10" (25.4cm) + ½" or ¾" (1.9cm) = 10 ¾" (27.3cm) (+ 1"–2" [2.5–5.1cm] menswear)
Crotch Length: 25" (63.5cm)

Knee: 13 ½" (34.3cm) + 1" (2.5cm) ease = 14 ½" (36.8cm) ÷ 2 = 7 ¼" (18.4cm)
  Front: 7 ¼" (18.4cm) − ½" (1.3cm) = 6 ¾" (17.1cm)
  Back: 7 ¼" (18.4cm) + ½" (1.3cm) = 7 ¾" (19.7cm)
  (@ a depth of 24" [61cm])

Thigh: 18 ½" (47cm) + 1" (2.5cm) ease = 19 ½" (49.5cm) ÷ 2 = 9 ¾" (24.8cm)
  Front: 9 ¾" (24.8cm) − ½" (1.3cm) = 9 ¼" (23.5cm)
  Back: 9 ¾" (24.8cm) + ½" (1.3cm) = 10 ¼" (26cm)
  (@ a height of 8" [20.3cm] from mid-knee)

Calf: 12 ½" (31.8cm) + 1" (2.5cm) ease = 13 ½" (34.3cm) ÷ 2 = 6 ¾" (17.1cm)
  Front: 6 ¾" (17.1cm) − ½" (1.3cm) = 6 ¼" (15.9cm)
  Back: 6 ¾" (17.1cm) + ½" (1.3cm) = 7 ¼" (18.4cm)
  (@ a depth of 5" [12.7cm] from mid-knee)

Ankle: 9 ½" (24.1cm) + 1" (2.5cm) ease = 10 ½" (26.7cm) ÷ 2 = 5 ¼" (13.3cm)
  Front: 5 ¼" (13.3cm) − ½" (1.3cm) = 4 ¾" (12.1cm)
  Back: 5 ¼" (13.3cm) + ½" (1.3cm) = 5 ¾" (14.6cm)
  (@ a height of 3" [7.6cm] above full length)

Base: 15" (38.1cm) + 0 ease = 15" (38.1cm) ÷ 2 = 7 ½" (19.1cm)
  Front: 7 ½" (19.1cm) − ½" (1.3cm) = 7" (17.8cm)
  Back: 7 ½" (19.1cm) + ½" (1.3cm) = 8" (20.3cm)

Above Knee: 22" (55.9cm)
Capri Length: 30" (76.2cm)

PANTS GUIDELINES

Begin with front guidelines when drafting a pants sloper. A pants guideline block is a rectangle measuring the **full pants length** and the width of the **front low-hip calculation**. It includes guidelines showing the waist, high hip, low hip, crotch depth, knee, thigh, calf, and base. Mark the center front and side. The back pants sloper is drafted off the front sloper so a back guideline block is not needed (*Fig. 9.3*).

1. Draw a line the full length of the pants sloper. Do not use the edge of the pattern paper for the center front. Leave about 4" (10.2cm) open from the edge of the paper to draw the crotch.
2. Square a line out from the top of the pants length for the waist guideline. The guideline should be as wide as the **front low-hip calculation**.
3. Draw the high-hip depth at 4½" (11.4cm) from the waist guideline. This guideline should measure as the **front low-hip calculation**. *Skip this step in menswear.*
4. Draw the low-hip depth, less 1" (2.5cm), from the waist guideline. For example, if the low-hip depth is 8½" (21.6cm), draw the line at 7½" (19.1cm). This will give more room to draw the crotch curve. This guideline should measure as the **front low-hip calculation**.
5. Mark the crotch depth as calculated. Square a guideline out at this depth measuring the **front low-hip calculation**.
6. Draw the placement of the knee guideline from the waist. Check the measurements sheet to find the depth of the knee from the waist at side. The guideline should measure as the **front low-hip calculation**.
7. Measure 8" (20.3cm) up from the knee guideline and draw the thigh guideline. The guideline should measure as the **front low-hip calculation**.
8. Measure 5" (12.7cm) down from the knee guideline. Draw the calf guideline. The guideline should measure as the **front low-hip calculation**.
9. Square a guideline out at the base of the pants. The guideline should measure as the **front low-hip calculation**.
10. Label the center front and side.
11. Mark the four corners of the rectangle **A**, **B**, **C**, and **D**.

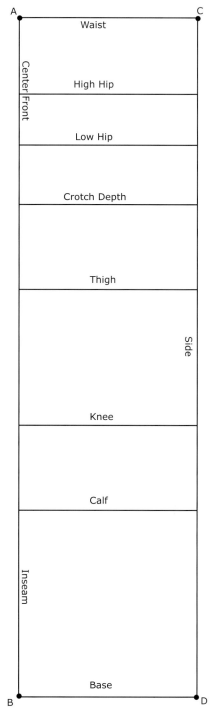

Figure 9.3

212   Building Patterns

Exercises

SLACKS SLOPER

This works for both womenswear and menswear. The slacks sloper has a foundation in between a tight jeans fit and a looser trouser fit. It is helpful to draft a middle fit for a sloper because it is easy to manipulate it larger or smaller for different looks. Note that the instructions cycle through the alphabet twice: first with uppercase letters, then with lowercase letters.

1. **AE** = ½" (1.3cm) in at center front (*Fig. 9.4*)
2. **F** = the low-hip guideline at center front
3. **EG** = dart distance from center front (see Front Dart Distance Formula). *Skip any reference to the front waist dart in menswear.* For more about darts, refer to Skirts—Darts (page 29).
4. **GH** = dart width (see Front Dart Width Chart)

Front Dart Distance Formula

Divide the front waist calculation in half, then add 1" (2.5cm).

For example, if the front waist calculation is 7" (17.8cm), divide 7" (17.8cm) by 2 = 3½" (8.9cm) + 1" (2.5cm) = 4½" (11.4cm).

Front Dart Width Chart

If in between, round down.

- If the difference between the **full**-waist and low-hip measurements (with ease) is 14"–16" (35.6–40.6cm), use a 1½" (3.8cm) dart width.
- If the difference is 10"–13" (25.4–33cm), use a 1¼" (3.2cm) dart width.
- If the difference is 8"–9" (20.3–22.9cm), use a 1" (2.5cm) dart width.
- If the difference is 7" (17.8cm) or less, use a ¾" (1.9cm) dart width.

Take the difference between the full-waist and low-hip measurements with ease, not the difference between the waist and hip calculations.

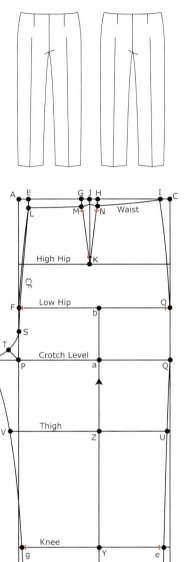

Figure 9.4

5. **HI** = remainder of the front waist calculation after subtracting the dart distance (**EG**). Make sure **EG** + **HI** equals the front waist calculation.
6. **J** = center of the dart width
7. **JK** = length of dart (see Dart Length Chart)
8. **EL** = ½" (1.3cm) waist shaping

Dart Length Chart

- If the dart width is 1 ½" (3.8cm), use a dart length of 5 ¾" (14.6cm).
- If the dart width is 1 ¼" (3.2cm), use a dart length of 5" (12.7cm).
- If the dart width is 1" (2.5cm), use a dart length of 4 ½" (11.4cm).
- If the dart width is ¾" (1.9cm), use a dart length of 3 ½" (8.9cm).

9. Connect **L-I** for the waist shaping in a shallow curve. Square off at **L** for ¾" (1.9cm) before shaping to **I**.
10. **MN** = bring the dart legs **G** and **H** straight down to meet the waist shaping, keeping the dart width the same as **GH**. Mark **M** and **N** on the **LI** line as shown (*Fig. 9.4*).
11. Connect **M-K-N** for the dart legs. Check the legs to make sure they are even. Adjust at **N** as needed and redraw **N** to **I**. Push the dart bulk toward the side and trace the shape, so it is flush with the waistline.
12. Measure **LI**, excluding the dart width **MN** (as that width will be sewn out) to check the front waist measurement.
13. Connect **L-F**.
14. **FO** = low-hip guideline
15. Connect **I-O** to shape the side. Make sure the front high-hip calculation is cleared. Raise the waist dart point or increase at the side as necessary to get the high-hip calculation.
16. **PQ** = mark the crotch level guideline
17. **PR** = extension to the crotch point (see Front Crotch Extension Chart)
18. **PS** = 2" (5.1cm) guide for shaping the crotch on the **FP** line. If **S** ends up higher than **F**, bring **S** down to **F** making **F** and **S** the same point.
19. Redraw the center front from **L** to **S**.
20. **PT** = ⅝" (1.6cm) guideline at 45-degree angle for shaping the crotch
21. Connect **R-T-S** for the crotch shape. It is okay to lengthen or shorten at **T** to get a smooth curve. **PT** can ultimately measure anywhere from ½"–1" (1.3–2.5cm).
22. Connect **L-S**, bypassing **F**.
23. **U** = thigh guideline at the side
24. **UV** = front thigh calculation. It is okay if the thigh calculation extends beyond the pants block in the inseam.
25. **W** = center of **BD** (base guideline)
26. **X** = center of the calf guideline
27. **Y** = center of the knee guideline
28. **Z** = center of the original thigh guideline (not necessarily the center of **UV**)

Front Crotch Extension Chart

If the low hip (with ease added and rounding up if in between) is:

- 31"–32" (78.7–81.3cm), the front crotch extension is ¾" (1.9cm)
- 33"–34" (83.8–86.4cm), the front crotch extension is ⅞" (2.2cm)
- 35"–36" (88.9–91.4cm), the front crotch extension is 1" (2.5cm)
- 37"–38" (94–96.5cm), the front crotch extension is 1 ⅛" (2.9cm)
- 39"–40" (99.1–101.6cm), the front crotch extension is 1 ¼" (3.2cm)
- 41"–42" (104.1–106.7cm), the front crotch extension is 1 ⅜" (3.5cm)
- 43"–44" (109.2–111.8cm), the front crotch extension is 1 ½" (3.8cm)
- 45"–46" (114.3–116.8cm), the front crotch extension is 1 ⅝" (4.1cm)
- 47"–48" (119.4–121.9cm), the front crotch extension is 1 ¾" (4.4cm)
- 49"–50" (124.5–127cm), the front crotch extension is 1 ⅞" (4.8cm)
- 51"–52" (129.5–132.1cm), the front crotch extension is 2" (5.1cm)
- 53"–54" (134.6–137.2cm), the front crotch extension is 2 ⅛" (5.4cm)
- 55"–56" (139.7–142.2cm), the front crotch extension is 2 ¼" (5.7cm)
- 57"–58" (144.8–147.3cm), the front crotch extension is 2 ⅜" (6cm)
- 59"–60" (149.9–152.4cm), the front crotch extension is 2 ⅝" (6.7cm)

For every 2" (5.1cm) over 60" (152.4cm), add ⅛" (3.2mm).

29. **a** = center of **PQ**
30. **b** = center of the low-hip guideline
31. Connect **W-X-Y-Z-a-b** for the grainline and crease line of the pants leg.
32. **cd** = front base calculation centered over **W**
33. Connect **Q-d** in a straight line. A fraction might be cut off at **U** by doing this. Move **U** over to meet the **Qd** line. Move **V** beyond the guideline if necessary to get the front thigh calculation.
34. Mark **e** at the knee guideline at the side seam on the **Qd** line.
35. Mark **f** at the calf guideline at the side seam on the **Qd** line.
36. **Yg** = as the measurement of **Ye** on the knee guideline
37. Connect **R-g** in a shallow curve. Make sure **V** is cleared. It is okay if the **Rg** line extends beyond **V**. Re-mark **V** on the inseam line. Connect **g-c** in a straight line.
38. Smooth the inseam at **g**. It is okay to adjust **g** in or out ⅛" (3.2mm) for a smoother line. Mark **h** on the **gc** line as it crosses the calf guideline.

39. Note the distance between **C** and **I**. If the distance is more than 2½" (6.4cm), consider adding another waist dart to get the **CI** distance in the 2½" (6.4cm) range. If **CI** is ½" (1.3cm) or less, reduce the dart until **CI** is ½" (1.3cm). Curve is needed from waist to low hip, but too much curve could add unnecessary bias.

40. Note the measurement of the front crotch length (**LSTR**).

41. Note the measurement of the inseam (**RVghc**).

Back

1. Trace the front pants pattern outline including the guidelines and grainline (see dotted outline on *Fig. 9.5* for reference). Transfer point **P** on the front (this point will be needed for the back crotch extension). Flip the pattern as shown, so the crotch point is on the opposite side. Mark the traced pattern **A, B, C, D, E** (**E** is where **P** was on the front), and **F** as shown. Draft the back pants pattern on top of the traced front pants outline.

2. **GH** = extend the entire side ½" (1.3cm) from waist to base and draw the guidelines to meet the new side line

42. Pattern: **L-M-N-I-O-Q-U-e-f-d-W-c-h-g-V-R T-S-L**, including the dart (**M-K-N**)

43. Notch the low hip at the side and center front (**F** and **O**). Notch the knee (**g** and **e**). Notch and awl-punch the dart. Awl-punch the crotch point (**R**). Draw the grainline: **W-X-Y-Z-a-b**. Add ½" (1.3cm) seam allowance and a 1½" (3.8cm) hem allowance. Drag the notches to the perimeter. Cut (2) self.

3. **AI** = extend the center back 1½" (3.8cm), continuing the slant of the line

4. Connect **G-I** in a straight line.

5. **GJ** = half the back waist calculation measured on the **GI** line

6. **JK** = dart width as front. (*For menswear pants, use a 1"* [2.5cm] *back dart.*)

7. **KL** = remainder of the back waist calculation (as **GJ**)

8. **M** = half the dart width

9. **MN** = length of dart as chart (see Dart Length Chart). The center of the dart should be squared off the high-hip guideline.

Drafting Tip:

Break the back dart width into two equal darts (example: a 1½" [3.8cm] dart can be broken into two ¾" [1.9cm] darts). Divide the back waist calculation into three equal parts, and place the darts in between the sections. Be sure to shorten the dart length based on the Dart Length Chart. Consider breaking up the front darts into two, especially if they are puckering at the vanishing point. In front, space the darts 1½" (3.8cm) apart between the second leg of the first dart and the first leg of the second dart. Consider moving the first dart toward the center front 1" (2.5cm) to make more room for two darts. The vanishing point (apex) of a dart can be tilted ¼" (6.4mm) toward the side seam to give the illusion of a smaller waist. Experiment!

---

10. Connect **J-N-K** for the dart legs. Adjust at **K** so **NK** equals **NJ**. Fold the dart bulk toward the center-back seam, and trace the shape so it is flush with the waistline.

11. **OP** = back low-hip calculation. Note that the measurement starts from **O**.

12. **EQ** = ½" (1.3cm) down for the back crotch level

13. **QR** = half the back low-hip calculation, less ¾" (1.9cm). For example, if the back low-hip calculation is 9½" (24.1cm), divide that in half for 4¾" (12.1cm) and subtract ¾" (1.9cm) for 4" (10.2cm) (**QR**).

14. Draw the back crotch level line from **R** to **Q** to the side seam.

15. **QS** = 1" (2.5cm) guide at a 45-degree angle from **Q**.

16. Connect **L-P-S-R** for the back crotch shape. Adjust the **QS** guideline as needed for a smooth shape.

17. **BT** = ½" (1.3cm) extension of the inseam at the base

18. Extend the calf ½" (1.3cm) at the inseam and mark **U**.

19. Extend the knee ½" (1.3cm) at the inseam and mark **V**.

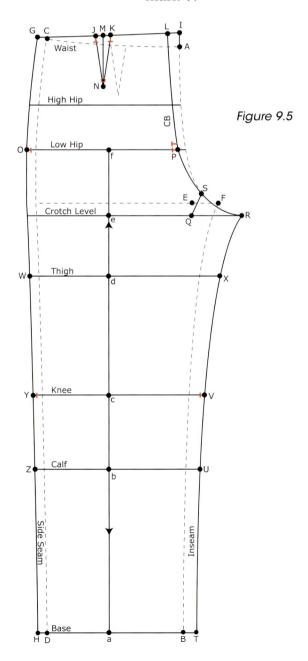

Figure 9.5

20. Connect **R-V** in a shallow curve for the back inseam.

21. Connect **V-U-T**. Extend the thigh guideline to meet the inseam.

22. Mark the thigh guideline **W** and **X** as shown.

23. Mark the knee guideline at side **Y**.

24. Mark the calf guideline at side **Z**.

25. Mark the grainline and center of the pants leg **a-b-c-d-e-f**. This line should have been transferred from the front sloper pattern.

26. Measure the back inseam. Compare the measurement to the front. The back inseam can measure up to ⅜" (1cm) shorter than the front. Keep this discrepancy in the pattern. It will create the slight cupping needed in the seat of the pants to prevent sagging. If the front and back inseams measure the same, do not make any adjustments. True the shape of the front and back patterns from the knee guideline to the crotch points and from the knee guideline to the base. Do this in two passes.

27. Pattern: **L-K-J-G-O-W-Y-Z-H-a-T-U-V-X-R-S P-L**, including the dart (**J-N-K**)

28. Notch the low hip at the side (**O**) and double notch the center back (**P**). Notch the knee (**Y** and **V**). Notch and awl-punch the dart. Awl-punch the crotch point (**R**). Draw the grainline: a-b-c-d-e-f. Add ½" (1.3cm) seam allowance and a 1½" (3.8cm) hem allowance. Drag the notches to the perimeter. Cut (2) self.

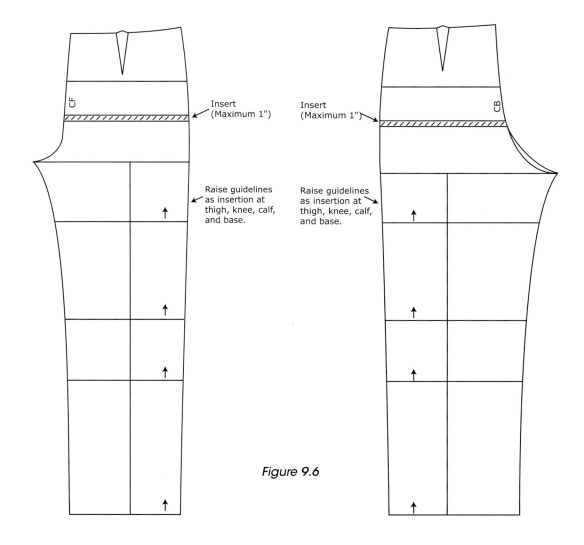

Figure 9.6

Front and Back Pants Sloper

Measure the back crotch length (**LPSR**). Add the front crotch length to the back crotch length. If it measures within 1" (2.5cm) bigger than the amount noted on the crotch length measurement sheet, then no adjustments are needed before sewing. If it measures shorter by more than 1" (2.5cm), split the amount needed and add half to the front and half to the back at the low-hip guideline. Do this by separating both the front and back patterns at the low-hip guidelines and insert across each pattern. Raise the thigh, knee, calf, and base guidelines the amount that was inserted to get them back to the original level (*Fig. 9.6*). This can be done by folding up at the thigh guideline. Smooth the perimeter.

If there is strain or wrinkling at the inseam after the first fitting, cut horizontally at the knee guideline and slide the base of the pattern (from the knee down) toward the inseam 1" (2.5cm) on both the front and back (*Fig. 9.7*). Blend the crotch points to the knee on the inseam, and blend from crotch level line to the knee on the side seam. This adjustment is recommended in womenswear even before the first fitting. The adjustment gives more curve to the hip area.

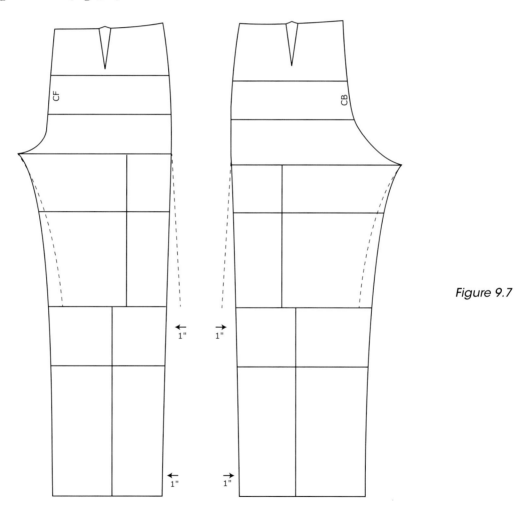

Figure 9.7

Truing Tip:

Pants patterns can be difficult to true. The side shapes are often different at the hips with the front straighter than the back. The back inseam can be up to ⅜" (1cm) shorter than the front inseam. There might be a dart in the back, but not the front, which can skew the side seam. True seams by walking them. Make sure connection points are smooth. If the pants sews up easily and fit well, don't force the truing.

TRANSFERRING THE PANTS SLOPER TO TAG

Once the sloper fit is adjusted, true the pattern on more time. Make sure there is a smooth transition from the front to back crotch point by butting the front and back inseams together; note the transition at the crotch point. Make sure the shape is not forming a peak or a dip. If so, trim or fill in as necessary.

Awl-punch the crotch extension points on the front (**P**) and back (**Q**) (*Fig. 9.8*). These points are needed to draft jeans and trouser foundations. Trace the front and back pieces onto tag without seam or hem allowances.

The sloper is not a garment. It is a template. Think of the sloper as having up to 70 percent of the work done. The remaining 30 percent is about design, fabric choice, adjusting fit, silhouette and details to reflect the designer's sketch.

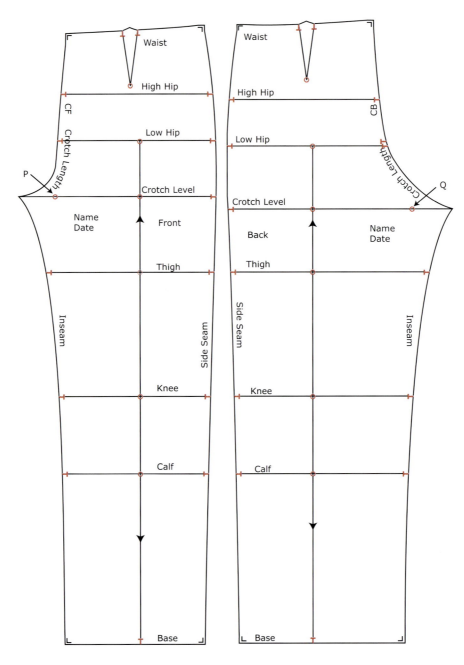

Figure 9.8

TROUSERS

A trouser sloper has a looser fit and a full leg.

Styling Tip:

Many pants styles do not have a front waist dart. Not having a front waist dart allows for a minimalist look on the front and looks less crowded when adding a front pocket or a zipper or button fly. Shave the front dart by splitting the difference of the dart width between the front and the back waist at side. For example, if the front sloper has a 1" (2.5cm) dart, shave ½" (1.3cm) off the front side seam at waist and back side seam at waist and bend into the low hip. Keep the dart on the back waist. The back waist dart is needed for a smooth fit over the rear.

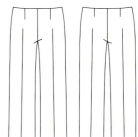

Front

1. Trace the front slacks sloper. For the looser trouser fit, lower the crotch by cutting across the low-hip guideline and inserting ½"–1" (1.3–2.5cm). Raise the leg guidelines at the thigh the amount of the low-hip insertion. Then mark **A**, **B**, **C**, **D**, **E**, and **F** as shown (*Fig. 9.9*). The dotted outline shows the slacks sloper.
2. Mark the center of the base **G**.
3. **FH** = one-fourth the front low hip as measured on the sloper, less ¼" (6.4mm). For example, if the front low hip on the sloper measures 10" (25.4cm), divide that by one-quarter for 2½" (6.4cm), then subtract ¼" (6.4mm) for 2¼" (5.7cm) (**FH**). Increasing will give a looser fit. Note that this extension is from F to H, not E to H.
4. **I** = front crotch level at side
5. **HA** = connect for the new crotch curve. The crotch point might extend slightly, but the curve is kept the same.
6. **KJ** = the adjusted front base. Extend from **C** and **D** 1"–1½" (2.5–3.8cm) on each side. Adding 1" (2.5cm) will increase each pants leg base by 4" (10.2cm) total; 1¼" (3.2cm) will increase each pants leg base by 5" (12.7cm) total; and 1½" (3.8cm) will increase each pants leg base by 6" (15.2cm) total.
7. Connect **I-J** for the side seam.
8. Connect **H-K** for the inseam keeping the curve shallow.
9. Mark **L** and **M** on the knee guideline as shown.
10. Pattern: **A-B-I-M-J-G-K-L-H-A**, including the dart
11. Notch the low hip at the side and center front. Notch the knee at the inseam and side seam. Notch and awl-punch the dart. Awl-punch the crotch point (**H**). Draw the grainline. Add ½" (1.3cm) seam allowance and a 1½" (3.8cm) hem allowance. Drag the notches to the perimeter. Cut (2) self.

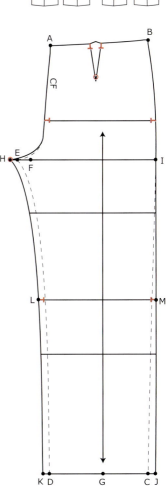

Figure 9.9

Back

1. Trace the back slacks sloper. Lower the crotch as front by cutting across the low-hip guideline and inserting ½"–1" (1.3–2.5cm). Raise the leg guidelines at the thigh the amount of the low-hip insertion. Then mark **N**, **O**, **P**, **Q**, **R**, and **S** (*Fig. 9.10*).
2. Mark the center of the base **T**.
3. **SU** = half the back low hip as measured on the sloper, less ¼" (6.4mm). For example, if the back low hip on the sloper measures 9½" (24.1cm), divide that in half for 4¾" (12.1cm), then subtract ¼" (6.4mm) for 4½" (11.4cm) (**SU**). Increasing the back crotch extension will give a looser fit. Note that the extension is from **S** to **U**, not **R** to **U**.
4. **V** = back crotch level at side
5. **UN** = connect for the new crotch curve. Notice how the crotch point might extend slightly, but the curve is kept the same.
6. **WX** = back base extended as front
7. Connect **U-W** for the inseam in a shallow curve.
8. Connect **V-X** for the side seam.
9. Mark **Y** and **Z** on the knee guideline as shown.
10. True the front and back patterns.
11. Pattern: **N-O-V-Z-X-T-W-Y-U-N**, including the dart
12. Notch the low hip at the side and the center back. Notch the knee at the inseam and side seam. Notch and awl-punch the dart. Awl-punch the crotch point (**U**). Draw a length grainline. Add ½" (1.3cm) seam allowance and a 1½" (3.8cm) hem allowance. Drag the notches to the perimeter. Cut (2) self.

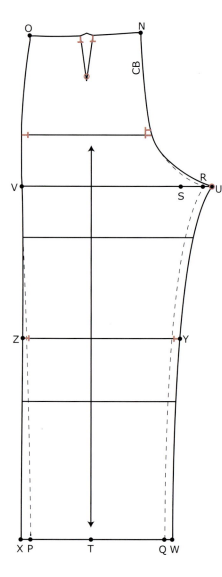

Figure 9.10

JEANS

A jeans foundation has a close fit and a narrow leg. Note that the instructions cycle through the alphabet twice: first with uppercase letters, then with lowercase letters.

Front

1. Trace the front slacks sloper. For a tighter fit with a higher crotch, cut across the low-hip guideline and overlap ¼" (6.4mm) to shorten the crotch length. Mark **A**, **B**, **C**, **D**, **E**, and **F** as shown (*Fig. 9.11*). The dotted lines show the slacks sloper.
2. Mark the center of the base **G**.
3. **EH** = decrease the crotch extension ¼" (6.4mm) from **E**. Decreasing the front crotch extension will give a tighter fit.
4. **I** = front crotch level at side seam
5. **HA** = connect for the new crotch curve
6. **KJ** = reduce the base by ½"–1" (1.3–2.5cm) on both the inseam and side seam. Reducing ½" (1.3cm) will decrease the base 2" (5.1cm) total; reducing ¾" (1.9cm) will decrease by 3" (7.6cm) total; and reducing 1" (2.5cm) will decrease 4" (10.2cm) total.
7. **IL** = 2" (5.1cm) along the existing side seam
8. Reduce the knee by ½" (1.3cm) on both the inseam and side seam (1" [2.5cm] total). Mark **M** and **N**.
9. Connect **L-N-J** for the side seam.
10. Connect **H-M-K** for the inseam.
11. Pattern: **A-B-I-L-N-J-G-K-M-H-A**, including the dart
12. Notch the low hip at the side and center front. Notch the knee at the inseam and side seam. Notch and awl-punch the dart. Awl-punch the crotch point (**H**).
13. Draw the length grainline. Add ½" (1.3cm) seam allowance and a 1" (2.5cm) hem allowance. Drag the notches to the perimeter. Cut (2) self.

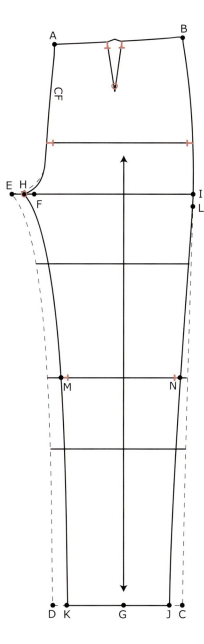

Figure 9.11

Back

1. Trace the back slacks sloper. Adjust the crotch level up ¼" (6.4mm) if it was adjusted in front. Mark **O**, **P**, **Q**, **R**, **S**, and **T** as shown (*Fig. 9.12*).
2. Mark the center of the base **U**.
3. **TV** = one-quarter of the back low hip as measured on the sloper, plus ½" (1.3cm). For example, if the back low hip measures 9½" (24.1cm), divide that by one-quarter for 2⅜" (6cm), then add ½" (1.3cm) for 2⅞" (7.3cm) (**TV**). Decreasing the back crotch extension will give a tighter fit.
4. **W** = back crotch level at side
5. **VO** = connect for the new crotch curve
6. **XY** = reduce the base as front
7. **WZ** = 2" (5.1cm)
8. Reduce the knee as front on both the inseam and side seam. Mark **a** and **b**.
9. Connect **Z-b-Y** for the side seam.
10. Connect **V-a-X** for the inseam.
11. True the pattern.
12. Pattern: **O-P-W-Z-b-Y-U-X-a-V-O**, including the dart
13. Notch the low hip at the side and center back. Notch the knee at the inseam and side seam. Notch and awl-punch the dart. Awl-punch the crotch point (**V**). Draw a length grainline. Add ½" (1.3cm) seam allowance and a 1" (5.1cm) hem allowance. Drag the notches to the perimeter. Cut (2) self.

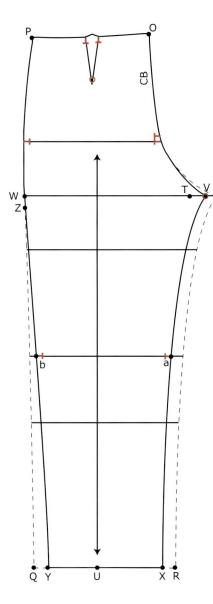

Figure 9.12

Fitting Tip:

The more fitted the pant is through the rise, the more slanted the back rise can be. More slant equals more bias in the rise, allowing for more give and comfort when sitting down. This also means the back side seam will shift out. Experiment with slanting the back rise.

PANTS VARIATIONS

Now that three basic pants foundations (slacks, trousers, and jeans) have been drafted, use the appropriate foundation to create other pants styles.

Capri Pants

Capri pants can use the slacks, trouser, or jeans foundation, depending on the design. The example uses the jeans foundation and slits; or zippers are added at the base of the side seams for ease. This silhouette can be used when drafting slim **cigarette pants** (*Fig. 9.13*).

Flare Pants

Flare pants use the slacks or the trouser foundation. *Fig. 9.14* uses the slacks foundation as a starting point. When drafting generously flared pants, it is best to cut into the center of the pants leg (front and back) and add an insertion. Adding into the center of the pants allows the flare to distribute more evenly. Note the Y-shaped cut. This type of cut will keep the upper foundation intact, and the flare will start below the crotch. If a design calls for the flare to start lower, simply draw the cut lines lower.

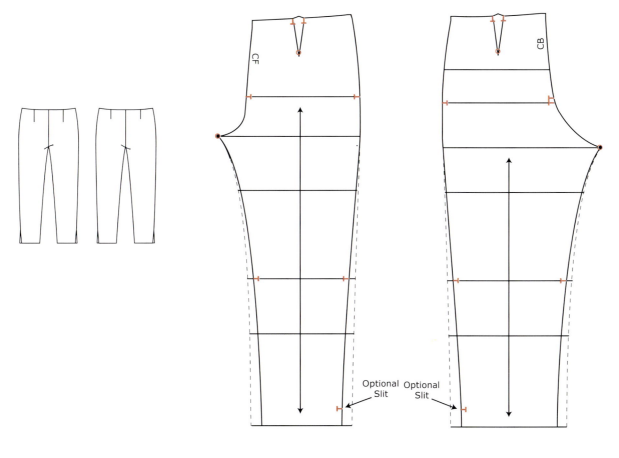

Figure 9.13

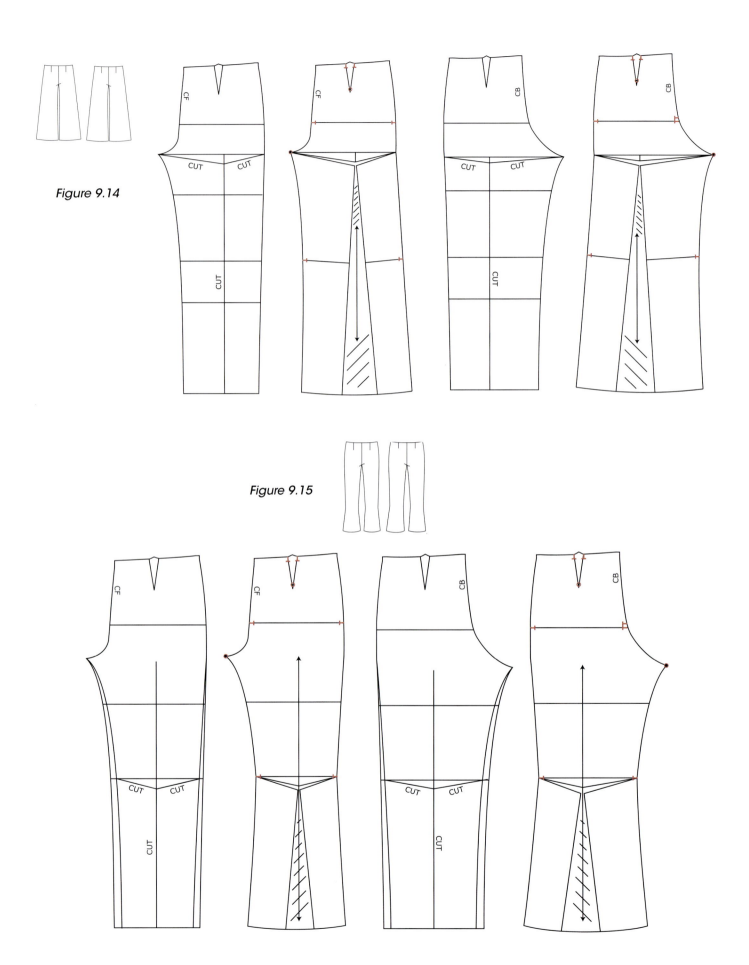

Figure 9.14

Figure 9.15

Bootcut Pants

Bootcut pants use the jeans foundation. A bootcut follows the same instructions as flare pants, only the cut lines stop at the knee guideline or slightly lower on the front and back (*Fig. 9.15*).

Pleated Pants

Pleated pants use the slacks or trouser foundation. Using the trouser foundation will give a looser, more drapey look to the pants. The crotch points on the front and back can be dropped even further for a baggier look. The example starts with the trouser foundation. Pleated pants can have one, two, or three pleats on each front panel. The example shows two pleats. Each pleat can be up to 3" (7.6cm) in width, with the average pleat width being 2" (5.1cm). The pleat insertion is brought all the way down to the perimeter at the base; therefore, note that the front leg is widening as well. Pleats are not added to the back, but the back crotch point should be lowered if it was lowered in front (*Fig. 9.16*).

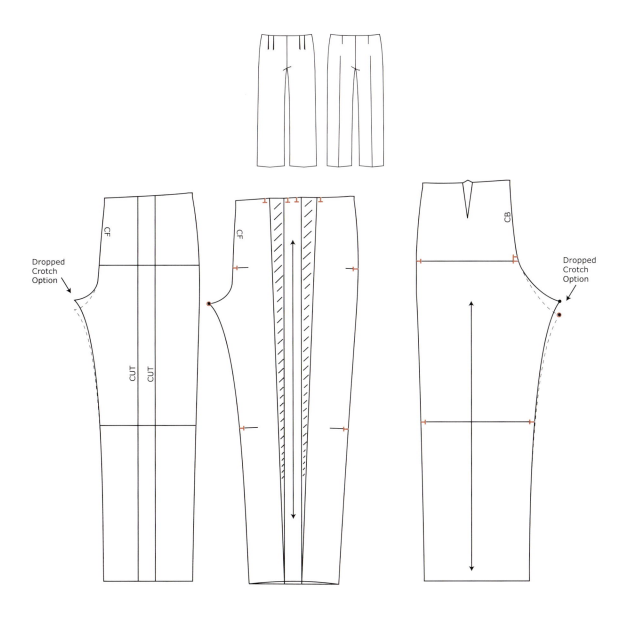

Figure 9.16

JUMPSUIT

For a fitted jumpsuit in a stretch woven or knit, start with the jeans foundation. For a semifitted jumpsuit, start with the slacks foundation. For a looser jumpsuit, start with the trouser foundation. Regardless of the foundation, at least 1½" (3.8cm) needs to be added in length for ease when sitting (*Fig. 9.17*).

1. Take the pants foundation front and back, and line up the bodice sloper at the waist. It will not be a perfect fit across the waist. Most likely, the bodice pieces will hang over the side because there is more ease and wider darts. Line up the center front of the pants and bodice and the center back of the pants and bodice. Keep center front and center back straight, and shave off any excess from the bodice at the side seam. Or adjust the darts so the pieces fit together better.

2. Draw a line 2" (5.1cm) up from the waist guideline on the front and back bodice. Cut the line and insert ½"–1" (1.3–2.5cm) into the cut. Use ½" (1.3cm) for a closer fitting jumpsuit and 1" (2.5cm) for a looser, baggier jumpsuit.

3. Cut at the low-hip guideline on the front and back pants, and insert 1"–2" (2.5–5.1cm) into the cut. Use 1" (2.5cm) for a closer fitting jumpsuit and 2" (5.1cm) for a looser, baggier jumpsuit. If these insertions are not included with a woven fabric, sitting will be uncomfortable. If the jumpsuit is made in a stretchy knit, these insertions may not be necessary.

4. Mock up the jumpsuit before drafting a collar, sleeves, pockets, plackets, or other design details. Fit the jumpsuit foundation so those details do not need to be redone if the silhouette changes.

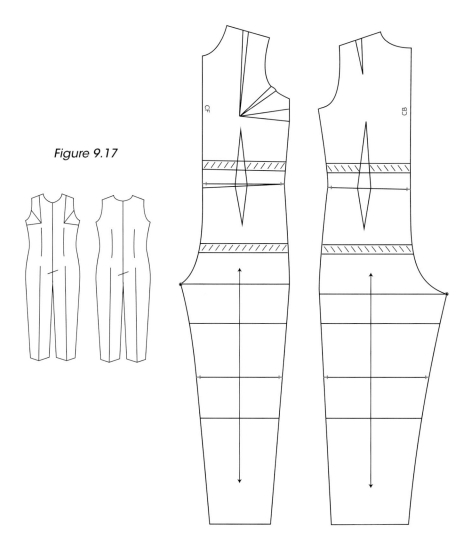

Figure 9.17

DRAWSTRING PANTS

Use the trouser foundation for drawstring pants. Note that this pattern does not have a side seam. To try something different, the front and back pieces are merged for one pattern piece. Mock up the pattern in a soft sweatshirt fleece or a drapey woven fabric.

1. Draw a vertical guideline on a piece of pattern paper the length of the pants sloper. Draw a horizontal line at the base of the vertical line. The horizontal guideline should be centered on the vertical guideline and should measure about 20" (50.8cm) total.
2. Place the base of the front and back pattern pieces flat on the horizontal guideline and bring the widest part of the patterns to the vertical guideline. The widest part is usually the crotch level line. Adjust the base out or in at **E** and **D** if desired. Mark **A**, **B**, **C**, **D**, **E**, and **F** (*Fig. 9.18*).
3. Lower the waist 2" (5.1cm). Ignore the darts.
4. Draw the casing depth as desired (example: 2" [5.1cm]). Mark **G** and **H**. Mark a ½" (1.3cm) vertical buttonhole ¾" (1.9cm) in from the center front and centered within the casing depth. For example, with a 2" (5.1cm) casing depth, the buttonhole will start ¾" (1.9cm) down from the top, and end ¾" (1.9cm) up from the bottom of the casing. The buttonholes are needed to thread the drawstring through the casing. (Think about marking and sewing a channel around the drawstring to keep it from moving up or down.)
5. Cut the casing off the pants pattern on the **GH** line. Note center back.
6. Casing Pattern: **A-B-H-G-A**
7. Notch side top and bottom. Notch the base to keep track of the orientation of the casing when sewing. Draw a grainline at center front. Add ¼" (6.4mm) seam allowance. Drag the notches to the perimeter. Cut (2) self on fold at center front. Cut (2) interfacing.
8. Pants Pattern: **G-H-C-D-E-F-G**
9. Notch the side. Notch to show casing orientation and notch the knee. Awl-punch the crotch points. Draw a length grainline on the vertical guideline at side. Add ¼" (6.4mm) seam allowance at **GH**. Add ½" (1.3cm) seam allowance everywhere else. Add a 1" (2.5cm) hem allowance. Drag the notches to the perimeter. Cut (2) self.
10. The drawstring should measure as A-B plus about 20" (50.8cm).

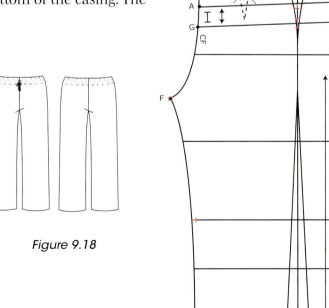

Figure 9.18

Tips:

- **Ease Tip:** For a looser pants, add 1"–2" (2.5–5.1cm) at the vertical guideline to give an additional 2"–4" (5.1–10.2cm) of ease.
- **Design Option:** Cut the pattern apart at the vertical guideline for separate front and back legs, so pockets can be added at the side seam. If side pockets are not included, keep the pattern as one piece and think about adding patch pockets.
- **Construction Tip:** Use the same approach for elastic-waist pants. The casing height for an elastic waist should be elastic width plus ¼" (6.4mm). Buttonholes are not needed in an elastic casing.

Stretch Classifications

- **Stable** knits stretch up to 15% (10" [25.4cm] stretches to 11 ½" [29.2cm])
- **Moderate** knits stretch up to 25% (10" [25.4cm] stretches to 12 ½" [31.8cm])
- **Stretch** knits stretch between 25%–50% (10" [25.4cm] stretches to 15" [38.1cm])
- **Super-stretch** knits stretch between 50%–100% (10" [25.4cm] stretches to 20" [50.8cm])

LEGGINGS

Leggings work best with a thicker, super-stretch knit fabric. Because of the stretch, the circumference and length measurements need to go into negative ease. Remove 4" (10.2cm) from the circumference measurements and 4" (10.2cm) from the ankle length measurement before drafting. To keep the stretch consistent around the leg, draft leggings without a side seam (*Fig. 9.19*).

1. **AB** = ankle length − 4" (10.2cm). Example: 37" (94cm) − 4" (10.2cm) = 33" (83.8cm).
2. **AC** = waist calculation (example: 26" [66cm] − 4" [10.2cm] = 22" [55.9cm] ÷ 4 = 5½" [14cm])
3. **AD** = **AC**
4. **BE** = ankle calculation (example: 9½" [24.1cm] − 4" [10.2cm] = 5½" [14cm] ÷ 2 = 2¾" [7cm])
5. **BF** = **BE**
6. **AG** = crotch depth − 2" (5.1cm). Example: 10" (25.4cm) − 2" (5.1cm) = 8" (20.3cm).
7. **GH** = front crotch level (example: 25" [63.5cm] − 4" [10.2cm] = 21" [53.3cm] ÷ 2 = 10½" [26.7cm] / Front 10½" [26.7cm] − 1½" [3.8cm] = 9" [22.9cm])
8. **GI** = back crotch level (example: 10½" [26.7cm] + 1½" [3.8cm] = 12" [30.5cm])
9. **AJ** = knee depth less 4" (10.2cm). Example: 24" (61cm) − 4" (10.2cm) = 20" (50.8cm).
10. **JK** = knee circumference calculation (example: 13½" [34.3cm] − 4" [10.2cm] = 9½" [24.1cm] ÷ 2 = 4¾" [12.1cm])
11. **KL** = as **JK**
12. **JM** = 7" (17.8cm) from **J** for thigh guideline
13. **MN** = thigh calculation (example: 18½" [47cm] − 4" [10.2cm] = 14½" [36.8cm] ÷ 2 = 7¼" [18.4cm])
14. **MO** = as **MN**

Leggings Calculation Worksheet

Ankle Length: _____ − 4" (10.2cm) = _____

Waist Circumference: _____ − 4" (10.2cm) = _____ ÷ 4 = _____

Crotch Depth: _____ − 2" (5.1cm) = _____

Crotch Length: _____ − 4" (10.2cm) ÷ 2 = _____

    Front: _____ − 1½" (3.8cm) = _____

    Back: _____ + 1½" (3.8cm) = _____

Knee Depth: _____ − 4" (10.2cm) = _____

Knee Circumference: _____ − 4" (10.2cm) = _____ ÷ 2 = _____

Thigh Circumference: _____ − 4" (10.2cm) = _____ ÷ 2 = _____

Calf Circumference: _____ − 4" (10.2cm) = _____ ÷ 2 = _____

Ankle Circumference: _____ − 4" (10.2cm) = _____ ÷ 2 = _____

15. **JP** = 3" (7.6cm) down for the calf guideline
16. **PQ** = calf calculation (example: 12½" [31.8cm] − 4" [10.2cm] = 8½" [21.6cm] ÷ 2 = 4¼" [10.8cm])
17. **PR** = **PQ**
18. **DS** = 1" (2.5cm) to raise the center back
19. **CT** = ½" (1.3cm) for front waist shaping
20. Connect **T-S** in a shallow curve. Square off at **T** for ¾" (1.9cm) and make a right angle at **S** for 1" (2.5cm).
21. Flatten the back crotch at **I** for 1" (2.5cm).
22. Connect **T-H-N-K-Q-E** for the front shape. Smooth any points or edges.
23. Connect **S-I-O-L-R-F** for the back shape. Smooth any points or edges.
24. **UV** = 2" (5.1cm) down from **TS** for a casing
25. Pants Pattern: **T-S-I-O-L-R-F-B-E-Q-K-N-H-T**
26. Notch the knee. Double notch the low hip. Mark the grainline in the direction of the most stretch in the knit. Add ¼" (6.4mm) seam allowance. Cut (2) self.
27. Trace the casing pattern: **T-S-V-U-T**
28. Mark center front and center back on the casing pattern. Use the same grainline as the pants. Add ¼" (6.4mm) seam allowance. Cut (2) self on fold at center front.

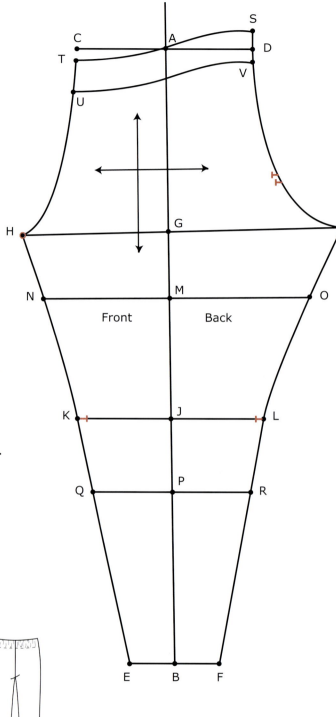

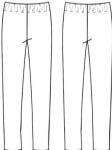

Figure 9.19

Fitting Tip:
For added mobility, use the gusset pattern drafted in the Sleeves chapter (page 199) as a gusset for the crotch seam.

Fabric Tip:
With so many knits on the market and each with a different stretch ratio, it is best to mock up a knit pattern in the knit fabric that will be used for the final garment.

BUTTON FLY
Pants (for both zipper and button fly)
1. Trace the front of a pants pattern or use the front slacks sloper (*Fig. 9.20*).
2. **AB** = length from waist to low hip
3. **BC** = ¾" (1.9cm)
4. **AD** = 1½" (3.8cm)
5. **BE** = 1½" (3.8cm) as **AD**
6. Connect in a straight line from **D** to **E**, then curve from **E** to **C**.
7. Draw a double top stitching line. The first line at 1⅛" (2.9cm) from the center front guideline and another line ¼" (6.4mm) away at 1⅜" (3.5cm).
8. Notch **B** and **C**. Include a length grainline. Add ¼" (6.4mm) seam allowance at the waist and ½" (1.3cm) everywhere else. Drag the notches to the perimeter. Cut (2) self.

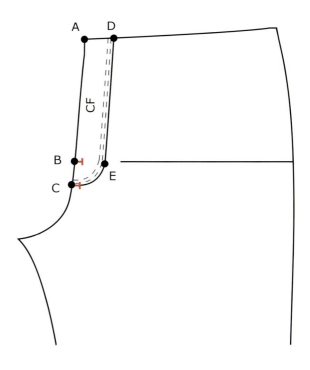

Figure 9.20

Drafting Tip:
When drafting a waistband with a button fly or zipper fly, the extension on the waistband is 1½" (3.8cm).

Right-Side Button Placket

1. Trace **A-D-E-C-B-A** with **D-E** on a folded piece of pattern paper (*Fig. 9.21*). Mark **DE** as a fold line.
2. Mark button placement. Use ½" (1.3cm) flat buttons. Draw a line ½" (1.3cm) away from **AC**. The buttons should be centered on this line. The center of the first button should be ½" (1.3cm) down from the waistline of the pants.
3. Space the rest of the buttons 1" (2.5cm) apart. (The center of each button should be spaced 1" [2.5cm] apart.)
4. Notch **D** and awl-punch **E**. Draw a length grainline. Add ¼" (6.4mm) seam allowance at the waist (**A-D-A**) and ½" (1.3cm) everywhere else. Drag the notches to the perimeter. Cut (1) self. Cut (1) interfacing.

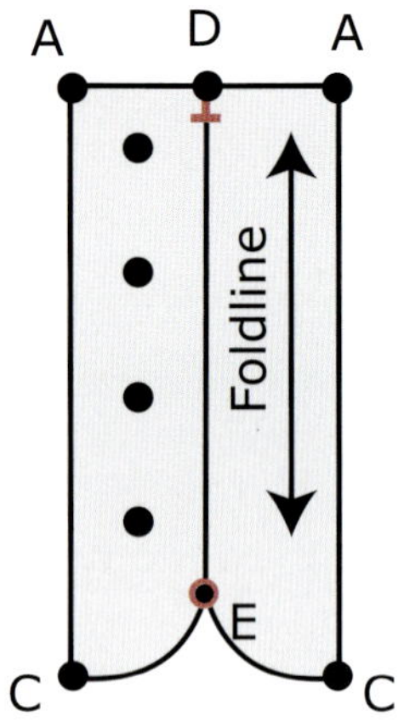

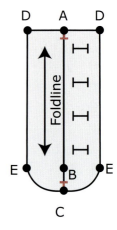

Figure 9.21

Left-Side Buttonhole Placket

1. 1. Trace **A-D-E-C-B-A** with **A-B-C** on a folded piece of pattern paper (*Fig. 9.22*). Mark **A-B-C** as the fold line.
2. 2. Draw a line ⅜" (1cm) in from **A-B-C**. Mark buttonhole placement to correspond with button placement.
3. 3. Notch **A** and **C**. Draw a length grainline. Add ¼" (6.4mm) seam allowance at the waist (**D-A-D**) and ½" (1.3cm) everywhere else. Drag the notches to the perimeter. Cut (1) self. Cut (1) interfacing.

Figure 9.22

ZIPPER FLY

Pants

Use the same pants pattern from the Button Fly exercise (page 233).

Right-Side Facing

1. Trace **A-D-E-C-B-A** with **D-E** on a folded piece of pattern paper (*Fig. 9.23*). Mark **DE** as a fold line.
2. Notch **D** and **E**. Draw a length grainline. Add ¼" (6.4mm) seam allowance at the waist (**A-D-A**) and ½" (1.3cm) everywhere else. Drag the notches to the perimeter. Cut (1) self. Cut (1) interfacing.

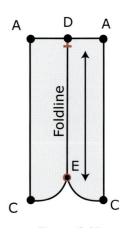

Figure 9.23

Left-Side Extension

1. 1. Trace **A-D-E-C-B-A** (*Fig. 9.24*).
2. 2. Draw a length grainline. Add ¼" (6.4mm) seam allowance at the waist (**AD**) and ½" (1.3cm) everywhere else. Drag the notches to the perimeter. Cut (1) self. Cut (1) interfacing.

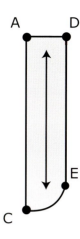

Figure 9.24

Seam Allowance Tip:
When attaching a waistband or a casing to pants, the standard seam allowance is ¼" (6.4mm).

CONTOURED WAISTBAND

Use a contoured waistband on pants with a lowered waistline. Pants with a high waistline can have a straight, fold-over waistband. The height of either waistband is generally 1¼" (3.2cm) finished.

1. Trace a pants foundation and draft a pants front and back with a lowered waistline (*Fig. 9.25*).
2. At a depth of 1¼" (3.2cm) from the lowered waistline on both the front and back, draw a line following the waistline curve.
3. Cut on the lines drawn in Step 2 for front and back waistband pieces. Fold out the darts if they appear in the waistband.
4. Tape the pieces together at the side seam and smooth the edges. After smoothing, adjust the height of the waistband to a consistent 1¼" (3.2cm) throughout. This usually involves adding to the top of the waistband.
5. Add an extension to the right side on the center front guideline. Add ¾" (1.9cm) for a button, snap, or hook closure; add 1½" (3.8cm) for a zipper- or button-fly closures. Fold the extension back and true it. Mark for the intended closure. Most button- and zipper-fly patterns lap left over right.
6. Notch the center front, sides, and center back. Draw a length grainline parallel to the center front extension to stabilize the closure. Add ¼" (6.4mm) seam allowance around the piece. Drag the notches to the perimeter. Cut (2) self. Cut (2) interfacing.

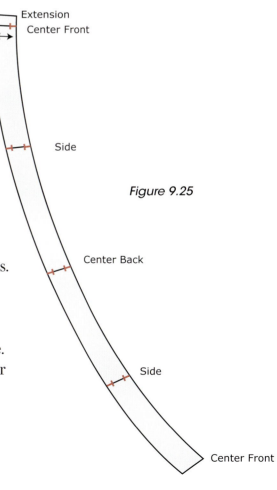

Figure 9.25

BELT LOOPS

Commonly, there are five belt loops on pants. One belt loop is placed at the center back; two belt loops are placed 1½"–2" (3.8–5.1cm) from the side seam, toward the back; and two more are placed about 2¾" (7cm) from the center-front line. Placement of belt loops on a pants pattern and waistband should be marked with drill holes.

A single belt loop pattern piece is 1½" (3.8cm) wide (later folded into a ½" [1.3cm] wide finished belt loop) x 3¼" (8.3cm) long, 2¾" (7cm) finished with ¼" (6.4mm) seam allowance at both top and bottom (*Fig. 9.26*). A 1½" x 3¼" (3.8 x 8.3cm) pattern piece will produce a finished belt loop of ½" wide x 2¾" long (1.3 x 7cm). Experimenting with the size, shape, and placement of belt loops is encouraged.

Instead of trying to keep track of one tiny belt loop pattern piece, make all five belt loops in a row on one pattern piece. The cutting and construction are quicker if belt loops are made in a row, then cut apart during construction.

BACK YOKE

Back yokes are found on traditional jeans. Mark down from the waistband 1½" (3.8cm) at the back side seam. Mark 3" (7.6cm) down from the center back below the waistband. Connect the two points. Cut the yoke pattern away from the rest of the pants pattern, and fold out the back waist dart in the yoke pattern. If part of the waist dart remains below the yoke, either shave it off at the center back or sew the remainder. If there is ¼" (6.4mm) or less of the dart remaining, shave it off ⅜" (1cm) or more remaining, sew it. Yokes are cut on the same grainline as the pants. Extend the pants grainline through the yoke. Cut (2) self (*Fig. 9.27*).

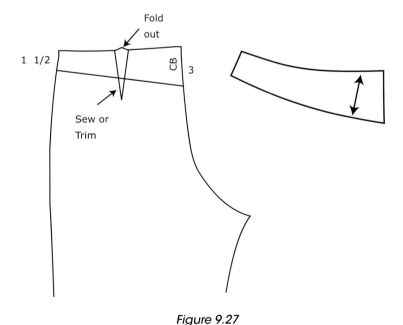

Figure 9.27

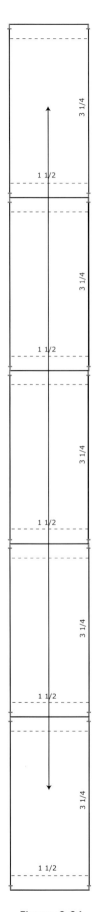

Figure 9.26

CUFFS

Draw a dotted line up from the base of the front and back pants leg the desired height of the cuff (example: 1½" [3.8cm]). Draw three guidelines down from the base the same measurement as the cuff height cuff (example: 1½" [3.8cm]) (*Fig. 9.28*). Fold the cuff sections up, down, then under and trace the pants side seam and inseam over the over the cuff bulk. Unfold and draw the traced outline on the cuff. Mark the fold lines and notch the edges as shown.

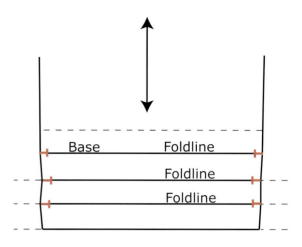

Figure 9.28

Drafting Tip:
Use the same approach when adding a folded cuff on a sleeve base.

 ## Test Your Knowledge

1. What are some differences when drafting a menswear pants sloper versus a womenswear pants sloper?

2. Why is it better to insert a flare into the middle of a pants leg rather than add the amount to the side seam?

3. When is a contoured waistband used instead of a straight, fold-over waistband?

4. Briefly describe how a jumpsuit foundation pattern is drafted.

5. Describe the four categories of knit fabric stretch.

This chapter starts by teaching students pocket terminology and how to differentiate between pocket styles. Students learn to draft a variety of patch pockets, pockets in seams, and welt pockets.

OBJECTIVES

Upon completion of this chapter, you will be able to

- Differentiate between patch, in-seam, and welt pockets
- Confidently choose the right pocket for a garment
- Correctly identify the names of pockets and pocket pieces

CHAPTER 10
Pockets

Patterning Pockets

TYPES OF POCKETS

Before designing and drafting a pocket, consider the type of pocket needed and the size, shape, and placement. A pocket can be functional as well as decorative. It can be sewn into a seam as a hidden pocket or sewn onto a garment as a prominent feature.

There are three types of pockets: (1) **patch pockets** are sewn on the outside of a garment; (2) **in-seam pockets** are sewn into a garment seam; and (3) **welt pockets** have welts or flaps of fabric visible on the outside of the garment with the pocket bag hanging inside the garment. Note: A welt pocket can also be referred to a **jetted pocket**.

POCKET TERMS

- **Pocket**—A pouch with an open top or side.
- **Pocket Opening**—A functional pocket opening is usually about 5"–7" (12.7–17.8cm), depending on hand size and how functional the pocket is. Smaller patch pocket openings tend to be about 3"–5" (7.6–12.7cm).
- **Pocket Bag**—The pouch of a pocket.
- **Pocket Front**—The front of the pocket bag (toward the front of the garment).
- **Pocket Back**—The back of the pocket bag (toward the body).
- **Pocketing**—Pocketing is the fabric used for the bag of a pocket. Pocketing fabric is thin, strong, tightly woven cotton or polyester. Lining can also be used for a pocket bag, but it is not as strong.
- **Facing**—The top of a pocket can have a facing that cleans up the opening and provides stability. Facings are usually 1" (2.5cm) deep. Facings should be interfaced.
- **Pocket Stay**—A pocket stay is placed behind a pocket opening to provide additional support to prevent a pocket from stretching out of shape. Pocket stays are cut from fusible interfacing.

GRAINLINE

A pocket is often cut on the same grain as the garment (which is usually the length grain).

SEAM ALLOWANCE

Seam allowance on pocket pieces should be ¼"–¾" (0.6–1.9cm), depending on the type of pocket. Seam allowances will be addressed with each exercise.

MARKING POCKET PLACEMENT ON PATTERNS

Pocket placement should be drafted onto the garment pattern. Patch pocket and welt pocket placement should be marked with drill holes (*Fig. 10.1*). Denote placement by punching ⅛" (3.2mm) inside the finished shape of the pocket on the garment the pocket will be sewn to. With a welt pocket, awl-punch ⅛" (3.2mm) in from either side of the pocket opening.

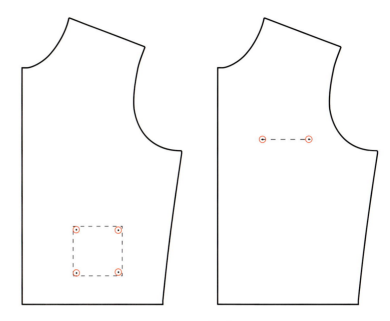

Figure 10.1

Tips:

- **Design Tip:** Consider cutting a pocket on bias or cross grain for **surface interest** on the face of a garment if the garment fabric is a stripe or plaid cut on length grain.
- **Helpful Tip:** The following exercises give instructions on cutting just one of each pocket pattern piece during the learning phase, but if the garment calls for two pockets, then cut two of each.
- **Drafting Tip:** When a pattern piece is shaded, it means the piece should be interfaced for added support and structure.

Exercises

PATCH POCKET

1. Draw the desired finished size and shape of the pocket. Mark **A**, **B**, **C**, and **D** as shown (*Fig. 10.2*).
2. Draw a guideline showing the depth of the facing at 1" (2.5cm) below **AB**. Mark **E** and **F**.
3. Fold on the **AB** line and trace **A-B-F-E** for the facing. Unfold and mark **G** and **H** as shown. Mark **AB** as the fold line.
4. Pocket: **G-H-B-C-D-A-G**
5. Notch the fold line (**AB**). Interface the facing. Draw the grainline. Add ⅜" (1cm) seam allowance around the pocket pattern (more than ⅜" [1cm] will create bulk and less than ⅜" [1cm] is harder to fold in and press). Drag the notches to the perimeter. Cut (1) self.

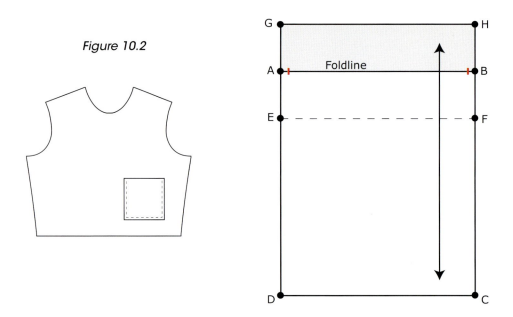

Figure 10.2

Design Tip:

Rectangular patch pockets are more flattering than square. Rectangular shapes visually lengthen the body. Place the long side of the rectangle vertically. Designers are not limited to rectangular-shaped patch pockets. Round the edges or create a point at the center of the base. Most pockets are symmetrical, but they don't have to be. Make pocket shapes and details your design signature.

CARGO POCKET

1. Draw the desired finished size and shape of the pocket without the flap.
2. Mark **A**, **B**, **C**, and **D** as shown (*Fig. 10.3*, Diagram 1). Mark **E** and **F** at the center of the pocket for the pleat placement.
3. Separate the pattern on the **EF** line and insert 2" (5.1cm) for a pleat, making sure **A**, **B**, **D**, and **C** stay on the same plane when the pleat is folded.
4. Mark the center of the pleat **G** and **H** as shown (*Fig. 10.3*, Diagram 2).
5. Draw a guideline showing the depth of the facing 1" (2.5cm) below **AB**. Mark **I** and **J**.
6. Fold on the **AB** line and trace **A-B-J-I** for the facing. Unfold and mark **K** and **L**.
7. Mark **AB** as a fold line.
8. Re-mark **E**, **G**, and **E** at the top of the facing pattern.
9. Pocket: **K-E-G-E-L-B-C-F-H-F-D-A-K**, including the pleat.
10. Notch the fold line (**AB**). Notch the pleat legs (**E**, **G**, **E**, **F**, **H**, and **F**). Note that the pleat should be sewn together through the facing at the top. Draw the grainline. Add ⅜" (1cm) seam allowance around the pocket pattern (excluding the **KL** at the facing edge) and drag the notches to the perimeter. Cut (1) self.

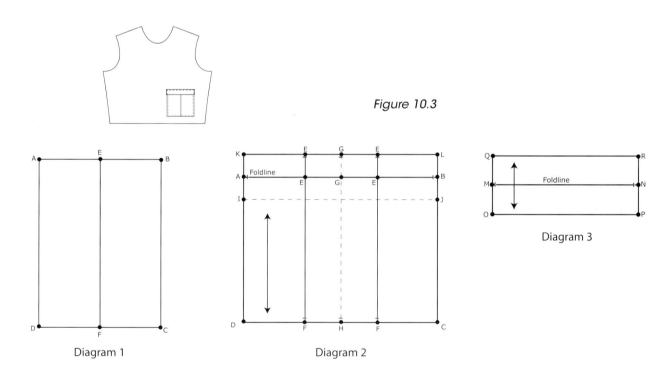

Figure 10.3

Diagram 1

Diagram 2

Diagram 3

Design Tip:

The pleat can fold to the correct side for a box pleat or to the wrong side for an inverted box pleat. Structurally, it does not make much of a difference, but it does change the look. A box pleat will be more prominent on the correct side, giving more surface interest to the garment.

Flap

11. For the flap, draw a line the finished width of the pocket without the width of the pleat (**AB** less **EE**).
12. Add ⅛" (3.2mm) to either side of the line and mark **M** and **N** (*Fig. 10.3*, Diagram 3). The flap is slightly wider, so it covers the edges of the pocket.
13. Draw the desired depth of the flap from **MN** and mark **O** and **P** as shown.
14. Connect **M-N-P O-M**.
15. Fold on the **MN** line and trace **M-N-P-O-M** for the flap facing. Mark **Q** and **R**.
16. Flap: **Q-R-N-P-O-M-Q**. Interface the entire flap pattern for added support.
17. Notch the fold line (**MN**). Draw the grainline. Add ⅜" (1cm) seam allowance around the flap pattern and drag the notches to the perimeter. Cut (1) self.

Sewing Tip:

Place the top of the flap ½" (1.3cm) above the pocket. If the flap is sew at the pocket opening, it is difficult to access the pocket.

SWEATSHIRT PATCH POCKET

1. Draw half the desired finished size and shape of the pocket. Mark **A**, **B**, **C**, **D**, and **E** as shown (*Fig. 10.4*, Diagram 1).
2. Note the slant from **B** to **C**. **B** to **C** represents the pocket opening.

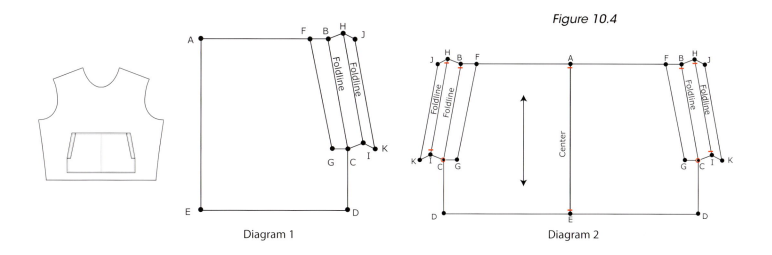

Figure 10.4

Diagram 1

Diagram 2

Design Tip:
A slant will give a more natural and comfortable pocket opening position for the hand.

3. Draw the reinforcement shape for the pocket opening as follows:
3a. **BF** = ¾" (1.9cm)
3b. **CG** = ¾" (1.9cm) squared off **CD**
3c. Connect **B-C-G-F-B**.
3d. Fold on the **BC** line and trace **B-F-G-C**. Unfold the pattern and mark **H** and **I** as shown.
3e. Fold at **H-I** and trace **H-B-C-I**. Unfold and cut ⅛" (3.2mm) along the edge to reduce bulk and mark **J** and **K** as shown. The triple fabric layer is to add more support and structure to the pocket opening.
3f. Interfacing can be added to **B-H-J-K-I-C** for more support.
4. Trace the pattern onto a folded piece of pattern paper for a full pocket pattern (*Fig. 10.4*, Diagram 2). The fold is on the **AE** line.
5. Pattern: **J-H-B-F-A-F-B-H-J-K-I-C-D-E-D-C-I-K-J**
6. Mark fold lines at **BC** and **HI**. Notch **B**, **H**, and **I**. Notch the center at **A** and **E**. Awl-punch the corners at **C**. Add the grainline. Add ⅜" (1cm) seam allowance around the pocket pattern, except along the **JK** line, and drag the notches to the perimeter of the pattern. Cut (1) self.

Structural Tip:
A jeans side pocket needs to anchor into a waistline seam for support. Without an anchor, the pocket bag and its contents will shift and strain the pocket opening, causing it to weaken and rip at the lower edge.

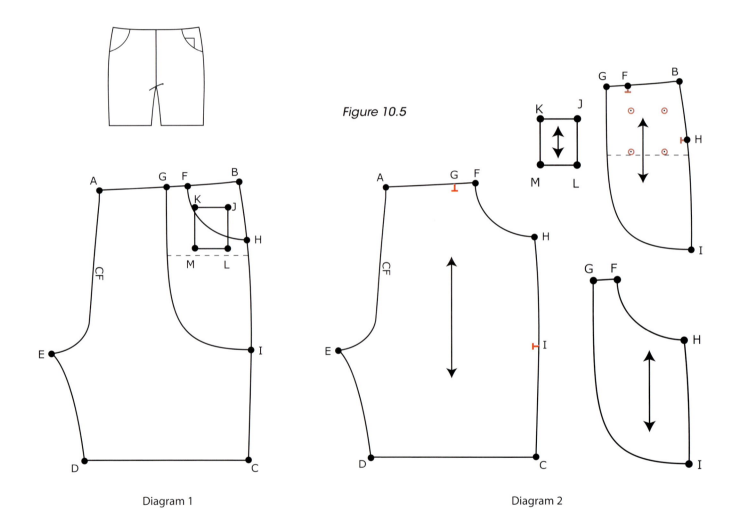

Figure 10.5

Diagram 1

Diagram 2

JEANS POCKET

1. Trace the front pants and mark **A**, **B**, **C**, **D**, and **E** as shown (*Fig. 10.5*, Diagram 1).
2. **BF** = mark where the pocket will start on the waistline (example: 3½" [8.9cm])
3. **FG** = 1" (2.5cm) as an anchor for the top of the pocket at the waistline
4. **BH** = depth at side for the pocket opening (example: 3"–4" [7.6–10.2cm])
5. Connect **F-H** in the curve for the pocket opening.
6. **HI** = depth of the pocket bag (example: 5" or 6" [12.7 or 15.2cm])
7. Connect **G-I** for the shape and size of the pocket bag.
8. Small Pocket (Right Side Only): At 1¼" (3.2cm) down from the waistline along the side seam, mark in 1" (2.5cm) and label that **J**.
9. **JK** = square over approximately 2"–3" (5.1–7.6cm) for the small pocket opening
10. **JL** = square down 3½" (8.9cm)
11. **KM** = as **JL**
12. Connect **K-J-L-M-K** for the small pocket rectangular shape.
13. Front Pants Pattern: **A-G-F-H-I-C-D-E-A**
14. Notch **G** and **I** (*Fig. 10.5*, Diagram 2). Draw the grainline. Add ½" (1.3cm) seam allowance and drag the notches to the perimeter. Cut (1) self.
15. Pocket Back: **G-F-B-H-I-G**
16. Notch **F** and **H**. Awl-punch for pocket placement of the small pocket ⅛" (3.2mm) inside each corner placement.
17. Option: To reduce bulk, the area below the dotted line on the pocket back can be cut from pocketing. Above the dotted line should be cut from self-fabric. Add ¼" (6.4mm) seam allowance to both pieces at this cut line to seam them together. The dotted line should be 1" (2.5cm) below the pocket opening so the seam does not show. Add ½" (1.3cm) seam allowance to the remainder of the piece and drag the notches to the perimeter. Cut (1) self and (1) pocketing.
18. Pocket Front Pattern: **G-F-H-I-G**
19. Draw the grainline. Add ½" (1.3cm) seam allowance. Cut (1) pocketing
20. Small Patch Pocket: **K-J-L-M-K**
21. Draw the grainline. Add ⅜" (1cm) seam allowance. Cut (1) self.

HIDDEN POCKET IN A SEAM

1. Trace the front bodice sloper and mark **A**, **B**, **C**, **D**, **E**, and **F** as shown (*Fig. 10.6*, Diagram 1).
2. Draw the cross-front guideline and mark **G** and **H**.
3. Decide the pocket placement and width of the pocket opening (example: 3" [7.6cm]) on the cross-front guideline. Mark as **I** and **J**. Pockets start 2"–3" (5.1–7.6cm) from the center front guideline.
4. **IK** = desired depth of pocket (example: 3½" [8.9cm])
5. **JL** = **IK**
6. Connect **I-J-L-K-I** for the pocket shape.
7. Trace the upper portion: **A-B-C-H-J-L-K-I-G-A**
8. Trace the lower portion: **G-I-J-H-D-E-F-G**
9. On the upper portion (*Fig. 10.6*, Diagram 2), fold at **KL** and trace the pocket shape again (**I-J-L-K-I**). Mark the fold line at **KL**.
10. Attach the upper portion to the lower portion at **IJ**. Note that this is an all-in-one pattern piece, which includes the upper portion, the pocket back, the pocket front, and the lower portion. The pocket front and back will be hidden behind the lower portion.
11. Pattern: **A-B-C-H-J-L-J-H-D-E-F-G-I-K-I-G-A**
12. Awl-punch **I** and **J**. Notch **K** and **L** for the fold line. Draw the grainline. Add ⅜" (1cm) seam allowance around the piece and drag the notches to the perimeter. Cut (1) self.

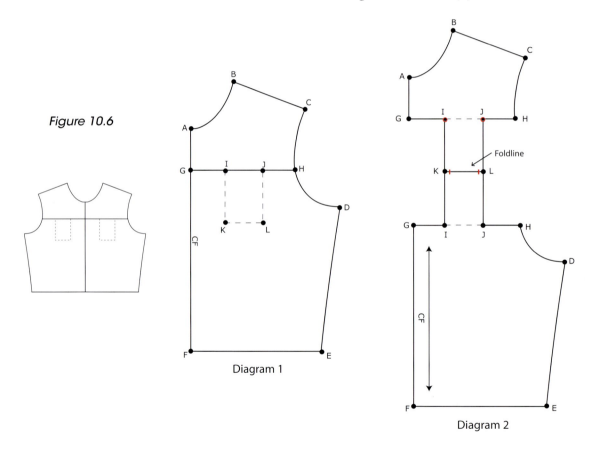

Figure 10.6

Diagram 1

Diagram 2

Design Tip:
A hidden pocket opening at the cross front is usually smaller because the hand will not be resting in the pocket.

POCKET IN A SIDE SEAM

1. Trace the front skirt (pants or bodice) sloper and mark **A**, **B**, **C**, and **D** as shown (*Fig. 10.7*, Diagram 1).
2. Decide the placement of the top of the pocket opening at the side (example: 1½" [3.8cm] down from the waistline on the side seam). Mark **E**.
3. Decide the width of the pocket opening from **E** on the side seam (example: 5½" [14cm]). Mark **F**.
4. **EF** = pocket opening
5. **BH** = top of the pocket to anchor it at the waistline (example: 3" [7.6cm])
6. **FG** = desired depth of the pocket bag anchor beyond the opening at side (example: 1" [2.5cm])
7. **I** = mark the desired width and depth of the corner of the pocket bag from the side seam (example: 4"–6" [10.2–15.2cm]). Round out the corner at **I** if desired.
8. **BJ** = 1" (2.5cm) for width of the pocket facing
9. Square over 1" (2.5cm) from **G**, mark **K** and then connect **H-I-K-G** for the shape of the pocket bag.
10. Connect **J-K**, maintaining a 1" (2.5cm) width from **BG**.
11. Trace the Pocket Front: **H-B-E-F-G K-I-H**
12. Notch the pocket opening at **E** and **F** (*Fig. 10.7*, Diagram 2). Add the grainline. Add ½" (1.3cm) seam allowance and drag the notches to the perimeter. Cut (1) pocketing (or lining)

Helpful Hint:
Unlike squared edges, rounded edges don't collect lint.

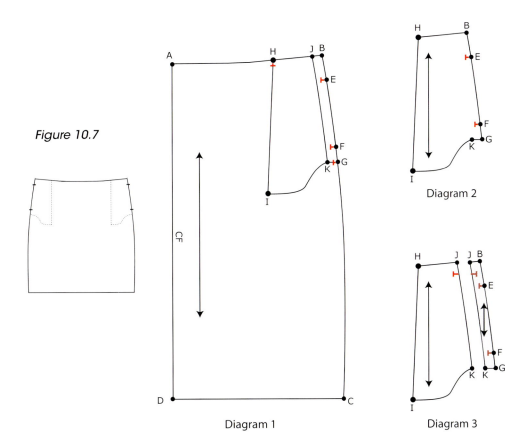

Figure 10.7

Diagram 1

Diagram 2

Diagram 3

13. Trace the Pocket Back: **H-J-B-E-F-G-K-I-H**. Separate into two pieces at **J** and **K** (*Fig. 10.7*, Diagram 3).
14. Put in a corresponding notch on both pieces on the **JK** line to keep track of how they sew together.
15. Pocket Facing: **J-B-E-F-G-K-J**
16. Notch at **E**, **F**, and on the **JK** line. Add the grainline parallel to the skirt grainline. Add ½" (1.3cm) seam allowance around the pieces and drag the notches to the perimeter. Cut (1) self. Cut (1) interfacing.
17. Pocket Back: **H-J-K-I-H**
18. Match a notch to the pocket facing along the **JK** line. Add the grainline. Add ½" (1.3cm) seam allowance around the piece and drag the notches to the perimeter. Cut (1) pocketing (or lining).
19. Skirt: **A-H-B-E-F-G-C-D-A**
20. Notch the pocket opening (**E** and **F**). Notch where the pocket anchors at the waistline (**H**) and at the side (**G**). Draw the grainline. Add ½" (1.3cm) seam allowance around the piece and drag the notches to the perimeter. Cut (1) self.

Structural Tip:

If a garment does not have a waist seam as with a dress or jacket, the top of the pocket cannot anchor at the waist; therefore, connect **J** to **I** in a convex shape. The pocket will anchor at the side seam.

---

21. Draft a back skirt pattern piece and include corresponding notches at **E** and **F** on the back side seam. Match a notch to the pocket facing along the **JK** line. Add the grainline. Add ½" (1.3cm) seam allowance around the piece and drag the notches to the perimeter. Cut (1) pocketing (or lining).
22. Skirt: **A-H-B-E-F-G-C-D-A**
23. Notch the pocket opening (**E** and **F**). Notch where the pocket anchors at the waistline (**H**) and at the side (**G**). Draw the grainline. Add ½" (1.3cm) seam allowance around the piece and drag the notches to the perimeter. Cut (1) self.
24. Draft a back skirt pattern piece and include corresponding notches at **E** and **F** on the back side seam.

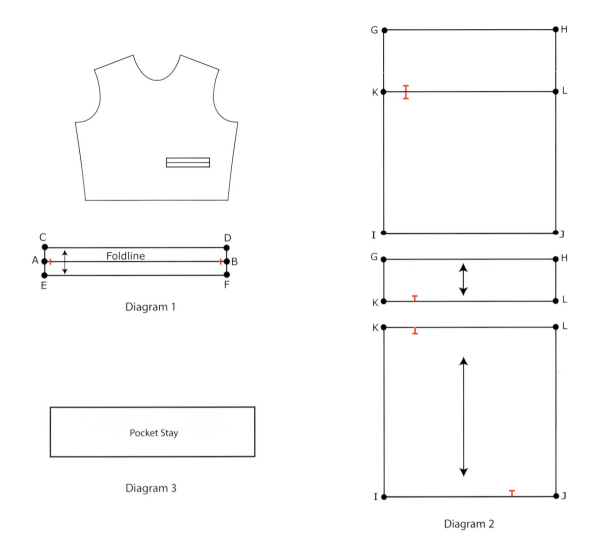

Figure 10.8

Design Tip:
Welt (jetted) pockets are used on jackets, coats, pants, skirts, and occasionally dresses. They work best on medium to heavier-weight fabrics.

DOUBLE-WELT POCKET WITH FLAP VARIATION

Welt
1. **AB** = draw a line the width of the pocket opening as desired (example: 5"–7" [12.7–17.8cm]) (*Fig. 10.8*, Diagram 1)
2. **AC** = ¼" (6.4mm)
3. **BD** = ¼" (6.4mm)
4. **AE** = ¼" (6.4mm)
5. **BF** = ¼" (6.4mm)
6. Connect **C-D-F-E-C** for the welt.
7. Mark a fold line and notch at **AB**. Draw the grainline. Add ¾" (1.9cm) seam allowance to the sides and ¼" (6.4mm) seam allowance to the top and bottom of the welt, and drag the notches to the perimeter. Cut (2) self. Cut (2) interfacing.

Design Tip:
Try cutting the welts from a different fabric or on a different grainline than the garment to give more surface interest to a garment. For a more subtle look, match the fabric pattern and grainline to the garment.

Pocket Bag and Facing
8. **GH** = draw a line the width of the pocket opening (as **AB**) (*Fig. 10.8*, Diagram 2)
9. **GI** and **HJ** = draw the depth of the pocket bag, times two since it will fold up. For example, if the pocket bag will be 5" (12.7cm) finished, **GI** and **HJ** should measure 10" (25.4cm).
10. Connect **I-J** for the pocket bag rectangle.
11. **GK** and **HL** = 1" (2.5cm) down for pocket facing.
12. Connect **K-L**. Add a notch as shown to help match these two pieces when sewing.
13. Pocket Bag: **K-L-J-I-K**
14. Draw the grainline. Add ¾" (1.9cm) seam allowance to the sides and ¼" (6.4mm) seam allowance to the top and bottom of the pocket bag, and drag the notch to the perimeter. Cut (1) pocketing (or lining).
15. Pocket Facing: **G-H-L-K-G**
16. Draw the grainline. Add ¾" (1.9cm) seam allowance to the sides and ¼" (6.4mm) seam allowance to the top and bottom of the pocket facing, and drag the notch to the perimeter. Cut (1) self. Cut (1) interfacing.

Pocket Stay
17. Draw a rectangle the width of the pocket opening plus 1½" (3.8cm), with the depth 1" (2.5cm) (*Fig. 10.8*, Diagram 3). For example, if the pocket opening is 5" (12.7cm), the stay will be 6½" wide x 1" long (16.5 x 2.5cm). The stay is cut from fusible interfacing and is placed behind the welts on the wrong side of the fabric to stabilize the fabric behind the welts. Cut (1) interfacing.

Flap Variation
The pocket can remain as a visible double welt, or a flap can be added as a variation.
18. **MN** = pocket opening (as **AB** on the welt) (*Fig. 10.9*, Diagram 1)
19. **MO** = depth of flap as desired (example: 2" [5.1cm]) squared off **MN**
20. **NP** = **MO** squared off **MN**
21. **OQ** = ¼" (6.4mm) out to shape flap
22. **PR** = ¼" (6.4mm) out to shape flap
23. Connect **M-N-R-Q-M**.

24. Fold a piece of pattern paper, place **QR** on the fold, and trace **Q-M-N-R** for the all-in-one flap and the flap facing (*Fig. 10.9*, Diagram 2).

25. Flap: **M-N-R-N-M-Q-M**

26. Mark the fold line at **QR** and notch. Draw the grainline. Add ¼" (6.4mm) seam allowance around the piece and drag the notches to the perimeter. Cut (1) self (or contrasting). Cut (1) interfacing.

Design Tip:

A pocket flap is both functional and decorative. It is used to keep the contents in a welt pocket bag from falling out. Depending on the shape and fabric choice, it adds surface interest as well.

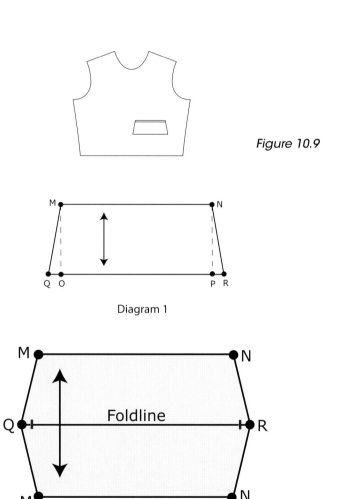

Figure 10.9

Diagram 1

Diagram 2

Design Tip:

Single-welt pockets are often drafted horizontally for chest pockets (and can hold pocket squares) on suit jackets or applied diagonally on jackets and coats for waist or hip pockets.

SINGLE-WELT POCKET

For the pocket bag, pocket facing, and pocket stay, use the pattern pieces drafted in the Double Welt exercise (page 252).

1. **AB** = width of the pocket opening as desired (example: 5"–7" [12.7–17.8cm]) (*Fig. 10.10*)
2. **AC** = height of the welt as desired (example: 1" [2.5cm]) squared off **AB**
3. **BD** = as **AC** squared off **AB**
4. **CE** = ⅛" (3.2mm) out to shape the welt
5. **DF** = ⅛" (3.2mm) out to shape the welt
6. Connect **A-E-F-B-A**.
7. Fold a piece of pattern paper, place **EF** on the fold, and trace **F-B-A-E** for an all-in-one single welt and facing.
8. Single Welt: **A-B-F-B-A-E-A**
9. Mark the fold line at **EF** and notch. Draw the grainline. Add ¼" (6.4mm) seam allowance around the piece and drag the notches to the perimeter. Cut (1) self (or contrasting). Cut (1) interfacing.

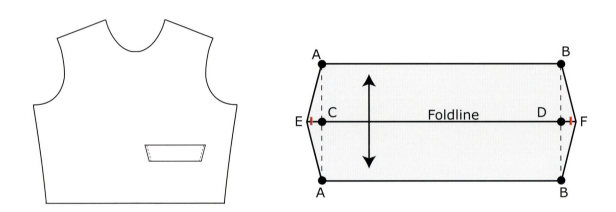

Figure 10.10

Template Tip:
After perfecting a pocket pattern, commit it to tag. That way, you are building a pocket template library that you can draw from again and again. Drawing from template libraries saves a lot of time when drafting patterns.

✓ Test Your Knowledge

1. Identify the three main types of pockets.

2. Why would a patternmaker cut a pocket on a different grainline rather than the grainline used for the garment?

3. What is the purpose of a pocket anchor?

4. Explain how using a pocket template is beneficial.

5. What is another name for a welt pocket?

This final chapter includes step-by-step instruction on how to combine the exercises in Chapters 2–10 to draft full garments. It teaches the order of operation when drafting skirts, pants, shirts, blouses, tops, dresses, jackets, and coats.

OBJECTIVES

Upon completion of this chapter, you will be able to

- Understand the order of operations when drafting complete garments
- Combine exercises confidently to create full garment patterns
- Enhance your patternmaking and design instincts

CHAPTER 11
Garments

How to Work with This Chapter

— — — — — — —

This chapter includes the order of operations to draft specific garments. Depending on the garment style, the order could vary and details can be added or taken away. Think of these lists as generic and for consideration only. Once you become a skilled patternmaker, the drafting order will become more intuitive. Garment diagrams are intentionally omitted so as not to dictate style. Use your experience, imagination, and artistry. Experiment!
Instruction in this chapter is given with the assumption that the student has worked through the earlier chapters of this book. Always make a primary pattern. Pattern pieces are then traced from the primary. Primary patterns make it easier to make changes and to trace off facings, linings, pocket pieces, etc.

— — — — — — —

Exercises

DRAFTING SKIRTS

Front
1. Trace the front skirt sloper. Adjust the length by squaring down from the low-hip guideline, making a rectangle from the low hip to the desired length. Lower the waist if desired.
2. Draft the skirt pattern.
3. Mark pocket placement and draft pocket pieces on the primary pattern.
4. Note the measurement of the waistline.
5. Draft facing and lining pieces on the primary pattern as needed.

Back
6. Trace the back skirt sloper. Adjust the length as front. Lower the waist if lowered in front. The center-back waist can be higher than the center-front waist, but they should match at the side seams.
7. Draft the skirt pattern.
8. Decide on a closure and draft accordingly.
9. Mark pocket placement and draft pocket pieces on the primary pattern.
10. Note the measurement of the waistline.
11. Draft facing and lining pieces on the primary pattern as needed.

Pockets (Optional)
12. Trace or draft the pocket pieces.

Waistband (Optional)
13. Draft a waistband if that is part of the design. Choose either a waistband or facings.

Facings and Linings (Optional)
14. Trace the facing and lining pieces.

Front and Back
15. Trace the pattern pieces from the primary pattern.
16. Cut the traced pattern apart at the style lines and manipulate the darts if necessary.

Entire Pattern
17. True the pattern.
18. Include notches and drill holes.
19. Draw grainlines on all pieces.
20. Trace any interfacing pieces.
21. Mark all pattern pieces with a style name or number, piece, how many to cut, and out of which fabric.

Final Pattern
22. Once the pattern has been finalized, include hem and seam allowances on the pattern. Drag the notches to the perimeter.
23. Include a pattern record card showing all the pattern pieces as well as the trims.

DRAFTING PANTS

Front
1. Trace the front pants sloper. Adjust the length. Lower the waist if desired.
2. Draft the pants pattern.
3. Mark pocket placement and draft pocket pieces on the primary pattern.
4. Decide on the closure. Draft a zipper fly or button fly. Or chose to have the pants close at the side or center back with a zipper or buttons/buttonholes and draft accordingly.
5. Note the measurement of the waistline.
6. Draft a facing on the primary pattern as needed.

Back
7. Trace the back pants sloper. Adjust the length as front. Lower the waist if lowered in front. The center-back waist can be higher than the center-front waist, but they should match at the side seams.
8. Draft the pants pattern.
9. Draft a yoke if that is part of the design.
10. Mark pocket placement and draft pocket pieces on the primary pattern.
11. Note the measurement of the waistline.
12. Draft a facing on the primary pattern as needed.

Fly
13. Draft the fly shields, facings, or extension pieces.

Pockets (Optional)
14. Trace or draft the pocket pieces.

Waistband (Optional)
15. Draft a waistband if that is part of the design. Choose either a waistband or facings.

Facings (Optional)
16. Trace the facing pieces.

Front and Back
17. Trace the pattern pieces from the primary pattern.
18. Cut the traced pattern apart at the style lines and manipulate the darts if necessary.

Entire Pattern
19. True the pattern.
20. Include notches and drill holes.
21. Draw grainlines on all pieces.
22. Trace any interfacing pieces.
23. Mark all the pattern pieces with a style name or number, piece, how many to cut, and out of which fabric.

Final Pattern
24. Once the pattern has been finalized, include hem and seam allowances on the pattern. Drag the notches to the perimeter.
25. Include a pattern record card showing all the pattern pieces as well as the trims.

Ease Tip:

Ease is usually added or taken away at the side seam. However, if ease is to be added in the shoulder also, draw a vertical line on the front and back patterns from the base up to the shoulder (see dotted line in *Fig. 11.1*), cut the pattern apart, and add a rectangular insertion from base to shoulder. To avoid distortion, the insertion amount should max out at 1" (2.5cm). Commonly, the insertion amount is ¼"–½" (0.6–1.3cm). Remember, you are adding ease to four quarter panels, so adding ½" (1.3cm) will give an additional 2" (5.1cm) ease. More ease can still be added to the side seam.

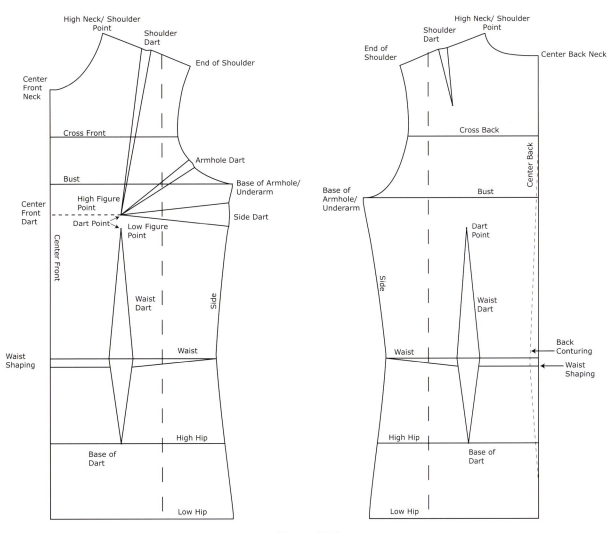

Figure 11.1

DRAFTING SLEEVELESS TOPS AND TUNICS

Front

1. Trace the front sloper to the low hip. Adjust the length by squaring down from the low-hip guideline, making a rectangle from the low hip to the desired length.
2. Adjust the ease at the bust. A sleeveless garment should not have more than 1" (2.5cm) total around the bust (bust circumference + 1" [2.5cm]). Adjust the ease at the waist and hips.
3. Decide the depth at the center-front neck. Decide the placement of the high-neck/shoulder point. Draw the neckline. With low necklines, include a neckline dart to prevent gaping.
4. Will the shoulder dart be sewn, ignored, or manipulated?
5. Adjust the end of shoulder in or out. Adjust the cross front in or out half the amount the end of shoulder was adjusted. Lower the base of the armhole if desired. Redraw the armhole. Redraw the side seam. The armhole dart should be sewn or manipulated to prevent gaping in sleeveless garments.
6. Decide if there will be interior seamlines, such as princess seams or a dart manipulation, and draft that in.
7. How will the side dart be handled? Sewn or manipulated? There isn't an option to ignore the side dart (or the front and back sides will not line up).
8. How will the waist dart be handled? Sewn, ignored, or manipulated?
9. Draw waist shaping if the garment is fitted or semifitted. Waist shaping can be taken at the waist or at the neck and shoulder if the garment does not have a waist seam, empire seam, or a princess seam. Waist shaping is not needed in loose garments.
10. If needed, draw in a button extension and facing. Or include a button placket. Mark the placement of the buttons and buttonholes.
11. Show pocket placement. Draft pocket pieces over the primary pattern.
12. Shape the base as desired.
13. Note the measurement of the neckline for a bias-binding finish or to draft a collar.
14. Note the measurement of the armhole for a bias-binding finish unless the armhole will be faced.
15. Draw facing and lining pieces as needed.

Back

16. Trace the back sloper and adjust the length as front.
17. Include back contouring if the garment has a center-back seam.
18. Adjust the ease at the bust, waist, and hips as front.
19. Decide the depth at the center-back neck. Often, sleeveless tops have a slit opening at a depth of 4" (10.2cm) from the center-back neck to pull the garment over the head. The closure can have a button and fabric loop.
20. Decide the placement of the high-neck/shoulder point.
21. Will the shoulder dart be sewn, ignored, or manipulated?
22. Adjust the end of shoulder. Check that the front and back shoulder widths are the same. Adjust the cross back in or out half the amount the end of shoulder was adjusted.
23. Lower the base of the armhole if lowered in front. Redraw the armhole. Redraw the side seam.
24. Decide if there will be a princess seam or other style line and draft that in.
25. How will the waist dart be handled? Sewn, ignored, or manipulated?
26. Include waist shaping if the garment is fitted.

27. Shape the base to be compatible with the front. Make sure there is a smooth transition from front to back.
28. Note the measurement of the neckline for a bias-binding finish or to draft a collar.
29. Note the measurement of the armhole for a bias-binding finish unless the armhole will be faced.
30. Draw facing and lining pieces as needed.

Collar (Optional)
31. Draft the collar.
32. Trace an upper and undercollar.

Pocket (Optional)
33. Trace or draft the pocket pieces.

Facings and Linings (Optional)
34. Trace the front and back facing and lining pieces from the primary pattern.

Front and Back
35. Trace the pattern pieces from the primary pattern.
36. Cut the traced pattern apart at the style lines and manipulate the darts as desired. Fold or cut away the waist shaping if necessary.

Entire Pattern
37. True the pattern.
38. Include notches and drill holes.
39. Draw grainlines on all pieces.
40. Trace any interfacing pieces.
41. Mark all the pattern pieces with a style name or number, piece, how many to cut, and out of which fabric.

Final Pattern
42. Once the pattern has been finalized, include hem and seam allowances on the pattern. Drag the notches to the perimeter.
43. Include a pattern record card showing all the pattern pieces as well as the trims.

Drafting a Vest

The steps for drafting sleeveless tops is a starting point for drafting vests. Traditional vests have either a notched collar or roll collar on a V-neckline, which needs to be drafted onto the front pattern piece. Vests have buttons down the center front. Face the center-front opening, neckline, and the armholes with an all-in-one facing. Vests are fitted with darts or princess seams. Often there is a belt or a tie between the back darts or princess seams that helps to tighten the waist. Traditional vests have a shaped base and end around the high hip. Of course, vests can also be long, loose, and flowy without a collar or have a simple band collar.

DRAFTING BLOUSES AND BUTTON-DOWN/BUTTON-UP SHIRTS

Front

1. Trace the front sloper to the low hip. The entire neckline can be raised ⅛"–¼" (3.2–6.4mm) if a tighter-fitting collar is needed. Adjust the garment length as desired.
2. Adjust the ease at the bust, waist, and hip. A shirt or blouse with sleeves should have at least 2"–3" (5.1–7.6cm) ease around the bust (bust circumference + 2"–3" [5.1–7.6cm]).
3. Will the shoulder dart be sewn, ignored, or manipulated?
4. Leave the end of shoulder point or extend it. Shirts or blouses can have a slightly dropped shoulder. Adjust the cross front out half the amount the end of shoulder was adjusted. Lower the base of the armhole ¼"–1" (0.6–2.5cm) for a looser fit. Redraw the armhole. Redraw the side seam.

Drafting Tip:
If the design calls for a puff sleeve, pleats, darts, or any fullness at the sleeve cap, bring the end of the shoulder in ½" (1.3cm) so the fullness sits on top of the shoulder. Bring the cross front and cross back in half the amount the end of shoulder was brought in.

5. The armhole dart is usually ignored when sleeves are included, or half the dart width can be sewn or manipulated. Don't manipulate the entire armhole dart out or the sleeve will feel too tight.
6. Decide if there will be interior seamlines, such as princess seams or a dart manipulation, and draft that in.
7. How will the side dart be handled? Sewn or manipulated? There isn't an option to ignore the side dart (or the front and back sides will not line up).
8. How will the waist dart be handled? Sewn, ignored, or manipulated?
9. Take waist shaping if the garment is fitted. Ignore it if the garment is loose.
10. Decide on button size and draft a standard or hidden-button placket. Mark the placement of the buttons and buttonholes.
11. Show pocket placement. Draft pocket pieces on the primary pattern.
12. If the shirt is designed with a yoke, the yoke line on the front is often drawn 1"–2" (2.5–5.1cm) down and parallel to the shoulder seam.
13. Shape the base as desired.
14. Note the measurement of the neckline to draft the collar.
15. Note the measurement of the armhole to draft a sleeve.

Back

16. Trace the back sloper and adjust the length as front.
17. Include back contouring if the garment has a center-back seam (not usually the case unless the blouse or shirt is fitted).
18. Adjust the ease at the bust, waist, and hips as front.
19. Adjust the end of shoulder as front. Check that the front and back shoulder widths are the same. Adjust the cross back in or out half the amount the end of shoulder was adjusted.
20. Lower the base of the armhole if lowered in front. Redraw the armhole. Redraw the side seam.
21. Draw the back yoke seam. Draw the yoke seam line perpendicular to the center-back level with the base of the shoulder dart. That way, the shoulder dart can be manipulated out when the yoke line is cut.
22. If the garment does not have a yoke, the back end of shoulder should be extended ¼"–⅜" (0.6–1cm) with that amount eased back into the front shoulder when sewing. Adding extra length to the back shoulder, then easing it back in, offers more mobility when moving the arms forward in a garment with sleeves.
23. Draft a pleat under the yoke seam. Add a 1" (2.5cm) extension down the center back from under the yoke to the base. Cut on a center-back fold to create a 2" (5.1cm) pleat at center back. Generally, a pleat is not added if there are back darts or a princess seam because the look is too cluttered. However, a pleat does add more ease and therefore more comfort.
24. Decide if there will be a princess seam or other style line, and draft that in.
25. How will the waist dart be handled? Sewn, ignored, or manipulated?
26. Include waist shaping if the garment is fitted.
27. Shape the base to be compatible with the front. Make sure there is a smooth transition from front to back.

Design Tip:

Shirt and blouse bases are traditionally curved with the center back slightly longer than the center front. The base of the side seam is higher than the center front and center back. The higher front and sides reduce bulk if the shirt is tucked in. The longer back keeps the shirt tucked in when the wearer leans forward. Make sure the transition from front to back is smooth at the side seams.

28. Note the measurement of the back neckline to draft a collar.
29. Note the measurement of the armhole to draft a sleeve.

Sleeves

30. Draft a sleeve.
31. Draft a placket, pleat, and cuff.

Collar

32. Draft a collar with band (or any other collar). Add buttons/buttonholes at the collar points to create a button-down shirt. Button-up shirts do not have buttons/buttonholes at the collar tips.

Pocket
33. Trace or draft the pocket pieces.

Front and Back
34. Trace the pattern pieces from the primary pattern.
35. Cut the traced pattern apart at the style lines and manipulate the darts as desired. Fold or cut away the waist shaping if necessary.
36. Attach the front and back yoke pieces at the shoulder line.

Entire Pattern
37. True the pattern.
38. Include notches and drill holes.
39. Draw grainlines on all pieces.
40. Trace any interfacing pieces.
41. Mark all the pattern pieces with a style name or number, piece, how many to cut, and out of which fabric.

Final Pattern
42. Once the pattern has been finalized, include hem and seam allowances on the pattern. Drag the notches to the perimeter.
43. Include a pattern record card showing all the pattern pieces as well as the trims.

Drafting a Shirt Dress

Use the drafting instructions for drafting Button-Down/Button-Up Shirts (page 264). Adjust the length longer, consider a shorter sleeve, and add a tie at the waist.

DRAFTING DRESSES
Front

1. Trace the front sloper to the low hip. Adjust the length by squaring down from the low-hip guideline, making a rectangle from the low hip to the desired length.
2. Adjust the ease at the bust. A sleeveless garment should not have more than 1" (2.5cm) total around the bust. A dress with sleeves should have a minimum of 2"–3" (5.1–7.6cm) ease around the bust but can have more. Adjust the ease at the waist and hips.
3. Decide the depth at the center-front neck. Decide the placement of the high-neck/shoulder point. Draw the neckline. With low necklines, include a neckline dart.
4. Will the shoulder dart be sewn, ignored, or manipulated?
5. Adjust the end of shoulder in or out. Adjust the cross front in or out half the amount the end of shoulder was adjusted. Lower the base of the armhole if desired. Redraw the armhole. Redraw the side seam.
6. The armhole dart is needed to prevent gaping on a sleeveless garment. Decide if it will be sewn or manipulated. On a garment with sleeves, usually half the width of the armhole dart is sewn or manipulated, or it can be ignored altogether on looser garments.
7. Decide if there will be interior seamlines, such as princess seams or a dart manipulation, and draft that in.
8. How will the side dart be handled? Sewn or manipulated? There isn't an option to ignore the side dart in womenswear (or the front and back sides will not line up).
9. Draft the lower portion or skirt to the dress as desired. Is it full or slim? If there is a seam at the waist, draw that in. Cut the pattern apart at the waist and draft the skirt. If there isn't a waist seam, leave the pattern intact.
10. How will the waist dart be handled? Sewn, ignored, or manipulated?
11. Include waist shaping if the garment is fitted or semifitted. Waist shaping can be taken at the waist or at the neck and shoulder if the garment does not have a waist seam, empire seam, or a princess seam. Waist shaping is not needed in loose garments.
12. Show pocket placement if pockets will be included. Draft pocket pieces on the primary pattern.
13. Shape the base as desired.
14. Note the measurement of the neckline for a bias-binding finish or to draft a collar.
15. Note the measurement of the armhole for a bias-binding finish or to draft a sleeve.
16. Draw facing and lining pieces as needed.

Back

17. Trace the back sloper and adjust the length as front.
18. Include back contouring if the garment has a center-back seam.
19. Adjust the ease at the bust, waist, and hips as front.
20. Decide the depth at the center-back neck.
21. Determine the placement of the high-neck/shoulder point.
22. Will the shoulder dart be sewn, ignored, or manipulated?
23. Adjust the end of shoulder. Check that the front and back shoulder widths are the same if the garment is sleeveless. Adjust the cross back in or out half the amount the end of shoulder was adjusted. If the garment has sleeves, draw the back shoulder ¼"–⅜" (0.6–1cm) wider at the end of shoulder and ease that amount back into the front when sewing. This will offer more mobility when moving the arms forward.
24. Lower the base of the armhole if lowered in front. Redraw the armhole. Redraw the side seam.
25. Decide if there will be a princess seam or other style line and draft that in.
26. Draft the lower portion skirt to the dress. The skirt in back should be compatible to the skirt in front. Is there a seam at the waist? Draw that in. Cut the pattern apart at the waist and draft the skirt. If there isn't a waist seam, leave the pattern intact. Include a slit if the base is tight.
27. How will the waist dart be handled? Sewn, ignored, or manipulated?
28. Draw the waist shaping.
29. Shape the base to be compatible with the front. Make sure there is a smooth transition from front to back.
30. Note the measurement of the neckline for a bias-binding finish or to draft a collar.
31. Note the measurement of the armhole for a bias-binding finish or to draft a sleeve.
32. Draw facing and lining pieces as needed.

Fitting Tip:
There can be a horizontal seam at the back waist and not the front waist. If a model has a sway back, including a back waist seam can be helpful in removing excess fabric so the center-back waist is smooth. Blend to zero at the side seam so the front and back sides line up.

Sleeves (Optional)
33. Draft a sleeve.

Collar (Optional)
34. Draft the collar.
35. Trace an upper and undercollar.

Pocket (Optional)
36. Trace or draft the pocket pieces.

Facings and Linings (Optional)
37. Trace the front and back facing and lining pieces off the primary pattern.

Front and Back
38. Trace the pattern pieces from the primary pattern.
39. Cut the pattern apart at the style lines and manipulate the darts as desired. Fold or cut away the waist shaping if necessary.

Entire Pattern
40. True the pattern.
41. Include notches and drill holes.
42. Draw grainlines on all pieces.
43. Trace any interfacing pieces.
44. Mark all the pattern pieces with a style name or number, piece, how many to cut, and out of which fabric.

Final Pattern
45. Once the pattern has been finalized, include hem and seam allowances on the pattern. Drag the notches to the perimeter.
46. Include a pattern record card showing all the pattern pieces as well as the trims.

DRAFTING JACKETS AND COATS
1. Trace the front sloper to the low hip. Adjust the length by squaring down from the low-hip guideline, making a rectangle from the low hip to the desired length.
2. Adjust the ease at the bust. A jacket or coat has a minimum of 3" (7.6cm) ease around the bust but can have more. Adjust the ease at the waist and hips.
3. Consider grading the waist down ¼"–½" (0.6–1.3cm). Mark a line 2" (5.1cm) above the waist guideline. Cut the line and insert ¼"–½" (0.6–1.3cm) to lower the waist guideline.
4. Decide the depth at the center-front neck. Decide the placement of the high-neck/shoulder point—should it be graded out ⅛"–¼" (3.2–6.4mm)? Draw the neckline.
5. Will the shoulder dart be sewn, ignored, or manipulated?
6. Adjust the end of shoulder out. Adjust the cross front out half the amount the end of shoulder was adjusted. Lower the base of the armhole ½" (1.3cm) or more. Redraw the armhole. Redraw the side seam.
7. On a garment with sleeves, usually half the width of the armhole dart is sewn or manipulated out, or it can be ignored altogether for more armhole ease on looser garments. Decide how the armhole dart will be handled.
8. Decide if there will be interior seamlines, such as princess seams or a dart manipulation, and draft that in.
9. How will the side dart be handled? Sewn or manipulated? There isn't an option to ignore the side dart (or the front and back sides will not line up).
10. Decide button size and add the button extension. Mark the placement of buttons and buttonholes.
11. Draft a notched collar or a roll collar on a V-neckline. (These two collars need the measurement of the drafted back neckline before beginning the collar draft.) Include the roll line. The roll line is usually built up in jackets and coats with fusible interfacing or a stitch pattern.
12. Draft the lower portion of the coat as desired. Is it full or slim? If there is a seam at the waist, draw that in. Cut the pattern apart at the waist and draft the lower portion. If there isn't a waist seam, leave the pattern intact.

Drafting/Fitting Tip:
Because a jacket or coat is layered over other garments and is therefore sitting higher on the shoulder over those garments, the waist guideline and base raise up slightly. Counter that by grading the waistline down. The same principle applies to the high-neck/shoulder point. On a jacket or coat, the high-neck/shoulder point is often moved out ⅛"–¼" (3.2–6.4mm) so that high-neck/shoulder points do not stack on top of one another when layering garments. Grade the end of shoulder out as well. Armholes should be lowered at least ½" (1.3cm) and side seams should be extended at least ¼" (6.4mm) as garments layer. Think about how garments layer when pattern drafting and if edges, or guidelines need to be graded out or down.

13. How will the waist dart be handled? Sewn, ignored, or manipulated?
14. Include waist shaping if the garment is fitted or semifitted. Waist shaping is not needed in loose garments.
15. Show pocket placement if pockets will be included.
16. Shape the base as desired.

Back
20. Trace the back sloper and adjust the length as front.
21. Consider adding ¼"–⅜" (0.6–1cm) to the cross back at center back. Include back contouring if the garment has a center-back seam. Connect from zero at the center-back neck to the ¼"–⅜" (0.6–1cm) out at cross back and into back contouring. Taking the cross back out allows for added mobility when moving the arms forward in a jacket or coat.
22. Adjust the ease at the bust, waist, and hips as front.
23. Grade the high-neck/shoulder point and the waist guideline if they were graded in front.
24. Will the shoulder dart be sewn, ignored, or manipulated?

17. Note the measurement of the neckline to draft a collar if a notched or roll collar is not the intended collar.
18. Note the measurement of the armhole to draft a sleeve.
19. Draw facing and lining pieces as needed.

25. Adjust the end of shoulder. Extend the back shoulder ¼"–⅜" (0.6–1cm) at the end of shoulder, and ease that amount back into the front shoulder when sewing (ultimately the sewn shoulder will measure as the front shoulder). This will offer added mobility when moving the arms forward. Adjust the cross back in or out half the amount the end of shoulder was adjusted.
26. Lower the base of the armhole if lowered in front. Redraw the armhole. Redraw the side seam.
27. Decide if there will be a princess seam or other style line and draft that in.
28. Draft the lower portion of the jacket or coat to be compatible with the front. Is there a seam at the waist? Draw that in. Cut the pattern apart at

Fitting Tip:
Jackets and coats usually do not need a front neckline dart to prevent gaping even if the garment is low because it is not the base layer.

the waist and draft the base. If there isn't a waist seam, leave the pattern intact. Include a slit if the base is tight.

29. How will the waist dart be handled? Sewn, ignored, or manipulated?

30. Include waist shaping if the garment is fitted or semifitted. Waist shaping is not needed in loose garments.

31. Shape the base to be compatible with the front. Make sure there is a smooth transition from front to back.

32. Note the measurement of the neckline to draft a collar.

33. Note the measurement of the armhole to draft a sleeve.

34. Draw facing and lining pieces.

Front Stay

35. Draft a front stay onto the primary pattern (*Fig. 11.2*). A front stay supports the front opening, shoulder, and armhole areas of a jacket or coat. Using a front stay gives a jacket or coat a more tailored look. It is drafted in from the front extension about 2½"–3" (6.4–7.6cm), curves above the high figure point, then down from the armhole about 1"–2" (2.5–5.1cm).

It is cut in two layers. One layer is cut from batiste with ½" (1.3cm) seam allowanced added. The second layer is cut from **hair canvas** (aka **hymo**) without seam allowance and is sewn to the batiste layer. Since hair canvas is stiff and bulky, it is not sewn into the seam allowance. The batiste layer is there for support and to create a barrier between the self-fabric and the rougher hair canvas. Lining covers both layers. Trace the front stay.

Cut (2) length-grain batiste with ½" (1.3cm) seam allowance. Cut (2) length-grain hair canvas without seam allowance. A quicker, ready-to-wear version is cut in one layer from fusible interfacing and is fused behind the self-fabric.

Front Shoulder Reinforcement

36. Draft a front shoulder reinforcement on the primary pattern (*Fig. 11.3*). A front shoulder reinforcement gives support to the shoulder seam and prevents the fabric from collapsing under the collar bone. Using this reinforcement gives a jacket or coat a more tailored look.

A front shoulder reinforcement is drafted from the high-neck/shoulder point down about 4" (10.2cm) along the neckline edge, and about 5" (12.7cm) down along the armhole from the end of shoulder. It includes the shoulder and is slightly curved at the base. No seam allowance is added as it is sewn on top of the front support.

Cut (2) from hair canvas on a bias grainline. A quicker version is cut from fusible interfacing and is fused onto the front support.

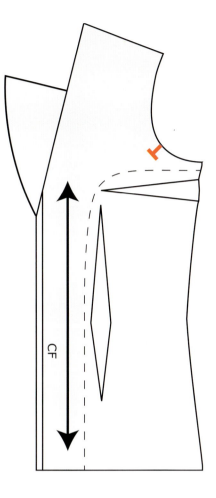

Figure 11.2

Back Stay

37. Draft a back stay on the primary pattern (*Fig. 11.4*). A back stay supports the shoulder and armhole seams, and it prevents collapsing between the shoulder blades. Using a back stay gives a jacket or coat a more tailored look.

A back stay is drafted about 6" (15.2cm) down from the center-back neck and about 3" (7.6cm) down from the underarm seam. The shoulder dart is eased into the shoulder rather than sewn. It is cut from cotton batiste or broadcloth. Add ¼" (6.4mm) seam allowance at the neckline. No seam allowance is added to the base, as it just hangs between the self-fabric and the lining. Add ½" (1.3cm) seam allowance everywhere else.

Cut one on a center-back fold, even if the garment has a center-back seam. A quicker version is cut from fusible interfacing and is fused to the back of the self-fabric.

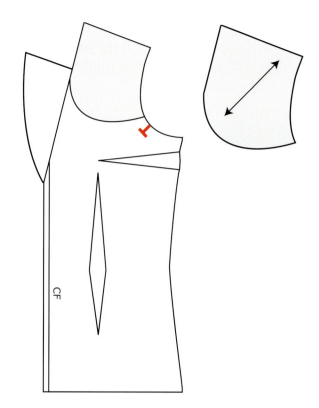

Figure 11.3

Sleeves

38. Draft a tailor sleeve or a two-piece sleeve, or a sleeve that is compatible with your design. A jacket or coat should have about 1"–1½" (2.5–3.8cm) ease at the cap.

39. Add a vent to the sleeve base.

Collar

40. Draft the collar if not already drafted as a notched or roll collar.
41. Trace an upper and undercollar.

Pocket

42. Trace or draft the pocket pieces.

Front and Back

43. Trace all pattern pieces from the primary pattern, including the collar pieces, pockets pieces, facings, linings, front support, front shoulder reinforcement, and back stay.
44. Cut the patterns apart at the style lines and manipulate the darts as desired. Fold or cut away the waist shaping.

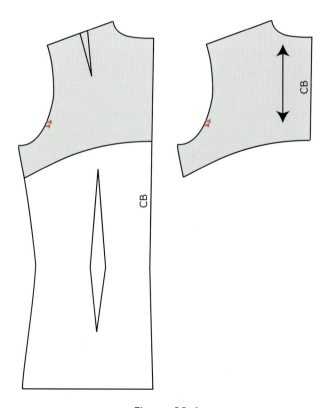

Figure 11.4

Lining

45. Add a 1" (2.5cm) pleat down the center back of the lining (for a 2" [5.1cm] finished pleat). This pleat will give the lining fabric more give and will offer added mobility when moving the arms forward (*Fig. 11.5*).

Entire Pattern

46. True the pattern.
47. Include notches and drill holes.
48. Draw grainlines on all pieces.
49. Trace any interfacing pieces.
50. Mark all the pattern pieces with a style name or number, piece, how many to cut, and out of which fabric.

Final Pattern

51. Once the pattern has been finalized, include hem and seam allowances on the pattern. Drag the notches to the perimeter.
52. Include a pattern record card showing all the pattern pieces as well as trims.

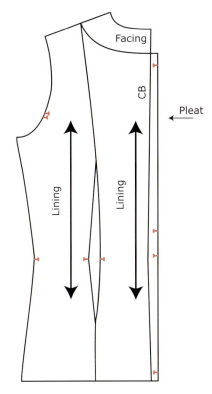

Figure 11.5

 Test Your Knowledge

1. Why is it important to draft a primary pattern?

2. What is the purpose of grading a high-neck/shoulder point or a waist guideline?

3. Describe some ways to get added mobility in the armholes when a garment has sleeves.

4. Describe a front support, front shoulder reinforcement, and a back stay. What is their purpose?

5. Choose a garment sketch or photograph. Draft a pattern for that garment using the steps in this chapter.

Glossary

80/20 Rule in Clothing—Consumers wear 20% of their wardrobe, 80% of the time.

Apex—Point of the dart (aka **vanishing point**).

Armscye—The armhole of the bodice.

As Worn—Refers to the pattern as it is placed on the body with correct side out.

Awl-Punch—To punch a drill hole on the pattern where a notch cannot reach.

Back Contouring—An adjustment on a pattern that allows a garment to fit closer to the body along the spine.

Back Stay—Supports the shoulder and armhole seams and prevents collapsing between the shoulder blades.

Backing Off a Dart—Moving the dart apex away from the high or low figure point.

Bias—Fabric cut at a 45-degree angle off the selvage.

Block Fuse—When fusible interfacing is adhered to fabric and then the pattern pieces are cut.

Break Point—Where the base of the lapel meets the bodice.

Cap Ease—The difference between the sleeve and the armhole measurements.

Correct Side Down—A term used with asymmetrical patterns where the pattern piece should be placed face down on the correct side of the fabric (aka **flip**).

Correct Side Up—A term used with asymmetrical patterns where the pattern piece should be placed face up on the correct side of the fabric.

Cross Grain—The yarns running perpendicular to the selvage edge.

Dart—Used to shape fabric into a three-dimensional shape that contours to the body.

Dart Bulk—The interior of a dart.

Dart-Equivalent Style Lines—Seam lines that cross over or near the bust points or dart points and control the fit.

Dart Take Up—The fullest part of a dart width.

Design Ease—An amount added to the body measurements to achieve the look of a desired silhouette.

Drill Hole—A punch on the pattern where a notch cannot reach.

Extension—The area from the center front guideline to the edge of a button placket, which correlates to button size.

Facing—A second layer of interfaced fabric, which supports a garment edge and adds structure to prevent stretching.

Fall—The distance from the height of a collar at center back, down to the neckline.

Fast Fashion—A fashion-industry model where trends are quickly interpreted and replicated using low-quality materials and some of the least expensive manufacturing to bring high-volume and inexpensive styles to the public.

First Pattern—The first draft of a pattern.

Fish-Eyed Dart—A dart with two points and a wide center (aka **double-pointed dart**).

Front Shoulder Reinforcement—Gives support to the shoulder seam and prevents fabric from collapsing under the collar bone.

Front Stay—Supports the front opening, shoulder, and armhole areas of a jacket or coat.

Gorge Point—The point where a collar splits off from a lapel.

Grainline—Shows how the pattern piece should be placed on the fabric when cutting in relation to the selvage.

Height—The height of a collar roll line at center back.
Hem Allowance—An amount added beyond the finished length of a pattern piece.
High Figure Point—Corresponds to the center of the breast.
High-Neck/Shoulder Point—The highest point of a neckline where the neck and shoulder meet.
Jogged Seam—An abrupt and distinct change in the width of the seam allowance.
Jump Pleat—A 1" (2.5cm) pleat added to the base of a lining pattern to absorb the movement of the wearer.
Length Grain—The yarns parallel to the selvage.
Low Figure Point—Corresponds to ¾" (1.9cm) below the high figure point; the apex of the front waist dart.
Moulage—A skintight fabric casing of the body.
Negative Ease—An amount reduced from the body measurements for a snug fit in knits.
Nondart-Equivalent Styles Lines—Style lines that do not control the fit of a garment.
Notch—A mark or set of marks on the perimeter of a pattern used to communicate how to join cut pieces when sewing.
Pattern Record Card—Lists pattern pieces, trims, and pertinent information for the production team and factory.
Pattern Stamp—A stamp used to identify pattern pieces, style, and cut information.
Pocket Bag—The pouch of a pocket.
Pocket Stay—Supports a pocket to keep it from stretching out shape.
Primary Pattern—A master pattern that shows all the pattern piece outlines.
Production Pattern—A final pattern that is ready for production.
Rise—The measurement from waist to crotch depth.
Roll Line—Where the collar peaks in height.
Seam Allowance—An amount added beyond the sew line of a pattern.
Seam Stretch—Adjustment at the neckline edge to account for bias stretch.
Self—Fashion fabric (aka **primary** fabric or **shell**).
Selvage—The finished edge running the length of a woven fabric.
Sleeve Cap—The top area on a sleeve pattern between the front and back notches.
Sleeve Head—A gathered piece of fabric that fills out the sleeve cap.
Sloper—A base pattern or template that is traced to begin a new pattern.
Slow Fashion—Clothing that is higher quality, is less trendy, has slower production schedules, and is produced in small batches with an eye on sustainability.
Stand—The distance on a collar from the neckline edge to the roll line.
Tag—Heavy manila paper used to make templates and slopers.
Truing—The process of establishing equal seam lengths on corresponding pattern pieces, making sure notches match and that connections at all seams are smooth.
Turn of the Cloth—Where a fabric switches direction at the roll line of a collar or on a lapel.
Vanity Sizing—Sizing clothes one or two sizes smaller than what the industry usually dictates.
Waist Shaping—A gentle curve that follows the waistline shape of the body.
Wearing Ease—An amount added to the body measurements for comfort.
Working Pattern—The first draft of a pattern or a pattern that is still being worked out.

Discussion Topics

SUSTAINABILITY IN FASHION

How does textile production affect the environment? Textile production has many steps, among them: growing, harvesting, softening fibers, milling, knitting, dyeing, finishing, transportation, etc. Each step in the process creates an opportunity for sustainability practices.

How much fiber is recycled? Which fibers are the easiest to recycle?

How much are clothing factory workers paid in different countries? How would you describe a sustainable living wage? What conditions need to be met for a healthy work environment?

FAST VS. SLOW FASHION

How much clothing does one really need? **80/20 Rule (in Clothing):** Consumers wear 20 percent of their wardrobe, 80 of the time.

Fast Fashion: Fast fashion is an industry model where trends are quickly interpreted and replicated using low-quality materials and some of the least expensive manufacturing practices to bring high-volume, inexpensive styles to the public.

Slow Fashion: Slow fashion is an industry model describing clothing meant to last and with an aim of reducing textile waste. Slow fashion adheres to a slower production schedule with less trendy styles created in small batches with a focus on sustainability, fair wages, healthy working conditions, and the environment.

UNDERSERVED AND EMERGING MARKETS IN FASHION

There are many underserved markets in fashion. Among them, people with disabilities, people of color, women over 50, plus-size customers, gender-nonconforming customers, and those that adhere to cultural or religious dress customs. How can the fashion industry better serve these markets? Pick one or more markets and discuss style, accessibility, colors, and fit. Also think about advertising and the in-person and online shopping experience for a customer in that market.

SIZING

Men's and children's sizing are fairly standard across brands. Currently, gender-neutral clothing is borrowing from menswear sizing while the market emerges. How can these markets improve sizing?

Given the varied shapes, curves, and sizes of women, womenswear sizing has not been standardized. Each womenswear label comes up with their own size chart. Should womenswear sizing be standardized? If so, how could the industry come up with standardized sizing for women? Is it possible?

Are there market advantages to **vanity sizing** (sizing clothing one or two sizes smaller than the industry usually dictates)?

Index

45-degree angle, 19

A-line skirt, 35
all-in-one facings, 131
apex, 29, 84
armhole dart, 89; when to use, 102
armscye, 180
awl, 10
awl-punch, 20

back contouring, 128
back dart manipulations, 97
back yoke (pants), 237
backing off a dart, 86
bagged lining (for skirt), 49
band collar, 161
belt loops, 237
bias flare skirt, 36
biceps level, 180
bishop sleeve, 195
block fuse, 47
block, 21
blouses, drafting, 264
boat neckline, 134
bodice sloper: armhole dart width chart, 64; calculation worksheet, 58, 74; center-front bust dart width chart, 67; drafting a knit, for the female figure, 68; drafting a knit, for the male figure, 81; drafting from moulage, 69; front waist dart width chart, 62; guidelines for, 59, 76; shoulder dart width chart, 61; side dart width chart, 63; transferring to tag, 71, 80
bodices, rules for well-fitting necklines and, 126
bootcut pants, 227
break point, 153
bust darts, 84

bust ease, deciding, 102
bust gathers with yoke, 93
button extensions, 155; facing, 155
button fly (pants), 233
button placket: hidden-, 158; standard, 156
button-down/button-up shirts, 264
buttonholes, 155
buttons, 154; ligne size, 154; sew-through, 154; shank, 154

camp collar, 159
cap ease, 180
cap sleeves, 191
capri pants, 225
cargo pocket, 243
center-front neck dart, 87
cigarette pants, 225
circle flare skirt, 38
circles template, 10
coats, drafting jackets and, 269
collar: band, 161; camp, 159; fall, 152, 153; height, 152; notched, 173; Peter Pan, 163; roll, 168; roll line, 152; seam stretch, 153; shawl, 166; stand, 152; trench coat, 170; trimming the under-, 153; with band, 159
collars, rules for drafting, 152
compass, 10
correct side down (CSD), 19
correct side up (CSU), 19
cross grain, 18
crotch, 204; depth, 204; extension, 204; length, 204; level, 204; point, 204; rise, 204
CSD (correct side down), 19
CSU (correct side up), 19
cuff, sleeve with placket, pleats, and, 189
cuffs (pants), 237

cutting order, 13

dart, backing off a, 86
dart bulk, 29, 84; changing, into seam allowance, 86; flush, 29
dart-equivalent style lines, 102
dart equivalents, 85
dart leg, 29
dart manipulations: for back, 97; for skirts, 99
dart, point of a, 29
dart take-up, 84
darts, 29
design ease, 17
diamond darts, 91
double princess lines, 112
double-pointed waist dart, 86
double-welt pocket with flap variation, 252
drafting curve, 10
drafting order, 17
drawstring pants, 229
dress: shift, 117; smock, 119; trapeze, 121
dress form, 10
dresses, drafting, 267
drill holes, 20
drop-shoulder bodice and sleeve, 200

ease, 17
eight gore skirt, 40
elbow level, 180
empire height, 24
empire line, 115
empire waistline, 40
eraser, 10

fabric scissors, 11
facings (for skirt), 47
facings, all-in-one, 131

facings, extension, 155
fall (collar), 152; adjustment, 153
fashion: sustainability, 276;
   underserved and emerging
   markets in, 276
fast fashion, 276
fast vs. slow fashion, 276
feminine figure, drafting a moulage
   for, 54
filling yarns, 18
final pattern, 17
first pattern, 17
fish-eyed dart, 86
flare pants, 225
flip, 19
flush, 29
French dart, 88
front waist dart, shaping the, 130
funnel neckline, 145

gigot sleeve, 196
grainline, 17
gusset, 199

height (collar), 152
hem allowance, 20
hidden-button placket, 158
hidden pocket in a seam, 248
high hip, 24
high-neck/shoulder point, 126
hip curve, 11
hood, 176
horizontal (line), 19
horizontal gathers at waist dart, 94

in-seam pockets, 240
inverted box pleat (skirt with), 44

jackets, drafting, and coats, 269
jeans pocket, 247
jeans sloper, 223. *See also* pants
jetted pocket, 240
jogged seam, 18
Juliet sleeve, 194

jump pleat, 49
jumpsuit, 228

knife pleats (skirt with), 45
knits: fabric tip, 99, 233; in slopers,
   35, 68, 81, 186, 231; stretch
   classifications, 230

leggings, 231
length grain, 18
ligne size (buttons), 154
lines and angles, 19
lining: (for skirt), 48; (for sleeve), 198
low hip, 24
L-squares, 15

masculine figure, drafting a moulage
   for, 72
meter stick, 16
moulage, 54; calculation worksheet,
   58; drafting a, for a feminine figure,
   54; drafting a, for a masculine
   figure, 72; measuring for, 54, 72
muslin, 11

neckline: boat, 134; dart chart, 128;
   funnel, 145; gathers, 96; lowered,
   128; scoop, 139; strapless, 143;
   surplice, 147; sweetheart, 141; V-,
   136
necklines, rules for well-fitting, 126
negative ease, 17
nondart-equivalent style lines, 102
notch, 20
notched collar, 173
notcher, 11

off grain, 18

pants: back yoke, 236; belt loops,
   236; bootcut, 227; button fly, 233;
   calculation worksheet, 210; capri,
   225; cigarette, 225; contoured
   waistband, 235; cuffs, 237; drafting,
   260; drawstring, 229; flare, 225;
   foundation, 204; guidelines for, 212;
   introduction to, drafting, 204; jeans,
   223; jumpsuit, 228; leggings, 231;
   measuring for, 205; pleated, 227;
   trousers, 221; zipper fly, 234
paper scissors, 11
patch pockets, 240, 242; sweatshirt,
   245
pattern, 17
pattern hook, 11
pattern, marking a, 19
pattern paper, 14
pattern punch, 14
pattern record card, 13
pattern stamp, 14
pattern, testing a, 21
pattern, truing a, 21
pencil line shape (skirt with), 40
pencils, 14
perpendicular line, 19
Peter Pan collar, 163
pivotal point, 85, 103
pleated pants, 227
pleats, shoulder, 95
pocket: cargo, 243; double-welt, with
   flap variation, 252; hidden, in a
   seam, 248; in a side seam, 249;
   in-seam, 240; jeans, 247; jetted, 240;
   patch, 240, 242; single-welt, 254;
   sweatshirt patch, 245; welt, 240
pocketing, 240
pocket bag, 240
pocket stay, 240
pockets, patterning, 240
primary pattern, 17
princess line to the armhole, 106
princess line to the shoulder, 106
princess line/side panel, 114
princess seams, drafting rules for,
   102
production pattern, 17
puff sleeve, 192

quartering a sleeve, 180

red pencil, 14
right angle, 19
roll collar on a V-neckline, 168
roll line (collar), 152

scoop neckline, 139
seam allowance, 20; changing dart bulk into, 86
selvage, 17
sew-through buttons, 154
shank buttons, 154
shawl collar, 166
shift dress, 117
short sleeves, 191
shoulder darts, asymmetrical, 92
shoulder pleats, 95
silhouette, 102
silhouettes, introduction to, 102
single-welt pocket, 254
sizing, 276
skirt: A-line, 35; bagged lining, 49; bias flare, 36; circle flair, 38; eight gore skirt, 40; empire waistline, 40; facings, 47; inverted box pleat, 44; knife pleats, 45; lining, 48; lowered waistline, 46; pencil line shape, 40; slit, 40; waistband, 51; wrap, 43
skirt sloper: back dart width chart, 33; calculation worksheet, 26; dart length chart, 31; drafting a knit, 35; fitting tip, 32; front dart distance formula, 31; front dart width chart, 30; guidelines for, 28; measuring for a, 24; transferring to tag, 34
skirts, dart manipulation for, 99
skirts, drafting, 259
slacks sloper, 213; dart length chart, 214; front crotch extension chart, 215; front dart distance formula, 213; front dart width chart, 213; transferring to tag, 220

sleeve: bishop, 195; cap (sleeve), 191; drop-shoulder bodice and, 200; gigot, 196; gusset, 199; Juliet, 194; lining a, 198; measuring for, 180; puff, 192; quartering a, 180; short, 191; tailor, 187; three-quarter, 191; two-piece, with vent, 187; with placket, pleats, and cuff, 189
sleeveless tops and tunics, drafting, 262
sleeve base, 180
sleeve cap, 180
sleeve ease, 180
sleeve notches, 180
sleeve sloper, basic, 182; formula, 182; knit, 187; square size chart, 183; transferring to tag, 186
slit (skirt with), 40
sloper, 21
slow fashion, 276
smock dress, 119
square a line, 19
stand (collar), 152
straight grain, 18
strapless neckline, 143
stretch classifications, 230
style lines, introduction to, 102
style number, 13
surplice neckline, 147
sustainability in fashion, 276
sweatshirt patch pocket, 245
sweetheart neckline, 141

tack, 14
tag, 14
tailor sleeve, 187
tape measure, 15
technical flat, 12, 13, 21
testing a pattern, 21
three-quarter sleeves, 191
thumbtack, 14
tops, drafting sleeveless, 262
tracing paper, 15
tracing wheel, 16

transparent ruler, 16
transparent tape, 16
trapeze dress, 121
trench coat collar, 170
trims, 13
trouser sloper, 221. *See also* pants
true bias, 18
truing a pattern, 21
T-squares, 15
tunics, drafting sleeveless tops and, 262
turn of the cloth (collar), 152, 153

vanishing point (dart), 29
vent, two-piece sleeve with, 187
vertical line, 19
vest, drafting, 263
V-neckline, 136; roll collar on a, 168

waist dart, 84; double-pointed, 86
waist dart, horizontal gathers at, 94
waistband, contoured (pants), 235
waistline, lowered, 24
warp yarns, 18
wearing ease, 17
weft yarns, 18
weight, 16
welt pockets, 240
working pattern, 17
wrap skirt, 43
wrist level, 180

yardstick, 16
Y-dart, 90
yoke, bust gathers with, 93

zipper fly (pants), 234

About the Author

Suzy Furrer has over 35 years of experience in the fashion industry. She is also the founder and director of Apparel Arts (established 1996), a successful fashion design training center in the San Francisco Bay Area. Suzy developed a comprehensive curriculum, giving students in-depth training to be strong candidates to enter the workforce in fashion or costume design or to build exceptional sewing and drafting skills for a personal sewing practice.

Apparel Arts has graduated students who currently work in the fashion and costuming industries and in education. She has been an instructor at Gap Inc.'s Product Development Immersion Program and speaks at sewing and craft conferences and guilds. She has conducted classes for CG artists at Pixar and Lucasfilm.

Suzy's popular patternmaking and sewing classes can be found at ApparelArtsProductions.com and Craftsy.com.

Acknowledgments

The invaluable feedback from Apparel Arts' students and faculty over the years has shaped the book you are holding today. I am grateful to all of them. I am especially grateful to Allison Page, a superior patternmaker, long-time Apparel Arts instructor, and my incredible friend.

For Pilar.